Between Two Worlds

Between Two Worlds

The Construction of the Ottoman State

Cemal Kafadar

UNIVERSITY OF CALIFORNIA PRESS

Berkeley / Los Angeles / London

University of California Press
Berkeley and Los Angeles, California

University of California Press, Ltd.
London, England

First Paperback Printing 1996

Library of Congress Cataloging-in-Publication Data
Kafadar, Cemal, 1954–
Between two worlds : the construction of the Ottoman state / Cemal Kafadar.
p. cm.
Includes bibliographical references and index.
ISBN 0-520-20600-2 (pbk. : alk. paper)
1. Turkey—History—Ottoman Empire, 1288–1918. 2. Turkey—History—Ottoman Empire, 1288–1918—Historiography. I. Title.
DR486.K34 1995
956.1'0072—dc20 94-21024

Printed in the United States of America

08 07 06 05 04 03 02
10 9 8 7 6 5 4 3

The paper used in this publication meets the minimum requirements of ANSI/NISO Z39.48-1992 (R 1997) (*Permanence of Paper*). ♾

bana okumayı sevdiren, sonra bu işi
abarttığımı araya giren gurbete rağmen
hiçbir zaman yüzüme vurmayan

Anneme ve Babama / To My Parents

Calabım bir şâr yaratmış
İki cihan âresinde
Bakıcak dîdar görünür
Ol şârın kenâresinde

Nâgihân ol şâre vardım
Anı ben yapılır gördüm
Ben dahı bile yapıldım
Taş ü toprak âresinde
Hacı Bayram Velî (d. 1429–30)

My Lord has created a city
In between two worlds.
One sees the beloved if one looks
At the edge of that city.

I came upon that city
And saw it being built.
I too was built with it
Amidst stone and earth.

Contents

PREFACE xi

CHRONOLOGY xvii

Introduction 1

Background and Overview 1
Identity and Influence in the History of Nations 19

1
The Moderns 29

The Rise of the Ottoman State in Modern Historiography 29
The Wittek Thesis and Its Critics 47

2
The Sources 60

Gaza and Gazis in the Frontier Narratives of Medieval Anatolia 62
The Chronicles of the House of Osman and Their Flavor: Onion or Garlic? 90

3
The Ottomans: The Construction of the Ottoman State 118

Strategizing for Alliances and Conflicts: The Early Beglik 122
Into the Limelight and the Rise of Tensions 138

Epilogue: The Creation of an Imperial Political Technology and Ideology 151

LIST OF ABBREVIATIONS 155

NOTES 157

SELECTED BIBLIOGRAPHY 193

INDEX 209

Preface

After decades of relative consensus and silence on the issue, the rise of the Ottomans, who established one of the longest-lived (ca. 1300–1922), yet least studied or understood, dynastic states in world history, is back on the agenda of historians as an open question. Until the twentieth century, no attempt was made to delineate the underlying factors or causes (in the postpositivist sense of the term) behind the fascinating development of the political enterprise headed by a certain ʿOṣmān in the western Anatolian marches of the late thirteenth century into a centralized and self-consciously imperial state under the House of ʿOṣmān in a few generations. The former occupied a tiny frontier outpost between the worlds of Islam and Byzantium, not only physically but also politically and culturally beyond the pale of established orders in either world; the latter, upon conquering Constantinople in 1453, represented itself as heir to the Eastern Roman Empire and leader of the Muslim world. Historians basically reiterated the legendary accounts received from frontier narratives that were first written down in the latter part of the fifteenth century—a century and a half later than the appearance in the historical record of ʿOṣmān (d. 1324?), the eponymous founder of the dynasty. With a controversial book in 1916, Herbert A. Gibbons initiated debate on the rise of Ottoman power, and this debate continued until the publication of two influential works in the 1930s by Fuat Köprülü and Paul Wittek.[1]

With these works, the gates of independent reasoning were closed, as it were. Wittek's "*ġazā* thesis" in particular—the thesis that assigned a crucial role to the spirit of ġazā ("Holy War ideology" in his unfortunate translation), which he claimed was prevalent among the early Ottomans—soon became textbook orthodoxy. This is not to say that there were no important studies whose coverage included that period in the context of broad developments in late Byzantine or medieval Turkish history. Except for a few cases that made no ripples, however, no direct discussion of the particular topic took place and no new hypotheses were presented until a flurry of publications in the 1980s took issue with the received wisdom, particularly on the basis of perceived contradictions between the ġazā thesis and early Ottoman behavior displaying inclusiveness and latitudinarianism. This book grew partly out of the author's joy in seeing a fascinating problem reincluded in the agenda of historians and partly out of his discomfort with some of the directions taken in these new works.

The decline and comeback of the topic parallels broad trends in world historiography and in Ottomanist scholarship. The waning of interest in the question coincided with the opening of the Ottoman archives to scholarly study and the ensuing fascination with archival research. For one thing, there is a phenomenal quantitative difference between the extant materials related to early Ottoman history and those pertaining to the sixteenth century and beyond. There is still not one authentic written document known from the time of 'Os̱mān, and there are not many from the fourteenth century altogether. Furthermore, the nature of the documents from later periods is such as to enable scholars to conduct social and economic studies of rare quantitative precision, while the prearchival sources are mostly legends, hagiographies, and annalistic chronicles. Naturally, this quality of the material coincided so well with the rising prestige of quantification-based social and economic history worldwide that the investigation of Ottoman "origins" lost its appeal, just as did historical linguistics (philology), which was among the most cherished areas of expertise for the generation of Wittek and Köprülü. Although the field of Ottoman studies did not and still is often reluctant to directly engage in a theoretical discourse, the victory of structure over progression of events indirectly made its impact on Ottomanists.[2]

However, more recent intellectual currents reveal heightened concern with issues like "origins," "genealogy," and "sequentiality of events" once again, though in a new manner. An example of this new spirit may be the popularity and esteem of Umberto Eco's *Name of the Rose* in the 1980s. I am not referring to the historical setting and flavor provided by a scholarly concern with authenticity but something more intrinsic to the novel: its plot. After all, had William of Baskerville, the detective-monk, inquired into the succession of head librarians in the abbey, had he pursued, as a traditional historian would have, the succession of events related to the library in chronological order, he would have discovered much sooner that Jorge of Burgos should have been the prime suspect.[3]

This trend is accompanied by a renewed interest in narrative sources, which were once seen as inferior to quantifiable records. Turning the tables around, historians now indulge in the application of literary criticism or narratological analysis to archival documents, to even such dry cases as census registers, which have been seen as hardly more than data banks in previous history-writing.[4]

It is not merely in the context of developments in world historiography that we should situate trends in Ottoman studies. For one thing, the two are hardly ever synchronized, since Ottomanists are often in the role of belated followers rather than innovators or immediate participants. Besides, history-writing, like any other kind of writing, needs to be viewed through its entanglements in the sociocultural and ideological context of its time and stands at a particular moment of an evolved intellectual/scholarly tradition. As the late classicist Sir Moses Finley has demonstrated in his *Ancient Slavery and Modern Ideology,* the temporal distance of the period under investigation does not necessarily provide it with immunity against the influence of present-day concerns.[5]

In Ottoman and Turkish studies, too, it is certainly true that the intensity of the ideological dimension in historical investigation does not diminish as one moves back in time. In fact, the period of Turkish migrations into and invasions of Anatolia and the eventual establishment of Ottoman power over what had been the Byzantine Empire must be one of the most ideologically laden, for reasons I hope will become apparent to the readers of this book. It may be due partly to such an awareness that lately more studies are published on the historiography of that formative period (pre- and early Ottoman) than straight histories. In fact the ongoing assessment of the ġazā thesis can be seen as part of the same historiographic stocktaking.[6]

This book itself is partly an extended historiographic essay on the rise of the Ottoman state and on the treatment of this theme in historical scholarship. It is also an attempt to develop, through this dialogue with Ottomanist scholarship, a new appraisal of the medieval Anatolian frontier setting, with its peculiar social and cultural dynamics, which enabled the emergence of Ottoman power and thus played a major role in shaping the destinies of southwestern Asia and southeastern Europe from the fourteenth to the twentieth century.

Transliteration is the perennial problem of historical scholarship in different branches of Islamic studies. Materials in pre-modern Turkish rendered in the Arabic script, as in almost all the sources used in this study, are particularly difficult to standardize, and any transliteration system is bound to be esthetically displeasing. But the shortcut of using modern spelling throughout feels anachronistic and thus even more displeasing to this author.

Still, I have decided to give place names (e.g., Konya) as well as the names of principalities (e.g., Karaman) and states (e.g., Abbasid) in their modern forms since that might make it easier to look them up in geographical and historical atlases or reference works. Words that appear in English dictionaries (such as sultan, kadi) are not transliterated unless they appear as part of an individual's name.

Otherwise, all individual names and technical vocabulary are transliterated according to a slightly modified version of the system used in the *Encyclopedia of Islam*. The transliteration of Arabic compound names is simplified when used in reference to the Turkish-speaking Anatolian/Balkan world: hence, Burhāneddīn instead of Burhān al-Dīn.

Like many other books, this one took shape as a long adventure for its author. Along the way, I was fortunate to receive comments, guidance, encouragement, or admonition from a number of friends and colleagues, among whom it is a pleasure to mention Peter Brown, George Dedes, Suraiya Faroqhi, Jane Hathaway, Halil İnalcık, Ahmet Karamustafa, Ahmet Kuyaş, Joshua Landis, Roy Mottahedeh, Gülru Necipoğlu, Nevra Necipoğlu, İrvin Schick, Ruşen Sezer, Şinasi Tekin, İsenbike Togan, and Elizabeth Zachariadou. I am particularly grateful to Cornell Fleischer, whose thorough reading of and thoughtful commentary on the manuscript were of immense help in giving the book its final shape. They are probably unaware how much they contributed to the development of this book through not only intentional interventions but also casual remarks or general observations that I appropriated, and possibly twisted, to my own ends. Plunder, as I hope the readers of this book will come to agree, can coexist in harmony with the assumption, or presumption, of serving some good cause in the end.

The critical tone of my historiographic evaluations should not obliterate the profound indebtedness I feel toward all those scholars whose works on the rise of the Ottoman state are surveyed here. Their findings and ideas, even when I disagreed with them, opened many pleasant vistas and doors for me.

I also appreciate having had the chance to try out some earlier and partial versions of my arguments on audiences whose responses enabled me to focus on formulations that needed to be refined and paths that needed to be abandoned. Such opportunities were provided at the Brown Bag Lunch series of Princeton University's Near Eastern Studies Department, at Washington University in Saint Louis, at the Istanbul center of the American Research Institute in Turkey, and at the Murat Sarıca Library workshop series in Istanbul.

Chronology

1071 The Battle of Mantzikert: Seljuks defeat Byzantine army; the first great wave of Turkish migrations into Asia Minor.

1176 The Battle of Myriokephalon: Seljuks of Rūm defeat Byzantine army.

1177 Dānişmendids subdued by the Seljuks of Rūm.

1204 The Fourth Crusade: Latins occupy Constantinople; Lascarids start to rule in Nicaea; Comneni start to rule in Trebizond.

1220–37 The reign of 'Alā' üddīn Keyḳūbād, peak of Seljuk control in Asia Minor.

1221 Shihāb ad-dīn 'Umar al-Suhrawardī brings insignia of *futuwwa,* sent by the caliph, from Baghdad to Konya.

1220s–30s Migrations from central Asia and Iran to Asia Minor due to Chingisid conquests; the ancestors of 'Oṣmān arrive in Anatolia according to some Ottoman sources.

1239–41 The Baba'ī Revolt of the Türkmen, led by Baba Ilyās and followers, crushed by the Konya government.

1243 The Battle of Kösedağ: Mongol armies defeat Seljuks of Rūm and render them into vassals.

1261 Byzantine capital moves from Nicaea back to Constantinople.

1276–77 Baybars leads Mamluk forces into Asia Minor.

1277 Mongols (Ilkhanids) take direct control of Asia Minor.

1298 The revolt of Sülemish against Mongol administration in Anatolia; seems to have allowed frontier lords to undertake independent action.

1298–1301 Likely dates of earliest conquests (Bilecik, Yarhisar, etc.) by 'Oṣmān.

1301	The Battle of Bapheus; ʿOsmān defeats a Byzantine contingent.
1304	Catalan mercenaries deployed by the Byzantine Empire against Turks (including the Ottomans) in Asia Minor.
1312	Ulu Cami built in Birgi by Aydınoğlu Meḥmed.
1324	The date of the earliest extant Ottoman document accepted as genuine: Orḫān is referred to as Şücāʿüddīn, "Champion of the Faith."
1326	Bursa conquered.
1331	Iznik (Nicaea) conquered.
1331?	The first Ottoman *medrese* (college) established (in Iznik).
ca. 1332	Ibn Baṭṭūṭa travels in Anatolia.
1337	Raiders from the Karasi and Ottoman principalities separately engaged in Thrace.
1337	Izmit (Nicomedia) conquered.
1337	The date on an inscription in Bursa that refers to Orḫān as *gazi;* authenticity and meaning controversial.
1341	The death of Emperor Andronikos III; beginning of civil war in Byzantium.
1344–46	Help sought by different factions from the Ottoman, Karasi, and Aydınoğlu principalities; Orḫān marries the daughter of John Kantakouzenos; Karasioğlu Süleymān marries the daughter of Batatzes. Karasi principality subdued and annexed.
1347	Kantakouzenos enters Constantinople and declares himself (co-)emperor.
1348, 1350, 1352	Kantakouzenos calls on Ottoman forces to be deployed in Thrace on his behalf.
1352	First Ottoman acquisition in Thrace: Tzympe.
1354	Kallipolis (Gelibolu) falls to the Ottomans following an earthquake.
1354	Gregory Palamas, archbishop of Thessaloniki, captured by the Ottomans, spends time in the emirate; his writings constitute important source on cultural life among early Ottomans.
1357	Prince Süleymān, Orḫān's son and commander of Thracian conquests according to Ottoman traditions, dies in accident.
1359 or 1361	Dhidhimoteichon (Dimetoka) conquered (by Ḥācī İlbegi).
1362	Orḫān dies, and Murād I succeeds him.
1366	Gelibolu lost to the Ottomans.
1361 or 1369	Dates suggested for the conquest of Edirne.
1371	The (Sırpsındığı) Battle by the River Maritsa: Serbian forces ambushed (by Murād's forces in one tradition, single-handedly by Ḥācī İlbegi in another).

1376 or 1377 Gelibolu recaptured.

1383–87 Suggested as the latest date by which point the imposition of *devshirme* had been initiated.

1385 or 1386 Nish conquered; Serbian king reduced to vassalage according to Ottoman tradition.

1389 The Battle of Kosovo; Ottoman victory over the Serbs, but with many losses; Murād I dies and is succeeded by Bāyezīd I.

1395? Sermon by the archbishop of Thessaloniki that includes the earliest known reference to the *devshirme* (which indicates that it had been practiced for some time).

1396 The Battle of Nicopolis (Niğbolu), in which Bāyezīd I defeats crusading army.

1402 The Battle of Ankara; Timur defeats Bāyezīd I.

1402–13 The Interregnum: Ottoman throne contested among brothers who rule over different parts of the realm.

1403 Süleymān Çelebi, Bāyezīd's eldest son, signs treaty with the Byzantine emperor ceding land.

1413 Meḥmed Çelebi ends up winner of internecine strife; Ottoman realm reunited.

1416 Civil war due to uprising led by Prince Muṣṭafā, a surviving son of Bāyezīd (or a pretender).

1416 The revolt of Sheikh Bedreddīn's followers crushed and Bedreddīn executed.

1421–22 The accession of Murād II, followed by rebellions of an uncle and a brother.

1430 Thessaloniki (Selanik) conquered.

1443 Army led by Janos Hunyadi descends deep into the Ottoman realm in autumn, is forced to return after the battle by the Zlatitsa Pass, where both sides suffer great losses.

1444 Murād II abdicates in favor of his son Meḥmed II; crusading army arrives in the Balkans; Murād, asked to lead the Ottoman forces again, triumphs in the Battle of Varna, returns to self-retirement.

1446 A Janissary revolt culminates in Murād II's return to the throne.

1451 Murād II dies; Meḥmed II's (second) reign begins.

1453 Constantinople (Istanbul) conquered.

1456 Unsuccessful siege of Belgrade.

1461 Trebizond (Trabzon) conquered; end of Comneni rule.

Regnal Years of Ottoman Begs and Sultans

ʿOs̱mān	?–1324?
Orḫān	1324–62
Murād I	1362–89
Bāyezīd I (the Thunderbolt)	1389–1402
Meḥmed I (Çelebi or Kyritzes)	1413–21
Murād II	1421–44 and 1446–51
Meḥmed II (the Conqueror)	1444–46 and 1451–81
Bāyezīd II	1481–1512

Introduction

Background and Overview

Osman is to the Ottomans what Romulus is to the Romans: the eponymous founding figure of a remarkably successful political community in a land where he was not, according to the testimony of family chronicles, one of the indigenous people. And if the Roman state evolved from a peripheral area to represent the center of the Graeco-Roman civilization, whose realm it vigorously expanded, so the Ottoman state rose from a small chieftainship at the edges of the abode of Islam eventually to become the supreme power within a much enlarged Islamdom. Once they came to rule, the Ottomans, like the Romans, gained a reputation as better administrators and warriors, even if less subtle minds, than the former representatives of their civilizations; they possessed less taste for philosophical finesse perhaps but had greater success in creating and deploying technologies of power. The "Romanesque" quality of the Ottoman political tradition has been noted before and was expressed recently by an eminent scholar of the Islamic Middle East: "The Ottoman empire . . . was a new and unique creation, but in a sense it also marked the culmination of the whole history of Muslim political societies. The Ottoman Turks may be called the Romans of the Muslim world."[1]

They were indeed called just that when they, like various other peoples of medieval Asia Minor, were referred to as Rūmī, that is, those of the lands of (Eastern) Rome.[2] This was a primarily geographic appellation, indicating basically where those people lived, but it did not escape the attention of geographers and travelers that the Turco-Muslim populations of Rūm, a frontier region from the point of view of the central lands of Islam, had their own peculiar ways that distinguished them from both the rest of the Muslim world and from other Turks. Namely, being a Rūmī Turk also implied belonging to a newly emerging regional configuration of Islamic civilization that was on the one hand developing its own habitus in a new land and on the other engaged in a competition to establish its political hegemony over a rival religio-civilizational orientation. The proto-Ottomans, of whom we know nothing with certainty before the turn of the fourteenth century, were a tiny and insignificant part of this new configuration at first but their descendants and followers eventually came to dominate it and to shape it toward the creation of a new imperial order under their rule.

According to most historical traditions, the immediate ancestors of Osman arrived in Anatolia with the second great wave of Turkish migrations from central Asia, which took place in the wake of the Chingisid onslaught in the early thirteenth century. Once in Anatolia, they would have encountered a variety of Turkish-speaking communities — some in urban centers, some settled down to agriculture, but the majority engaged in pastoral nomadism like Osman's ancestors, most but not all of them speaking the Oğuz dialect, most but not all of them Muslim, and even then divided into communities that understood different things about being Muslim — living in a complex ethnoreligious mosaic that included Christian and non-Turkish-speaking Muslim communities (especially Arab, Kurdish, and Persian).

The earlier wave, the tail end of the *Völkerwanderungen* in a way, had occurred in the eleventh century when large numbers of Turkish tribes, belonging primarily to the Oğuz dialect group and to the Oğuzid idiom of Inner Asian political discourse, crossed the Oxus and moved toward western Asia. While the Seljuk family from among these tribes soon became involved in politics at the highest levels in Baghdad and ended up as a dynasty that held the sultanate, many tribes moved further west and piled along the eastern borders of the Byzantine Empire. Their incursions into Asia Minor were independent of and at least occasionally contradictory to the will of the Seljuk sultanate.

The Byzantine Empire had faced a similar and at first more threatening pressure from a more southerly direction in the seventh century with the appearance of Arab-Muslim armies. While raids and counterraids continued to rage in the next few centuries, however, these were relatively localized in a fluid frontier zone that developed in southeastern Anatolia with its own borderland institutions, heroes, traditions, and lore. The Turkish-speaking settlers and conquerors of the later medieval era were to inherit a good deal of those traditions from both the Muslim and the Christian sides.

In any case, ongoing friction in eastern Anatolia in the eleventh century led to the fateful encounter of the Seljuk and Byzantine armies in Mantzikert in 1071, the same year that the Eastern Roman Empire lost Bari, its last possession in the Italian peninsula, to other tribal warrior bands led by the Normans. The Byzantine defeat at Mantzikert was to be followed by deeper and more frequent raids or plain migration by Türkmen tribes into Asia Minor. The political landscape of the peninsula started to change immediately and was not to fully stabilize for four centuries, until the Ottomans established unitary rule over it in the latter part of the fifteenth century.[3] Before the end of the eleventh century, most of Anatolia was divided up among petty potentates led by Turkish warriors, Armenian princes, Byzantine commanders, and Frankish knights arriving with the First Crusade (1096–99). The political configuration of the peninsula kept changing through mostly short-lived successes of different adventurers who were ready to enter into all sorts of holy and unholy alliances with others who were not necessarily of the same religious or ethnic background. Many an aspiring warrior seems to have enjoyed, to paraphrase Andy Warhol, fifteen days to fifteen years of glory before he disappeared or was sucked into the sphere of influence of a momentarily mightier one. The Byzantine Empire still held the coastline and some connected areas inland, especially after Çaka Beg, who was based in the Aegean, was murdered (in 1093, with the help of the Seljuk ruler) and the crusaders recaptured Nicaea from the Seljuks of Rūm for the empire (1097).

Among Turco-Muslims, who were largely restricted to the inner plateau after some very early excursions to the coastal areas and who were replenished by continued migrations of Türkmen tribes, two powers were able to acquire prominence and enjoy some longevity. An offshoot of the Seljuk family and the House of Dānişmend competed for the ultimate leadership of the Muslims of Anatolia for nearly a century. Melik Dānişmend, whose gests were to be woven into the epic cycle of Anatolian Muslims, and his family seem to have cared less for state building than for what they did better than anyone else for a while: namely, capturing towns and undertaking daring raids that brought them tremendous prestige. The Seljuks of Rūm, on the other hand, were keen to emulate more stable and structured modes of governing; they were particularly successful in that task after establishing Konya (ancient Iconium) as their capital during the reign of Mesʿūd I (r. 1118–55). The often violent competition between the Dānişmendids and the Seljuks of Rūm, both of whom sought the alliance of the Byzantine emperor or local Christian or Muslim powers when it seemed expedient, was ultimately resolved in 1177 in favor of the latter, who captured their rivals' last major holding, Malatya, and decisively reduced them to vassalage.

This feat was accomplished only one year after another Seljuk victory, this one over Byzantine imperial armies in Myriokephalon (1176). This was, in the words of one of the most prominent scholars of medieval Anatolia, "after an interval of a century, a replica of Mantzikert, which showed that henceforward there existed a Turkey which could never be further assimilated."[4] Although the word "Turchia" indeed appeared in Latin geographic designations in the twelfth century, from the point of view of the Turkish-speaking populations and polities of the area, there was no Turkey, either as a geographical or as a political entity, until the end of World War I, when the European designation was finally accepted by the locals themselves. Instead, there was a changing set of competing political enterprises, many of which were led by Turkish-speaking warrior elites but which were never organized along ethnic lines or with an eye to eventual ethnic unity. The land was known as the land of Rūm, and its people were divided into different communities of religious, linguistic, or political affiliation. The Ottoman ruling class eventually emerged as a combination of Muslims (some by conversion) who spoke Turkish (though not necessarily as a native tongue), affiliated (some voluntarily and some involuntarily) with the dynastic state under the rule of the House of Osman. And "Turk" was only one, and not necessarily a favored one, of the "ethnicities" ruled by that class.

With their victories in Myriokephalon and Malatya behind them, the Seljuks looked like they had accomplished, "from the Byzantine territories in the West almost to the further limits of the East, the political unity of Asia Minor."[5] But to a student of the later and much more solid Ottoman state, like this author, the rule of the Seljuks of Rūm in any period seems too fragile and ephemeral to be considered real political unity. All the major fault lines of those medieval Turkic states, built around the energies of tribal forces and ambitious warrior chieftains, were at work in the sultanate of the Anatolian Seljuks: there were many frontier zones of various sizes where the administrative apparatus hardly reached; there were many tribal groups that were not controlled; there were many ambitious warriors, some of them possibly made by the Seljuks, ready to imagine themselves independent of Seljuk authority; and when two or three of these came together, as they frequently did, they were able to shake, if not dissolve, state power. Finally, the Seljuks of Rūm also continued the practice of dividing up their land among the heirs of the dynast; the same Seljuk sultan who won the two victories mentioned above carved his realm into eleven pieces for his nine sons, a brother, and a nephew. The realm could still remain united in principle, under the leadership of a "senior partner" recognized by the others, but it proved only a matter of time before some of the heirs found support among Türkmen tribes or warrior bands, and rival foci of power emerged. As we shall discuss in later chapters, the Ottomans, as if or perhaps because they were good students of history, and under different conditions no doubt, proved themselves much more successful in confronting these fault lines and eventually steering their course clear of them on the way to creating one of the most durable states in history.

In all fairness to the Anatolian Seljuks, it must be admitted that they were approaching a firm consolidation of their power in the first four decades of the thirteenth century, and that their ultimate failure is closely related to an unforeseen external factor: the invincible Mongol armies. Even before the Mongols, however, a Türkmen rebellion under the leadership of Baba Ilyās and his followers presented a severe challenge to Seljuk authority between 1239 and 1241. It seems that the plight of the Türkmen tribes was due, among other things, to the squeeze for land that arose with the second big wave of migrations, which is said, as was mentioned above, in most sources to have brought the tribe of Osman's grandparents into Anatolia.[6] With the Seljuk defeat by the Mongol armies in Kösedağ (central Anatolia) in 1243, the tension-ridden pendulum of centripetal and centrifugal tendencies started to swing once again in favor of the latter. The political landscape was eventually, especially after the Mongols sent soldiers and horses to be fed in the name of establishing direct control over Anatolia (1277), thrown into turmoil with various forces waging a life-and-death struggle in a period of extreme violence and disarray. It is probably no coincidence that Yūnus Emre, *the* classical poet of the newly forged Anatolian Turkish dialect, emerged in that context and produced a corpus of poems that are distinguished by the profundity with which they looked death right in the eye. In any case, continued political disarray and demographic pressure pushed many Turkish tribes and warriors further into western Anatolia, especially since the Byzantine capital was moved back to Constantinople in 1261 after having been seated in Nicaea since 1204 (the Fourth Crusade) and having brought heightened security and prosperity to the area for half a century or so. Before the end of the thirteenth century, endemic political fragmentation had led to the emergence of numerous small chiefdoms and relatively autonomous tribal domains in various parts of Anatolia.

The political turbulences and human catastrophes of the thirteenth century should not prevent us from observing the tremendous possibilities unleashed by an unprecedented "globalization" of the Eurasian economy thanks, in good part, to the Chingisid conquests and the pax mongolica. It is for good reason that it has become a commonplace to refer to the travels of Marco Polo when speaking of the Chingisids. There were signs even before Chingis that Asia Minor, once the jewel in Byzantium's crown and then having suffered a series of depredations, had regained sufficient stability to serve as a long-distance trade link (along a North-South as well as an East-West axis) and to benefit from the new commercial potential created by the mixed economies of urban, agrarian, and pastoralist populations. The outburst of caravanserai building activity, the primary area of architectural patronage by the Seljuk elite, was initiated in the late twelfth century and was to increase its tempo no matter what the nature of political turbulences. The early thirteenth-century acquisition of the port towns of Sinop (by the Black Sea) and Alanya (by the Mediterranean) brought the Seljuk system and the Turco-Muslim-dominated economies of Anatolia that it controlled at the time into direct touch with the Levantine sea trade. By the end of that century, more than one hundred caravanserais in the peninsula provided lodging and protection to merchants (and other travellers).[7]

It is revealing, for instance, that what is no more than a remote backwater in modern Turkey, an obscure plateau between Kayseri and Maraş, once entertained a lively international fair where Middle Eastern, Asian, and European merchants exchanged commodities like silk textiles, furs, and horses. True, the fair does not seem to have survived long into the era of Mongol Ilkhanid direct rule, but trade is not known to have suffered in general. The chiefdoms that emerged in western Anatolia, where even Mongol power could hardly reach, to some extent built their power on raids and pillaging, but the western Anatolian coastline was integrated into a brisk Levantine trade around 1300, and the chiefs were signing commercial treaties with the likes of Venice in the early fourteenth century.[8] In fact, fragmentation and the emergence of small local powers may well have increased the possibility for a more local redistribution of resources that would otherwise have been siphoned off to distant imperial capitals.

One of those small chieftains, situated in the northwest in what was still partly Byzantine Bithynia, belonged to the clan of a certain Osman. He belonged to an exceptional generation (or two) of creative minds and social organizers who, either personally through their deeds or through their legacy as it was constructed and acted upon by followers, became the pivotal figures, the magnets, around whom the vibrant yet chaotic social and cultural energies of the Turco-Muslims of medieval Asia Minor ultimately found more-regular paths to flow. Since then, these figures, as embodied in the rich lore that has been built around them (whatever the relationship of such lore to their "real" or "historical" life), have represented the "classics" of western, or one might also say Roman, Turkish culture. Mevlānā Celāleddīn Rūmī and Ḥācī Bektaş Velī, for example, are the spiritual sources, respectively, of the two largest and most influential dervish orders in Ottoman lands. But their influence reaches far beyond any particular set of institutional arrangements, however large these may have been, and cuts across orders, social classes, and formal institutions. They have rather been fountainheads of broad cultural currents and sensibilities over the centuries. Yūnus Emre's appeal has been even more ecumenical, with his poetry considered by successive generations to be the most moving and unadulterated expression of piety in Anatolian Turkish; dozens of imitators tried to pass their own works off as those of Yūnus, and dozens of villages claimed to have his shrine. A certain Naṣreddīn of thirteenth-century Anatolia seems to have been at least the excuse for the creation of the lore of Nasreddin Hoca, the central figure of a corpus of proverbial jokes that now circulate, with many later embellishments of course, from the Balkans to central Asia. Aḫī Evren may be the least well known of these figures in the modern era, but his cult once played the most central role in the now defunct corporations of artisans and tradesmen, providing the basic structures and moral codes of urban economic and social life, at least for Muslims. Widely popular legends of a certain Ṣarı Ṣalṭuḳ, who also is honored at numerous burial sites, portrayed him as the most pivotal character in spreading Islam in the Balkans.

It is much more coincidental but still worthy of note that Osman was also a near contemporary of two figures, very remote from his sphere of action in thirteenth-century terms, whose descendants were to share with his house the limelight of international politics in the sixteenth century. One of these was Rudolf of Habsburg, who acquired his *Erb-*

lande in 1278. The Habsburg dynasty was to become the main competitor of the Ottomans on the central European and Mediterranean scenes, and the two states were to follow more or less the same rhythms until both disappeared as ruling houses in the aftermath of the First World War. And the other relevant member of the cohort, a much less likely candidate at that time for inclusion in our comparison here, was Sheikh Ṣafī al-Dīn (1252–1334) of Ardabil, whose own political role as a renowned Sufi may have been considerable but was primarily indirect. His legacy and the huge following of his order would eventually be shaped by late-fifteenth-century scions into the building blocks of the Safavid Empire, the main competitor of the Ottomans in the Muslim world in the early modern era.

Osman, a near contemporary of theirs, is the founder of a polity that rose over and above all its Anatolian and Balkan rivals to be eventually recognized, whether willingly or reluctantly, as the ultimate resolution of the political instability that beset Eastern Roman lands since the arrival of Turkish tribes in the eleventh century. He is a much more historical (i.e., much less legendary) character than Romulus of course. Nevertheless, he is equally emblematic of the polity that was created after his name and legacy. As Marshall Sahlins points out in his study of the stranger-king motif in Hawaiian and Indo-European political imagination, "it is not significant that the exploit may be 'merely symbolic,' since it is symbolic even when it is 'real.'"[9]

One of the most influential legends concerning Osman is the one that depicts his whole conquering and state-building enterprise as having started with an auspicious dream. Variants of this legend were retold in dozens of sources until the modern era, when the dream was dismissed in terms of its historicity but still, by some vengeful intervention of ancestral spirits perhaps, did not fail to occupy a central place in much of the debate among historians, as we shall see in the next chapter. According to one of the better-known versions, Osman was a guest in the home of a respected and well-to-do Sufi sheikh when he dreamt that

> a moon arose from the holy man's breast and came to sink in Osman Ghazi's breast. A tree then sprouted from his navel, and its shade compassed the world. Beneath this shade there were mountains, and streams flowed forth from the foot of each mountain. Some people drank from these running waters, others watered gardens, while yet others caused fountains to flow. [When Osman awoke] he went and told the story to the sheykh, who said, "Osman, my son, congratulations for the imperial office [bestowed by God] to you and your descendants, and my daughter Mālhūn shall be your wife." He married them forthwith.[10]

Thereafter, it is a story of success that culminated in the phenomenal expansion of the territories controlled by the House of Osman. In the early twentieth century, after various parts of the empire had been gobbled up or seceded throughout the eighteenth and nineteenth centuries, Ottoman forces were still defending what they considered to be their own territory in as diverse parts of the world as Macedonia, Libya, Yemen, and the Caucasus.

Phenomenal as it was, however, the Ottoman expansion was slow when compared to the empire-building conquests of some other Inner Asian/Turco-Mongol tribal formations, such as those led by Chingis and Timur, or when compared to the swift rise of the House of Seljuk to the sultanate in Baghdad, the fabled seat of the Islamic caliphate. That is probably why it was so much more durable. Relatively speaking, the Ottomans took their time building their state and it paid off. They took their time in constructing a coalition of forces and reconstructing it as it changed shape, while they were also keen on institutionalizing their political apparatus. It was a gradual and conflictual process of state building that took more than a century and a half from Osman's earliest ventures to the conquest of the Byzantine capital by his great-great-great-great-grandson, Meḥmed II (r. 1451–81), when the Ottomans can finally be said to have graduated to an imperial stage.

When Meḥmed the Conqueror visited Troy later in his reign as sultan, khan, and caesar, he seems to have been aware of the explanation of Ottoman successes by the theory, upheld by some in Europe, that Turks were, like the Romans before them, vengeful Trojans paying back the Greeks.[11] Standing at the fabled site, the sultan is reported to have inquired about "Achilles and Ajax and the rest" and then, "shaking his head a little," to have said: "It was the Greeks and Macedonians and Thessalians and Peloponnesians who ravaged this place in the past, and whose descendants have now through my efforts paid the right penalty, after a long period of years, for their injustice to us Asiatics at that time and so often in subsequent times."[12]

HISTORIOGRAPHY

Modern historiography, of course, has had little patience with dreams and legends as explanation. Still, both the dream story mentioned above and, even more so, the "true origins" of the proto-Ottomans have functioned as pivotal issues in twentieth-century discussions of Ottoman state building.

The first study devoted to the rise of the Ottoman state, published in

1916 by H. A. Gibbons, held that that successful enterprise could not have been built by "Asiatics." The dream story, contended Gibbons, though not to be taken at face value, implied that Osman and his tribe, who must have been pagan nomads of Inner Asian background, converted to Islam at some point and set out to Islamize their Christian neighbors in Byzantine Bithynia. Converts among the latter made up the majority of the proto-Ottomans and provided the expertise for setting up an administration.

In the charged environment of the early twentieth century, where nationalism was linked with racialism even more explicitly than it is today, this argument was obviously loaded. The emerging Turkish nationalism of the republican era (1923–), busily occupied with redefining the role of Turks in world history, was not entirely sympathetic to the later and "corrupt" phase of the Ottoman Empire that the Republic replaced; however, the same nationalists could not but proudly appropriate the earlier history of invasions, settlement, and state building, including the most successful case, represented by the Ottomans, that established the Turkish presence in the region.

In the formulation of M. F. Köprülü, the leading Turkish historian of his generation, who elaborated his views in the 1930s and framed them partly as a response to Gibbons, the military-political expansion of medieval Anatolian frontiers was primarily due to the demographic pressure of Turkish tribes fleeing the Chingisid armies. According to Köprülü, Osman's immediate entourage consisted of members of his tribe, who must have been of common descent as later Ottoman rhetoric claimed. As they set out to carve themselves a body politic, their numbers were replenished, on the one hand, by other Turkish elements of the same region and, on the other, by experienced representatives of the hinterland's sophisticated Turco-Muslim political-administrative culture. A number of conversions took place, but the Ottoman state was essentially a Turkish state; it was built by Turks, and almost all elements of Ottoman political culture can be explained by reference to their Turco-Muslim heritage deriving from central Asia and the Middle East. Tribal and ethnic cohesion as well as a sophisticated institutional legacy enabled the building of a state out of demographic pressure in a relative political void. Köprülü's vision was hailed and continues to serve as a building block of Turkish national historiography.

It was Paul Wittek's theory, however, formulated in the 1930s and partly as a response to Köprülü, that was to gain international recognition as the most convincing account of Ottoman success. Wittek found the rhetoric of tribalism unconvincing; nor did he dwell on the question of ethnicity as such, though he underlined continuities in Turco-Muslim culture without failing to note the occurrence of conversions and Christian-Muslim cooperation in some passages. For him, what fueled the energies of the early Ottoman conquerors was essentially their commitment to *gaza,* an "ideology of Holy War" in the name of Islam. Ottoman power was built on that commitment, as expressed in an inscription erected in Bursa in 1337, which referred to Osman's son as a "gazi, son of gazi." Wittek found the same spirit in the earliest Ottoman histories, none of which, however, dates from before the fifteenth century. While a shared ethos provided warriors who banded together with cohesion and drive, the realm they brought under their control was organized according to the administrative experiences of scholars and bureaucrats from the Islamic cultural centers. There was some tension between the two elements because the gazis belonged to a heterodox frontier culture; over time, orthodoxy prevailed as the Ottomans established a stable administration. Wittek's formulation, which has much in common with Köprülü's but avoids the ethnicist controversy and seems to place singular emphasis on religious motivation as the root cause of Ottoman power, was widely accepted and recycled in the pithy formula of "the gaza thesis."

Lawrence Stone, historian of early modern England, has described the fate of historical theses in terms of a tongue-in-cheek quasi-Hegelian spiral of generational cycles.[13] The dominant view of one generation is turned on its head by the next but is then reclaimed, hopefully in an improved version, by the next. It may be due to the ambiguous nature of "generation" as an analytical concept or the backwardness of Ottoman studies that the beat seems to have skipped a generation or two with respect to the gaza thesis, which was formulated in the 1930s. Alternative or supplementary explanations were occasionally aired in more-general studies, but there was no lively debate producing new research and ideas—until, that is, the 1980s, when many voices were raised, independently of each other, against the Wittek thesis.

The main tenor of those voices reflected a dissatisfaction with an explanation that put so much emphasis on "Holy War ideology" when early Ottoman behavior, it was claimed, displayed heterodoxy vis-à-vis Islam and accommodation vis-à-vis Christian neighbors. The early Ottomans could not have been driven by the spirit of gaza, because they were neither good orthodox Muslims nor zealous exclusivist ones. Ottoman sources that speak of gaza might as well be read as representatives of a later ideology, addressing Islamized audiences by putting a respectable religious veneer on earlier actions that had been driven by pragmatic considerations such as plunder and power.

No matter how radical a departure they claimed to represent from the consensus of the former generations, however, all of these critical voices still subscribed to the essentialism of earlier historiography. Its legacy, in other words, has proven sufficiently powerful even in the hands of critics to perpetuate a dichotomous analysis that wishes to see the early Ottoman conquerors and state builders as fundamentally Turkish, tribal, and driven by pragmatism and plunder or fundamentally Muslim and driven by zeal for holy war.

It is argued in this book that early Ottoman history and the state-building process cannot be properly appreciated within the framework of such dichotomous analyses. While the identities, beliefs, values, and actions of the early Ottomans are naturally bound to constitute the basic material for analysis and explanation, they do not need to be framed in terms of ahistorical either / or propositions. Human beings display many complex and even contradictory behaviors, and it is in that very complexity that explanations for historical phenomena must be sought. To be more specific, it is argued that the recent debate over the normative "Muslimness" of the gazis obscures the historical reality of the distinctive culture and ethos of the march environment within which the Ottoman state was born. Beyond reassessing the historiography, it is my aim to reconstruct that distinctive ethos as well as the social and political environment of the marches in late medieval Anatolia in order to reach a better understanding of the rise of the Ottoman state.

PLAN AND APPROACH

This book analyzes its problem and elaborates its perspective in three layers. Chapter 1 is a discussion of modern scholarship on the rise of the Ottoman state. It introduces, in a much more detailed canvas than the sketch given above, the specific issues that have been raised and the main perspectives developed with respect to that particular theme. It is not a survey of scholarship on medieval Anatolia, the way Norman Cantor, for instance, has recently examined the history of medieval European studies as a field.[14] Rather, this chapter is only a narrowly focused treatment of history-writing on the problem of the Ottoman state's emergence. It maps the wiring, as it were, of modern historiography on that problem in order to highlight the currents of tension and the nodes that are charged; any new conceptualization or reconstruction, including that of this author, will need to be assessed in terms of such a map.

Chapter 2 presents first a survey and analysis of the sources emanating from the Turco-Muslim frontier milieux of Anatolia, legendary accounts of the lives of warriors and dervishes, in order to illuminate how the people of the frontiers conceptualized their own actions and assigned meaning to them. This is the first attempt to reach a historicized understanding of the complex of values and attitudes embodied in or related to the notion of gaza, which both Wittek and his critics were more or less content to treat in terms of its dictionary definitions. This first part of the chapter demonstrates that the frontier ethos was intricately bound up with the gaza spirit, ubiquitous in the relevant sources, but nonetheless incorporated latitudinarianism and inclusiveness.

The second part of chapter 2 turns to a close reading and comparison of certain passages in a particularly relevant body of interrelated sources: the chronicles of the House of Osman, which were at least partly based on earlier oral narratives but were not rendered into writing before the fifteenth century, the more substantive compositions not emerging until the latter decades of that century. While enmeshed in frontier legends and myths, these sources at the same time present themselves as straight histories. As such, they have by and large suffered from either an uncritical adoption as factual accounts—a naive empiricism—or a nearly wholesale dismissal as myths—a hyperempiricism. The latter attitude or an outright neglect has severely limited the use of relevant hagiographical works that also develop their own historical arguments, in terms of the parameters of that genre of course, with respect to the early Ottomans.

Methodologically, my discussion is an attempt to transcend the positivistic attitude, still dominant in Ottoman studies, that every bit of information in the sources can and must be categorized as either pure fact or fiction. More specifically, my reading of the sources reveals that representatives of different political tendencies tried to appropriate the symbolic capital embedded in claims to success as gazis in their own ways through differing historical accounts. It is established through this discussion that the pertinent hagiographies and "anonymous" calendars and chronicles are far from being the inert products of accretion of oral tradition or chance coagulation of narrative fragments but rather represent internally coherent ideological positions articulated by authorial or editorial hands. By drawing out these several historiographical strands embedded in variants, the chapter enables an understanding of the gazi milieu as a social and cultural reality that sustained political and ideological debate. It identifies the major point of tension in the early Ottoman polity between centralizing and centrifugal tendencies, which shaped its trajectory until the conquest of Constantinople, when the triumph of centralized absolutism was sealed.

Chapter 3 proceeds to the old-fashioned task of reconstruction and is intended to be neither exhaustive nor definitive. It deals selectively with aspects of the process whereby the political enterprise headed by a certain Osman in the western Anatolian marches of the late thirteenth century was shaped into a centralized state under the House of Osman in a few generations. The discussion here moves from the gaza ethos to the gazis and other social agents in that scene and aims to re-present the pre-imperial Ottoman polity as the historically contingent product of a culturally complex, socially differentiated, and politically competitive environment rather than as the necessary result of a unitary line of developmental logic. It focuses on the sociopolitical plane, with particular emphasis on locating gazi warriors and dervishes, as well as their neighbors — tribal or settled, Christian or Muslim, rural or urban — within a matrix of shifting alliances and conflicts in late medieval Anatolia.

Insofar as it is a narrative of early Ottoman history, it is a highly selective treatment, intended only to highlight the process of coalition formation and dissolution and some of the most significant steps in the institutionalization of Ottoman power along a contested path that succeeded in circumventing the fault lines of medieval Turco-Muslim polities mentioned above.[15] A brief overview is provided here for the reader who may need an introduction to the orientation of the author and to the discussion of specifics before the third chapter. It might also be worthwhile to consult the chronology of events (pp. xvii–xix) after reading this introduction.

OVERVIEW

The scene is set in terms of the political wilderness and competition that characterized western Anatolia at the end of the thirteenth century. Byzantine, Mongol-Ilkhanid, and Seljuk powers still had some control over the region, but a number of chieftains or community leaders engaged relatively freely in acts that would determine their political future. A Turco-Muslim leader with a following and a recognized realm was called a ***beg*** or ***emir***, and his competitive, expansion-oriented enterprise was called a ***beglik*** or emirate. Some local Christian lords, called *tekvur* in Turkish sources, controlled fortified or naturally protected settlements and surrounding agricultural areas that constituted raiding territory for the forces of the begs. This frontier environment also witnessed a high degree of symbiosis, physical mobility, and religious conversions that facilitated the sharing of lore (legends about earlier heroes, for instance), ideas, institutional practices, and even warriors among inclusive political formations that were at the same time steeped in the ethos of championship of the faith.

Like his competitors, Osman Beg not only undertook raids with forces under his command and carried off booty (mostly slaves and precious objects) but also constructed a set of alliances with some of his neighbors with an eye to increasing his sphere of influence. Bonds of solidarity would be formed in joint raids or through neighborly relations that included trade and intermarriage. One of Osman's wives was the daughter of a rich and respected sheikh of a dervish community; one of Osman's sons married the daughter of a tekvur. The chieftain of a Christian village near Osman's base was a scout and an ally in some early expeditions. It cannot be imagined that other begs of the frontiers failed to appreciate the value of such ties and to forge similar alliances. Cliental relations with wonder-working dervishes, who indeed worked wonders in capturing the hearts and minds of tribesfolk as well as of Christian or ex-Christian peasants through syncretism, were not the monopoly of the Ottomans. Nor were the Ottomans the only ones who could claim to be "raiders in the name of the faith." Moreover, a policy of fiscal leniency (relative to late Byzantine practices), which worked well toward gaining Christian producers as subjects, was followed not only by the Ottomans but also by their rivals. They all benefited from the military potential in the restless energies and martial skills of the nomads and adventurers who had been "going West" in search of pastureland and other opportunities since around the mid thirteenth century.

Though it is difficult to assess whether the Ottomans had any comparative advantages in the use of any of these means toward expanding their sphere of control, it must at least be noted that Osman and his followers made effective use of them. Osman's political career seems to have started during the last years of the thirteenth century and to have carried him from the leadership of a community of nomadic pastoralists to the chieftainship of a beglik after he seized a few Bithynian fortresses. One particular advantage of his beglik was its location, since this base provided its forces with relatively easy access to poorly defended Byzantine territory. Successful military expeditions brought fame and riches, which were essential in attracting more warriors and dervishes as well as scholar-bureaucrats from the centers of Islamic culture. By the time of Osman's death (1323 or 1324), his small polity had the material and organizational means to strike coins, issue endowment deeds, and use siege tactics that required much more than competency in nomadic warfare. Particularly with the conquests of Bursa (1326) and Iznik (Nicaea) (1331) under Orḫān, Osman's son, the Ottomans controlled all the major towns of Bithynia and were in a position to build lasting institutions. Some recognized scholars, such as Çandarlı Ḳara Ḫalīl (d. 1387), seem to have arrived in Ottoman lands around this time, occupied top administrative positions (judicial and vezirial), and initiated new institutional mechanisms. The first Ottoman *medrese,* or college, was established in Iznik in 1331 and started to train scholar-scribes and judges. But the Ottomans were not the only ones who undertook lucrative expeditions, and at first they were not the most renowned of the emirates. Even their location right next to Byzantine territory to the southeast of the Marmara Sea was matched by that of the Karasi emirs, who controlled the southwestern half of the region. Insofar as the extension of gazi activity into southeastern Europe constituted the next significant step in the imaginations of the begs of western Anatolia, the Karasi were in fact more favored in terms of their location and more knowledgeable in military-strategic terms. Factional strife in Byzantine imperial politics in the 1340s invited both emirates to Thracian ventures, where the Ottomans and the Karasi were called to aid the factions, respectively, of Kantakouzenos and his rivals (including Batatzes, the father-in-law of a Karasi beg). The former won, and the Ottomans overran the Karasi emirate and incorporated its experienced gazis. By 1354, Gelibolu (Kallipolis), the strongest Byzantine fort across the Dardanelles, was captured, and the gazis could now hope that their engagements in Thrace would be more than temporary. The goal of permanent control in this new territory was buttressed by the colonization of kindred populations there.

In taking charge of the raiding and settlement in Thrace, which eventually paved the way for conquests in southeastern Europe, the Ottomans gained a decisive advantage over other emirates, since this role brought not only immense prestige but also access to substantial material resources in the form of booty and tax revenues. But they soon faced the quintessential Ibn Khaldunian predicament of tribal war-band leaders–turned–state builders: namely, the loosening of the bonds of solidarity among members of the war band as the administrative mechanisms and stately pomp of imperial polities are adopted by the leaders of the successful enterprise. In other words, as the House of Osman was being transformed into a dynasty at the head of an emerging administrative network of controls, the relatively egalitarian community of gazi commanders was giving way to a widening hierarchical space between central power and subordinate begs; not all of the latter were content with this role.

The disruption of communications between Asia Minor and Thrace for a decade after 1366, when Orḫān's son Murād I (1362–89) lost control of Gelibolu, encouraged some of the gazi warlords in Thrace to imagine themselves at the head of autonomous enterprises, especially because they could claim that many of the Thracian conquests were their own achievements. Many former states in the Muslim world, as Ibn Khaldūn observed, had begun a process of disintegration at a similar stage; the nature of the challenge might differ somewhat from case to case, but the basic problem was one of dissolving cohesiveness. The Ottomans rose to the challenge, however, not only by eliminating the challengers after Gelibolu was recaptured ca.1377 by also by creating an institution of artificial kinship, the Janissary standing army, that functioned as an extension of the royal household. This institution was the centerpiece of what hereafter would be a self-consciously centralizing administrative apparatus under "sultans" from the Ottoman family.

The goal of the sultanate thereafter was to enlarge its territory on the one hand and to control fissiparous dynamics on the other. Deftly making use of divisions among feudal polities, either by carrying out fierce raids or by gaining the loyalty of local populations through fiscal concessions and/or religious propaganda and of some of the local lords through incorporation, the Ottomans rapidly extended their power in the Balkans in the final decades of the fourteenth century. Of their major rivals, the Serbian kingdom was reduced to vassalage after the Battle of Kosovo (1389), and the Bulgarian one eliminated by 1394. Keeping almost a geometric sense of centralism, the Ottomans pursued a symmetrical expansion in Anatolia and reduced some of the weaker begs — first to unequal partnership, then to vassalage, and then to incorporation as removable appointees — just as they had done to many early Bithynian allies, gazi commanders, and Balkan local lords. It should be added that the forcefulness of Ottoman expansionism was also due to their extra-political logic in targeting important routes of commerce and sites of production.

In both the subjugation of gazi emirates and the building of bureaucratic mechanisms to buttress central government control over resources, Bāyezīd I (r. 1389–1402) was widely perceived, especially among gazi circles and the dervishes close to them, to have gone too far and to have relied too heavily on the help of scholar-bureaucrats like members of the Çandarlı family. The latter were in fact seen as the arch-enemies of a nostalgically reconstructed frontier ethos devoid of all imperial trappings. The last great conquering army of Inner Asia, led by Timur (Tamerlane), was drawn into Anatolia through the pleas of the leading families of subdued emirates. In the ensuing Battle of Ankara (1402), Bāyezīd was routed when his Anatolian Muslim vassals defected to the other side and his gazi commanders abandoned the battlefield, where the sultan was left with only his Janissaries, still a small force, and Balkan Christian vassals.

The Timurid debacle did not end the Ottoman empire-building project, especially since Timur soon left Asia Minor to pursue higher ambitions as a conqueror in Asia itself, but only led to temporary confusion until the whole realm was reunited under one heir after eleven years of internecine strife among Bāyezīd's sons. The gazi warlords, most of whom were based in the Balkans, were no longer powerful enough to challenge the House of Osman, but they did play a major role in the unfolding and outcome of events as the different princes negotiated for their support. For a few decades after the Interregnum, under Meḥmed I (r. 1413–21) and Murād II (r. 1421–44, 1446–51), state-controlled expansionism and raider activity coexisted with relatively little tension, partly due to pragmatism on both sides and partly due to the great success of the expeditions in enlarging the pie of redistribution. The new modus vivendi with the gazi warlords (and with formerly independent begs of gazi emirates who had been rendered Ottoman appointees) entailed their subordination but did not totally undermine their ability to take independent action or their access to booty and glory. Centralizing and fiscal policies were not abandoned, but neither were they pursued as aggressively as under Bāyezīd I.

Starting around 1440, strains emerged again between the level of Ottoman centralization and the empire-building project. A number of Hungarian-led "anti-Turkish" leagues undertook incursions that made the Ottomans feel on the brink of losing the Balkans; internal factionalism rose to the fore between a "war party," headed by gazi warlords, and a "peace party," headed by representatives of a central administration that was still led by the Çandarlı family. With the conquest of Constantinople, however, the young sultan Meḥmed II (r. 1444–46, 1451–81), who rode on the tremendous prestige of that feat, eliminated the leaders of both factions as well as the significance of both types of forces in Ottoman politics. A newly conceived imperial project was set in motion that spelled the ultimate victory, in terms of the internal dynamics of Ottoman state building, of the centralist vision.

Identity and Influence in the History of Nations

The larger story of medieval Asia Minor, within which the early history of the Ottomans would have been but one of many analogous episodes had they not turned out to be the ones who wrote the concluding chapter, had its counterpart in Iberia. From the eleventh to the fifteenth century, in the two peninsulas at the two ends of the Mediterranean, there raged a long series of confrontations that were fought between people who considered themselves, or found their means of legitimation as, representatives of their respective religio-civilizational orientations, Islam and Christianity.

It should be pointed out that this grand clash of two world religions did not determine each and every action of each and every actor on this scene. Nor were Muslims and Christians constantly engaged, in their actions or thoughts, in a struggle against each other. Coexistence and symbiosis were possible and probably more common. Besides, even these provisos set the scene in terms of a match between two teams, that is, in terms of two clearly designated different people who lived either at peace or at war with each other. This overlooks the fact that many individuals or groups changed sides and identities. Through conversion or enslavement, one could over time "become a Turk," within limits set by social and ideological structures, as in the case of "becoming an American." Furthermore, the sides were at any given moment divided within themselves into hostile camps or polities that did not think twice about establishing alliances with camps or polities from the other side.

Nonetheless, against these complex and shifting loyalties, a larger pattern over those four centuries can be reconstructed as a competition for political hegemony between powers that saw themselves as members of different religio-civilizational orientations. The periods of fragmentation in the political life of both peninsulas in the medieval era are in fact referred to by the same term, *mulūk al-ṭavā'if,*[16] by Muslim historians (Spanish, *taifas*), who clearly saw the structural affinities. In Asia Minor, the Muslims, whose own competition was won by the Ottomans, ended that struggle with the conquest of the last remnants of sovereign Christian power, Constantinople (1453) and Trebizond (1461), only slightly before the Catholic king of Spain captured the last stronghold of Muslim power in Iberia, namely, Granada (1492). The two victors, the Ottoman Empire and Spain (after passing into the hands of the Habsburgs), were soon to lock horns over what they would deem world supremacy, basically the old Roman world and its suburbs. Perhaps it was part of the same synchrony that Süleymān the Magnificent abandoned the use of luxury items and adopted a more pious orthodox image for the sultanate at around the same time that Charles V withdrew into a monastery. Maybe the emperors were just feeling the signs of strain that would become much more obvious in the public consciousness of their empires around the end of the sixteenth century when a decline and reform discourse appeared in both.

Like the Anatolian case, the Iberian one has been an ideological quagmire of modern historiography. The best example of this can be seen in the trials and tribulations of Américo Castro (1885–1972), the Spanish historian, who had to suffer disfavor and unpopularity in his homeland for writing of the Arabo-Muslim past of the peninsula as part of the Spanish heritage.[17] This is not the place, nor the author, to discuss the nature of the Spanish heritage, but it is impossible to overlook the parallels in the historiographies that have been forged in the age of national consciousness and nation-state building. In that context, the meaning of medieval Muslim invasions has been a particularly problematic one to deal with among many nations of Eurasia.[18] It does not seem so farfetched to imagine that long periods of coexistence, with both warlike and peaceful encounters (eight centuries in Spain, four centuries of instability in Anatolia followed by five centuries under relatively stable Ottoman rule), would shape peoples and cultures on either side in profound ways, and not just in the sense of developing a sense of enmity or in the mechanical sense of "influences" as cultural commodities taken from one side to the other. Taking one's commingling with the "other" seriously in the historical reconstruction of heritages, however, seems to demand too much of national historiographies.

National historiographies (indeed modern historiography in general, to the extent that it functions as the history of nations) have tended to assume more or less sealed cultural identities of peoples (Turks, Greeks, Spaniards, Arabs, etc.) who have come into contact within the framework of a larger bipolar division of equally sealed civilizational identities (East/West, Muslim/Christian, etc.). Spain was Spanish before the

Muslims and reverted to its "Spanishness" after expelling the invaders (after eight centuries!). Greece, Bulgaria, or any other post-Ottoman state did the same in terms of national history-writing, though the situation is not always as clear-cut as in Iberia, where systematic expulsions and forced conversions followed the reconquest. In the Balkans, as in India, it remains complex because of the intertwined existence of peoples who identify with different layers of a given country's past; so long as each layer remains exclusive of other layers in historical consciousness, such identification also has the potential of turning to exclusivism ("cleansing," to invoke the most notorious recent example) in reality. In terms of history-writing, all this implies that historicizing the identities of those peoples, and thus underlining their plasticity and multiplicity over time, is taken, as was the case for Castro with respect to "Spanishness," as questioning the essence of nationhood. That, I would argue, is precisely what needs to be done in understanding the Turkish invasions of and migrations into Asia Minor and in reconstructing the formation of the Ottoman state.

Most current historiography, however, tends to operate on the basis of a "lid model" whereby at least some empires (the oriental ones?) are conceived as lids closing upon a set of ingredients (peoples) that are kept under but intact until the lid is toppled and those peoples, unchanged (unspoilt, as nationalists would like to see it), simply reenter the grand flow of history as what they once were. They may have experienced changes in terms of numbers and material realities but not in essence. Readers may also be familiar with this view from the recent example of Soviet dissolution, which was widely analyzed in terms of history beginning again for the peoples of the former USSR. But can one see the expression of Kirghiz or Belarus national identities, for instance, in terms of a reassertion? Were they not constructed to a large degree, in terms of identifying with a particularly delineated territory as homeland, for instance, during the Soviet era, which was a formative *historical* experience for all of them?

A recent publication that appeared in the most authoritative encyclopedia in the field of oriental studies takes us closer to our specific subject matter. In the lead essay to the entry on "Othmanli" (= Ottoman), "the subject peoples of the Balkans" are described as "for centuries peoples without history" until the nineteenth century.[19] Where, in this depiction, could a historian fit the Muslim Slavs and Albanians, for instance? Or, how does one deal with the movement, under Ottoman rule, of Orthodox Slavs to areas now contested in Bosnia?

The Ottoman state/identity was not a lid that closed upon already formed national identities (of Arabs, Bulgarians, Turks, etc.) only to be toppled after a few centuries when those identities reasserted themselves. Some of these identities were formed to some extent, but they were reshaped (some might say, de-formed) under the aegis of, through the structures of, in response or reaction to, the Ottoman Empire. This is not a question of Ottoman influence but of a long and formative historical experience that shaped various communities and peoples under Ottoman rule through their interaction with each other as well as with peoples and ideas from neighboring civilizations. So the establishment of Ottoman rule in southwestern Asia and southeastern Europe, even if one sees it in black-and-white terms—namely, as either a yoke or a blessing—did mean much more than a lapse in what would otherwise have been the natural flow of the history of a given set of nations. Ottoman rule *is* part of the history of various communities, some of whom were able (and some unable) to shape and imagine themselves into a nation in the modern era thanks to a "historical consciousness" of their own (real or imagined) pre-Ottoman identity on the one hand and to that long and formative historical experience mentioned above on the other.

Specific issues of policymaking often do not require recourse to a historical argument, but the deeper matrix of orientations in which policy is made is inextricably linked with issues of national, that is, historical, identity in the political culture of nation-states. "Who we are," at least in political discourse, is taken to be a major determinant of "how we should act." Such linkages ultimately bring history-writing to the political sphere since national identity is defined and redefined through a historical discourse. "Who we are" is a culmination of "who we have been." While this is valid for all nation-states to some degree or other, it is particularly pointed in some which have not resolved their identity questions as successfully as others; and this is valid for most, if not all, of the Ottoman successor states.

This is not to say that any such resolution is ever final; I do not mean that France, for instance, has defined its national identity in a decisive manner, that its historiography has comfortably removed itself from the sphere of politics, and that younger nation-states will eventually do the same. There is nothing to warrant such optimism. There are similar problems in the "mature" nation-states as well, and we are constantly reminded by the reactions in Europe and North America to the growth of the numbers of Muslims or blacks or freedom- or opportunity-seeking refugees from the Third and Second Worlds that these problems can easily become more acute in the West. The assertion of regional identities across Europe is another reminder of the fact that the relative homogeneity of modern European nation-states, which arguably served as models in much of world politics and historiography, disguises a multilayered history. It now seems that that homogeneity is in part a cultural construction, built through not only historical exigencies and certain forms of exclusivism but also a linear narrative of the story of "our true nation, one united people across time."[20]

There is no doubt, however, that the question of identity is particularly acute in Ottoman successor states, including Turkey, a relatively young nation-state, the historiographical (and thus also political) discourse of which has been the major ingredient of Ottoman studies in this century. The thrust of political ideologies runs just as deep in the historical consciousness of the other post-Ottoman nation-states of the Balkans and the Middle East. But the Turkish case is the more significant one for our purposes because of its obvious, but not necessarily to-be-taken-for-granted, centrality in Ottoman studies.

Three major issues still make up the underlying currents of tension in different national interpretations of Ottoman state building, though versions of the near consensus reached among Turkish historians in the first half of this century are accepted by international scholarship at large.[21] These issues are not necessarily discussed any more — at any rate they do not inspire many original research projects — but one can still feel the tension generated by differences of opinion on them. First is the rather racially conceived question of numbers: how many Turks came to Asia Minor, how many Anatolian Christians converted, what is the ratio of "real" Turks to converts in the composition of the later "Turkish" society under the Ottomans? Although there was heated debate on this question in the earlier part of this century, as we shall see in the next chapter, it was resolved in favor of "real" Turks.[22] National historiographic discourses could hardly accommodate a different answer, whether one considers the Ottomans to be one's own or one's enemy. Thus, a nationalist Turkish and a nationalist Greek historian might easily agree that the Ottoman state was built by Turks, while the ethnic origins of a particularly favorable character such as an artist or a "good vezir" may be disputed.

Second is the issue of dislocation and violence caused by the migrations and the invasions; like the next question, it is one of respectability. There is a tendency on the one hand to portray them as sheer violence and, on the other, to see the migratory process as rather pacific. Here, most of the Turkish historians took the position that such disruption was minimal, while the nationalisms that defined themselves as liberation movements from the yoke of an alien people tended to emphasize the violence in the process that led to the rise of Ottoman power.[23] It is not only the desire to cater to the pacific values of the modern world that compels historians to magnify the level of violent power displayed by the other side or to reduce that displayed by their own. Some macho bravado is also involved here. Namely, it is also to portray defeat as due to the numerousness and violence of the enemy's military forces or to protect victory from being attributed to sheer numbers and brute power (rather than bravery, values, faith, tactics, etc.).

Whatever the motives, there are two main strategies here that can be mixed in varying degrees: to argue that the expansion was very or only minimally violent, or to argue that the rule of the conquerors or of the former regime was more tyrannical than the other and made violence legitimate. Thus Turkish historians, for instance, have gladly borrowed and chosen to focus on the modern European image of a "degenerate" Byzantium and of a rapacious feudalism before the Ottoman order: some violence may have been exerted but only for a good cause in the end.[24]

Third is the issue of influence whereby an otherwise hostile national tradition might recognize the good things in its foe only to then "demonstrate" that the good thing is actually of one's own but taken over by the other as an "influence." Here the burning issue was, and to some extent still is, whether and how much the Ottomans (read Turks) were influenced by the Byzantines (read Greeks), though on this issue the "Turkish consensus" is most deeply respected in the international scholarly community. As we shall see in the next chapter, the creation of the Ottoman administrative apparatus has been particularly controversial in this regard, with some historians arguing that it was all based on Byzantine models and others that the Ottomans could find all they needed in their Turco-Muslim heritage. In terms of broader cultural exchange or "lifestyles," too, various sides of nationalist polemics have tended to see the influence of their side in, say, shared musical or culinary practices. The problem with both sides of this debate stems partly from their adherence to a static notion of cultural "goods," whether one conceives of them in the realm of state building or cooking. In other words, "influence" is understood as a creative party giving one of its own "goods" to an imitating, uncreative other — a notion that needs to be recast now that historians realize influence is not possible without interaction, without a choice by the allegedly passive receiver. And even then, common cultural traits are not necessarily reducible to influence.

The issue of influence in cultural history is also skewed by its being understood in terms of a sexual act conceived as an unequal relationship. The influencer is like the one who penetrates and is proud, and the influenced is like the one who is penetrated and thus put to shame. A superior culture is naturally one that has more to be proud of in this manner. If "we" were the first ones to come up with the discovery of this (say, the dessert called baklava) and the invention of that (say, the shadow puppet theater called Karagöz) and "our" cultural possessions then infiltrated other cultures and gave birth to offspring, then "our" culture must have been superior and dominant the way a male is over a female. If you have been influenced by others, on the other hand, you have acted like a "passive" partner in intercourse; you have been "inseminated."

These are admittedly the more extreme versions of positions that are held much more moderately, if made at all explicit, by scholars who have developed a remarkable sensitivity to such issues and prefer to leave them alone. I feel, however, that we must recognize these issues as underlying currents of much of the historiographies (and of the historical consciousnesses that shape the scholars who create the historiographies) on the four centuries of turmoil and construction in Anatolia that led to the building of a world empire. I think these issues cannot be resolved as they are conceived; if there is any hope of transcending them, it is possible only through reformulating them, not through burying them.

Compared to the historiography on the rise of the Ottoman state, discussed in detail in the next chapter, that on the emergence of Norman power in medieval France does not run into the same sorts of complications, though there are striking parallels in the basic issues raised by their story. Did the Normans constitute a blood-tie society? Did they continue Carolingian practices and institutions or did they create their own?[25] These too are serious questions for the historian, but they lack the imbroglio of nationalist polemics, at least in a directly perceptible way. Had Normandy been a nation-state or a province with self-assertive Normans, the situation might have been different. Whereas, if in the questions posed above you were to replace Normans with early Ottomans, and Carolingian with Byzantine, you could have a whole range of settings for a politically charged discussion, from the corridors of a university to a coffeehouse in Istanbul or Thessaloniki. Charming as this may sound, there are drawbacks, as illustrated by the case of Petropoulos, who was persecuted under the Greek junta for, among other things, writing a book called *Ho tourkikos kaphes* ("Turkish coffee," which the junta ordered to be called "Greek coffee"). Similarly, under the Turkish junta of the early 1980s, an academician could suffer for writing about the presence of Armenian and other Christian fief-holders in the early Ottoman armies, whose existence is an undeniable fact. Such tensions may get more serious under military regimes but are not limited to them; even in "normal times," one can feel the heat generated by arguing whether Cyril and Methodius were Greek or Slavic, or by dealing with the ethnic origins of Sinān, that most accomplished of Ottoman architects who was recruited in the sixteenth century through a levy that was applied to non-Muslim subjects.

True, the majority of historians have scoffed at this sort of thing, but without directly tackling the assumption of a continuous national identity, a linear nationhood or national essence that underlies even their own nonchauvinistic historiography. If "we" (from the point of view of modern Turkish consciousness) or "the Turks" (from the point of view of non-Turkish historiography) have come on horseback from Inner Asia and established a state that replaced the Byzantine Empire of "the Greeks," it is only human that to be "one of us" (or "one of the Turks") one needs to assume, or in some cases feels compelled to "prove," that one's ancestry derives from the steppe nomads. And if one is of the Greeks, then one "knows" that one's ancestors have been oppressed by the Turks. Fortunately, such assumptions or presumptions can usually be made relatively easily at the individual level, where one slips into the role of citizen-as-member-of-the-nation (unless one is from a self-conscious minority, in which case one is a member of another "we" in a similarly linear story). It must have been rather traumatic, however, for a republican descendant of Köse Miḫal (Mikhalis the Beardless), one of the founding fathers of the Ottoman state, a Bithynian Christian who joined forces with Osman, converted, and started a minidynasty of raiders in the service of the House of Osman. The twentieth-century Turk, proud enough to take Gazimihal as his last name, at the same time felt compelled to write an article "proving" his glorious ancestor was also a Turk. In this fanciful account, Miḫal is one of those Christianized Turks employed by the Byzantines who eventually chooses to join his brethren on the right side.[26]

The essentialist trap cannot be avoided unless we, the historians, problematize the use of "the Turks" (or any other ethnonym for that matter), systematically historicize it and confront its plasticity, and study its different meanings over time and place. I certainly do not wish to imply that being a Turk or a Muslim or a Christian did not matter; for many, it was all that mattered in the grand scheme of things in the long run of the thirteenth to nineteenth centuries. In fact, individuals changed their identities presumably not only because they could but also because it mattered. Nor do I wish to imply that it is meaningless to speak of ethnic or national identities (Turks or others), but these should not be—and this is particularly clear in the case of medieval Anatolia, where religio-political affiliations and thus identities were in rapid flux—conceptualized as an original stock and descendants going through a linear series of adventures in time and, along the way, clashing with other original stocks and descendants going through similarly linear series of adventures. Historians tend to overlook the fact that (America is not the only case where) one is not necessarily born into a people; one may also become of a people, within a socially constructed dialectic of inclusions and exclusions.

It is not the purpose of this book to disentangle these questions of identity and influence embedded in varying degrees in any historical writing on the Ottomans. My purpose here is basically to problematize them before dealing with one specific era when identities were in particularly rapid flux.

We must note, however, that the issue is not an intellectual abstraction for those who consider Asia Minor their homeland and grapple with its heritage in terms of their own identity. Having grown up in a village which seems to have enjoyed continuous settlement for five millennia and where sprang up the cult of one of the Turkish colonizer-dervishes in the thirteenth century, a republican Turkish archaeologist muses that studying that village "would be a contribution to our national history since it is one of the earliest Turkish villages established in Anatolia in the 13th century," but he adds that "the cultural past of a village which has lived intertwined with the ruins of the prehistorical and the antique ages, which has not rejected those, which has appropriated and used the cave cemeteries, which has carved on its tombstones figures inspired by the wall paintings of those caves and used such figures in its embroideries, starts undoubtedly with the earliest human settlements on these lands."[27] Despite this openness to continuity at one level, the distinction between the "we who came from yonder" and "they who were here" is maintained with surgical precision. Turkish colonizers are immediately taken as the main actors when the archeologist moves to the analysis of some tombstone carvings that replicate designs seen in antique objects in the same region: "When the Turkish colonizers encountered such tombstones, they acquired and maintained the tradition." There is not even a doubt expressed that the tombstones of the "Turkish era" may have been carved by the very same people who had been producing the pre-Turkish stones, namely, by the locals who "became Turks." The liquidity and fluidity of identities in those centuries is hard to imagine in the national age.

It was not difficult for a sixteenth-century Ottoman intellectual, however, to appreciate the plasticity of identities that had gone into the making of the neo-Rūmīs:

> Those varied peoples and different types of Rumis living in the glorious days of the Ottoman dynasty, who are not [generically] separate from those tribes of Turks and Tatars . . . , are a select community and pure, pleasing people who, just as they are distinguished in the origins of their state, are singled out for their piety, cleanliness, and faith. Apart from this, most of the inhabitants of Rum are of confused ethnic origins. Among its notables there are few whose lineage does not go back to a convert to Islam . . . either on their father or their mother's side, the genealogy is traced to a filthy infidel. It is as if two different species of fruitbearing tree mingled and mated, with leaves and fruits; and the fruit of this union was large and filled with liquid, like a princely pearl. The best qualities of the progenitors were then manifested and gave distinction, either in physical beauty, or in spiritual wisdom.[28]

In that grand tableau, huge amounts of material—poetic, hagiographic, epigraphic, archeological—still await gathering and sifting. This is not the place to attempt such a tableau. It is the more modest ambition of this book to problematize the origins of the Ottoman state by engaging the historiography and thus hopefully opening early Ottoman history to wider debate. It is also my hope that some of the related questions will be taken up by future researchers to improve, alter, or disprove my suggestions.

CHAPTER I

The Moderns

If you have nothing to tell us except that one barbarian succeeded another on the banks of the Oxus and Jaxartes, what is that to us?
Voltaire, article on history, *Encyclopédie*

The Rise of the Ottoman State in Modern Historiography

Beginning in the fifteenth century, numerous historical accounts were composed, by Ottomans and others, that relate a series of events delineating the emergence and expansion of Ottoman power, but none of these would have passed Voltaire's test. From the point of view of modern historiography, they contain no explanation, no analysis of underlying causes or dynamics, and are only narratives of events in succession about successive dynasties and states. Naturally, a reader of Dumézil would be ready to trace implicit explanatory models in these sources, as literary or nonanalytical as they may seem, through an examination of their selection and ordering of events.[1] However, this would not change the fact that "the rise of the Ottoman state" was not problematized and explicit causal explanations were not sought until after the full impact of positivist and historicist thought on Ottoman studies at the turn of this century.

Ottoman histories from the earliest written works in the fifteenth century to the late imperial age tend to start off with Osman's genealogy and his dream against the backdrop of the physical and political turmoil caused by the Chingisids in western Asia. With Turks pouring into Asia Minor due to the onslaught of the Mongol armies and with Seljuk power disintegrating, a young warrior (son of so-and-so, son of so-and-so, etc.) has an auspicious dream that is read to imply the dreamer and his descendants are selected by God for rulership. There are various versions of this legend, and some attribute the dream to Ertoğrıl, Osman's father, but they all precede Osman's bid for political power and indicate that it was endowed with divine sanction. To the chroniclers and their audience, pedigree and divine sanction clearly played a crucial role in the rise of Ottoman power. These are accompanied by such personal qualities as sincere faith, righteousness, valor, and leadership.

Further, supplementary explanations could be woven into this model depending on the narrator's concerns. Just as genealogies could be reshaped or embellished through, say, remembrance of forgotten ancestors, divine blessing could easily accommodate some holy person who may be assigned intermediacy in its allocation or verification. If you wanted to make sure that you and yours got proper credit for their real or imagined contribution to Ottoman successes, you might include an episode or two to underline the nature of that contribution. In the vita of Ḥācī Bektaş, for instance, the patron saint of the Bektāşī order of dervishes, rulership is again a question of divine selection whereby God's sanction is removed from the House of Seljuk and transferred to that of Ertoğrıl.[2] However, the transfer does not take place through direct intervention by God. The news is broken by Ḥācī Bektaş, who, thanks to his *vilāyet* (proximity to God), has access to such divine secrets and power to intercede in the actual transmission of rulership. His blessing turns out to be another "factor" in the rise of Ottoman power.

In European sources, the question of origins again took up considerable space, but here the emphasis was on ethnicity or race rather than Osman's genealogy: are Turks indeed Trojans; or are they Scythians? What needed to be explained to European audiences was not so much the emergence of the Ottomans in particular but the arrival of the "Turkish menace" or "yoke" at large. Whether they were Trojans avenging Hector or Scythians out to destroy, or an Inner Asiatic people related to the Huns as it was later discovered, their superb military skills — a racial characteristic — would need to be underlined as well as the fact that they were now within the fold of Islam, thus armed with a "warlike religion." God's design, often in the form of a punishment for the sins of Christians, should not be neglected in this context.

Against this background, it is easy to understand why Samuel Johnson thought so highly of Richard Knolles (1550?–1610) as to call him "the first of historians," even though the good doctor was quick to add that the historian was "unhappy . . . in the choice of his subject." To explain the "beginning, progresse, and perpetuall felicity of this the Othoman Empire," Knolles referred to

such a rare unitie and agreement amongst them, as well in the manner of their Religion (if it be so to bee called) as in matters concerning their State (especially in all their enterprises to be taken in hand for the augmenting of their Empire) as that thereof they call themselves Islami, that is to say Men of one minde, or at peace amongst themselves; so that it is not to bee marvelled, if thereby they grow strong themselves, and dreadfull unto others. Joyne unto this their courage, . . . their frugalitie and temperatenesse in their dyet and other manner of living; their carefull observing of their antient Military Discipline; their cheerefull and almost incredible obedience unto their Princes and Sultans. . . . Whereunto may bee added the two strongest sinewes of every well governed Commonwealth; Reward propounded to the good, and Punishment threatened unto the offender; where the prize is for vertue and valour set up, and the way laid open for every common person, be he never so meanly borne, to aspire unto the greatest honours and preferments both of the Court and of the Field.[3]

Whatever the value of Knolles's explanations, however, they are clearly not targeted at the earlier phase of Ottoman history, or at the formative stages of the state, as such. This is also true of the more theoretical discourse on comparative political systems undertaken by various Renaissance European authors, such as Machiavelli and Jean Bodin, whose works must have been read by some of the authors of the abundant European historical literature on the Ottomans. It was in fact none other than Knolles who translated Bodin's *De la legislation, ou Du gouvernement politique des empires* into English just before writing his history of the Ottomans.[4] Like Knolles, the writers of comparative politics analyzed the strengths of the Ottoman system as it stood after the process of imperial construction but were not interested in that process itself. Nor is there anything specifically Ottoman in Knolles's account; all of the "factors" mentioned by him might apply to any of the Turco-Muslim polities the Ottomans competed with. Knolles was explaining the success not of the Ottomans in particular but of the "Turk"—a designation that was more or less synonymous with "Ottoman" and often also with "Muslim" among the Europeans of his age. Besides, as impressive as Knolles's precociously analytical attitude may be, it is submerged in hundreds of pages of traditional *histoire événementielle*.

This is also true for the most comprehensive and monumental narrative of Ottoman history ever written, *Die Geschichte des osmanischen Reiches* by the Viennese historian Joseph von Hammer-Purgstall (1774–1856), who represents the culmination of that tradition.[5] And it is true, though there are more than glimpses of a new historiography here, even for Nicolae Iorga (1871–1940), the Rumanian medievalist, whose neglected history of the Ottoman Empire is, on the one hand, a throwback to the mode of grand narrative with emphasis on politico-military events but, on the other, a product of the new *Kulturgeschichte*.[6] After all, he had been goaded to the task by his mentor, Lamprecht, the German historian whose anti-Rankean genetic method was meant to investigate not "how it actually was" but "how it actually came to be" (*wie es eigentlich geworden ist*). Not only was Iorga keen on underlining the significance of the Seljuk era as a formative background, but he also chose to include a nonnarrative chapter emphasizing "the military village life of the Turks" and the appeal of Ottoman administration to the Balkan peasantry by providing it protection, he argued, from seigniorial abuse.

It was not before the First World War, when the demise of the Ottoman state seemed imminent, that its emergence appeared as a specific question in historians' imagination. How was it that this state, now looking so weak and decrepit, so old-fashioned, still so oriental after many westernizing reforms, had once been so enormously successful? And the success, many realized, was not just in terms of expansion, which could be easily explained by militarism and violence. This state once ruled, without major unrest, over a huge population with a dizzying variety of religions, languages, and traditions.[7] How could some "barbarians," still nomadic at the outset of their empire-building enterprise, create such a sophisticated, even if ultimately "despotic," polity? The Ottoman patriot or Turkish nationalist would want to demonstrate, with a different wording of course, that this was not surprising, but he or she would be well aware that the question was of utmost weight for one's dignity or possibly the nation's very existence in the context of a new world order that clipped non-European empires into nation-states; these were in principle to be formed by peoples who could demonstrate through their historical experience that they were mature enough to govern themselves.

H. A. Gibbons (1880–1934), an American teaching at Robert College (Istanbul) in the 1910s, was the first to problematize and devote a monograph to the origins of the Ottoman state.[8] Pointing out that the earliest Ottoman sources—the basis for almost all speculation on the topic until then — were from the fifteenth century, he dismissed them as late fabrications. In fact, his assessment of Ottoman historiography is not very different from that of Busbecq, the Habsburg envoy to Süleymān the Magnificent (r. 1520–66). Echoing the sixteenth-century diplomat, who thought that "Turks have no idea of chronology and dates, and make a wonderful mixture of all the epochs of history," Gibbons wrote: "We must reject entirely the appreciations of Ottoman historians. None has yet arisen of his [Osman's] own people who has attempted to separate the small measure of truth from the mass of fiction that obscures the real man in the founder of the Ottoman dynasty."[9] He thus reached the conclusion that "in the absence of contemporary evidence and of unconflicting tradition, we must form our judgement of Osman wholly upon what he accomplished."[10] Oddly enough after this damning assessment, Gibbons not only used parts of the Ottoman historiographic tradition but even chose to rely on a particularly dubious element of it for his most pivotal argument.

One of his radically novel assertions was that Osman and his followers were pagan Turks living as nomadic pastoralists on the Byzantine frontier and pursuing successful predatory activities due to weakened defenses in that area. Converting to Islam at some stage of Osman's career, as the dream story implied according to Gibbons, these nomads were overtaken by a proselytizing spirit and forced many of their Christian neighbors to convert as well. The story of Osman's blessed reverie, Gibbons thought, may well have been a legend but it was meant to capture a particular moment in the young chieftain's real life, namely, his adoption of a new faith and of a politico-military career in its name.

Taking another piece of evidence from that "mass of fiction" that he otherwise deemed Ottoman histories to be, Gibbons "calculated" that the "four hundred tents" of Osman's tribe must have been joined by so many converts that the new community increased "tenfold" by this process. A new "race" was born — that of the Osmanlıs — out of the mixture of ex-pagan Turks and ex-Christian Greeks. The expansion of Osmanlı (the Turkish form of "Ottoman") power was accompanied not so much by fresh elements from the East but by more and more "defections and conversions from among the Byzantine Greeks; so, the creative force of the Ottoman Empire must not be attributed to an Asiatic people but to European" elements.[11]

This was after all a time when a historian did not even feel the need to be apologetic for making remarks like the following: "The government and the ruling classes of the Ottoman Empire are negatively rather than positively evil. There is nothing inherently bad about the Osmanli. He is inert, and has thus failed to reach the standards set by the progress of civilization. He lacks ideals."[12] Shrug or sigh as one might upon reading such comments today, when cultural domination is asserted and practiced in much subtler ways, Gibbons's self-satisfied lack of sensitivity for the "natives" allowed him to be free of neurotic caution and to make some daring suggestions. Whatever the weaknesses of his specific arguments, and despite his exaggerations and racialization of the issue, he was not altogether off the mark in underlining the emergence of a new political community out of some combination of people from diverse ethnic and religious backgrounds. It may also shed quite a bit of light on the possibly humble origins and enterprising nature of the early Ottomans to see Osman as a "self-made man." And even Gibbons's ardent critics agreed that Ottoman expansion in the Balkans must be seen not as the outcome of a series of booty-seeking raids but as "part of a plan of settlement" accompanied by such raids.

For more than two decades following Gibbons's book, the foundation of the Ottoman state and the identity of its founders were hot topics. His theory enjoyed some recognition outside the world of Orientalists especially since it could be superimposed on the theory of some Byzantinists at the time that the flourishing of early Ottoman administrative institutions and practices was due, not to a Turco-Islamic, but to a Byzantine heritage. As Charles Diehl, a French Byzantinist, put it, "the Turks . . . those rough warriors were neither administrators nor lawyers, and they understood little of political science. Consequently they modelled many of their state institutions and much of their administrative organization upon what they found in Byzantium."[13] While underlining the long historical evolution of the Turks as a background to the Ottomans, Iorga also held that the latter, "conquérants malgré eux," were almost totally assimilated into Byzantine life except in their religion. The empire they went on to build retained an element, to use his felicitous phrase, of "Byzance après Byzance."[14]

Nevertheless, most scholars of Ottoman or oriental history were critical of Gibbons, while some notable cases like Babinger and Grousset were inclined to accept that Osman converted to Islam at a later stage of his chiefdom. These were no more than exceptions however. Giese, for instance, criticized Gibbons's theories and use of evidence, particularly the construction of an argument around the dream legend, and suggested a new catalyst to the Ottoman conquests: Osman's relations with, or rather support among, the *aḫī* brotherhoods. These brotherhoods were the Anatolian version of the early Islamic *futuwwa* organizations, which comprised urban artisanal and mercantile milieux conforming to a quasi-chivalric, quasi-Sufi code of behavior and corporation.[15] Kramers took this suggestion a step further and argued that Osman was one of the leaders of the aẖīs from the Paphlagonian town of Osmancık—whence he supposedly drew his sobriquet.[16] Several prominent Orientalists such as Houtsma, Huart, Marquart, Massignon, and Mordtmann were eager to comment on issues related to Osman's ethnic or religious identity in those years. And identity—in a combination of ethnic, national, racial, and religious categories—was held to have a major explanatory value in historical understanding, especially in locating the rightful place of individuals and nations in the linear progression of civilization. While the minute differences of the arguments and speculations advanced by all these scholars need not be reproduced here in detail, it should be noted that a common underlying assumption characterized their positions and differentiated them from that of Gibbons; in one way or the other, they all tended to emphasize the "oriental" nature of the Ottomans and accepted the essentially Turco-Muslim identity of the founders of the state.

There was soon an attempt at synthesis by Langer and Blake, who breathed a new historiographic spirit into the debate by bringing in material and sociological factors, such as geography, changing trade patterns, and social organization of religious orders or artisanal associations. Though unable to use the primary sources in Middle Eastern languages, the two coauthors anticipated many of the points and perspectives that were soon to be taken up by two of the most prominent specialists in the field: Köprülü and Wittek. While recognizing the significance of conversions from Christianity to Islam, they were cautious enough not to draw any specific demographic configurations from all this. Nor would they accept that Osman had been born pagan on such flimsy evidence, but they were convinced that "religion played a part, perhaps an important part, in the story of Ottoman expansion." The "elan of the early Ottoman conquerors," they felt, could be explained by the presence of the dervishes around them. Underlining the growth of trade and the proliferation of the aẖī organizations as well, they reached the conclusion that "the first sultans had more than a mere horde of nomads to rely upon."[17]

THE KÖPRÜLÜ-WITTEK CONSOLIDATION

The elaboration of that last point, as well as the most direct and detailed criticism of Gibbons's views, had to wait until 1934 when Mehmet Fuat Köprülü (1890–1966), a Turkish scholar whose intellectual career spans the late Ottoman and early republican periods of imperial dissolution and nation building, delivered a series of lectures at the Sorbonne which were soon published as *Les origines de l'empire ottoman.*[18] Much more than a rebuttal of Gibbons's theories, this book contained a detailed discussion of methodology. Köprülü argued that the foundations of the Ottoman state could not be studied as an isolated Bithynian phenomenon, and that historians ought to concentrate not on detached politico-military incidents but on the social morphology, cultural traditions, and institutional structures of Anatolian Turks in general and of the late-thirteenth-century frontiers in particular. His primary conclusion after applying that method to a broad range of sources was that the material and cultural dynamics of Anatolian Turkish society were sufficiently developed to nurture the growth of a state like that of the Ottomans. A demographic push into western Anatolia in the latter part of the thirteenth century mobilized these dynamics. Even though various forces competed for control over these groups—and it is only here, in the last few pages of his book, that Köprülü turns his attention to the Ottomans specifically—Osman's beglik was favored due, primarily, to its strategic location and then to various other factors (to be discussed in chapter 3). In short, the Ottoman state was simply the culmination of certain dynamics, skills, and organizational principles that had been imported to or had developed in Anatolian Turkish society over more than two centuries. Osman just happened to be in the right place at the right time.

In the meantime, Paul Wittek (1894–1978), who had been to the Ottoman Empire as an officer of its Austrian ally during World War I and then moved on to a scholarly career, was working on the same period and asking similar questions. He published some of his findings in a 1934 monograph on the emergence and activities of another emirate, the Menteşe.[19] Soon after Köprülü, Wittek outlined his own ideas on the rise of the Ottoman state in a series of lectures delivered at the University of London in 1937 and published in 1938.[20] There were some significant differences between the views of the two scholars; in fact Wittek's work was partially intended to be a critique of Köprülü, as we shall see below. Yet on one basic point they were in agreement: the rise of the Ottoman state had to be studied against the background of centuries of warfare, cultural transformation, acculturation, and settlement of Muslims and Turks in medieval Anatolia.

Köprülü and Wittek did not always see the same things in the Anatolian-Turkish background. Yet again they were in agreement on another significant point: one had to distinguish between the hinterland and the frontiers in terms of both their social structure and their cultural characteristics. The two scholars also more or less concurred on the nature of this dichotomy; both of them found the hinterland to be composed of Persianate court circles and settled producers who essentially preferred peaceful relations (cohabitation) with the Byzantines or at least were not pleased to be in a state of continual hostilities, while the marches consisted of nomads, warriors, adventurers, and dervishes who were driven by their search for pasture, booty, glory, or religious vocation. Again, both of these scholars emphasized that frontier society allowed more room for heterodoxy, heterogeneity, and mobility.

As to their dissimilarities, Köprülü and Wittek held divergent opinions on the issue of the "tribal factor" in early Ottoman state building. Neither of them understood tribal formations in the sense utilized by modern anthropologists, however. For both historians (and all the Ottomanists of the time) tribalism entailed consanguinity; that is, a tribe would in essence have to be composed of blood relations whose ancestry ought to be traceable to a common origin, at least in principle. Given that, Köprülü was ready to accept that the Ottomans hailed from a tribe belonging to the Kayı branch of the Oġuz Turks, as most of the sources maintained and as eventually became official Ottoman dogma. However, Wittek pointed out, the earliest reports about the ancestry of Osman and his tribe are from the fifteenth century, and more significantly, there are a good many divergences in the genealogies different sources provide for the Ottomans. On the basis of these discrepancies, Wittek concluded that the early Ottomans cannot have been tribally associated; otherwise, they would have a consistent genealogy to show for it. In the same vein, Meḥmed II would have been unable to toy around with the idea of propagating a Comnenian lineage for his family. Even after Wittek's objections, Köprülü insisted on the validity of the Ottomans' Kayı identity, while at the same time maintaining that this was a secondary issue since, to him, the Kayı origins did not contribute anything specific to the rise of the state.

There was also a major difference of approach between the two scholars. Köprülü looked on the frontier society as a broad canvas composed of a variety of social forces (tribesfolk, warriors, dervishes, aḫīs, emigré scholar-bureaucrats), all of whom made their own significant contribution to the state-building potential of the Turco-Muslim principalities. All this eventually came under the domination of some descendants of the Kayı tribe because the latter happened to be located in a region that circumstances favored. Wittek, on the other hand, focused his attention on one specific element within the *uc* (term for *frontier* in medieval sources, pl. *ucāt*) society, the gaza milieu and its ethos, as being instrumental in the emergence of the principalities and ultimately of the Ottoman state, which overran the others. To him, the political history of the frontiers was made by bands of gazis, warriors of the faith, who spread across the frontier areas as Seljuk power diminished and formed aspiring emirates, among which the band led by Osman Gazi carried the day because of its fortunate position. The earliest Ottoman sources, an inscription from 1337 and Aḥmedī's chronicle, completed ca. 1410, both full of references to the House of Osman as gazis, confirmed in Wittek's opinion the significance of the gaza ethos for the early Ottoman thrust.

These gazi bands may have drawn members from some tribes but were not composed of tribal groups as such; rather, they consisted of warrior-adventurers from various backgrounds. In relation to the Menteşe emirate, for instance, he had argued that the "*gazi* pirates" who founded this stateling were "originally a mixture of Turks and indigenous elements from the neighborhood of Byzantine territory" who were soon joined by "a large number of Byzantine mariners . . . owing to their unemployment."[21] To borrow more recent terminology, gazi bands were "inclusive" entities for Wittek, and tribes were not. Since he held that tribalism required consanguinity (which, he argued, later Ottoman genealogies were unable to establish anyway), and since the warrior bands whom he deemed responsible for the creation of the principalities were anything but consanguineous, he rejected the notion that a tribe could have been instrumental in the foundation of the Ottoman state. The cohesiveness of the political-military cadres of the emirates came from shared goals and faith, not blood.

The differences between Köprülü and Wittek were never explicitly discussed in later scholarship because the issue was encumbered by nationalistic or counternationalistic considerations. From that viewpoint, the role of Byzantine "dissidents" and converts in one of the major political achievements of Turco-Muslim civilization was obviously a highly charged issue. The polemic against Western historiography, which often tended to show Turks as uncreative barbarians, should be an object of inquiry in itself as part of late Ottoman/early republican intellectual history. (And its intensity must be seen against the fact that Western historiography had been particularly aggressive in its attempt to barbarize and delegitimize the "Turkish" empire, with territories right within the European continent and lording it over Christian peoples.) Köprülü, from his youthful poetry to his postacademic career as a politician, was certainly part of that discourse as an outspoken nationalist (though his nationalism was different from the official version in many ways). Before his lectures on the rise of the Ottoman state, he had published what turned out to be a highly influential study criticizing then prevalent views with respect to Byzantine influences on Ottoman institutions, primarily in the administrative sphere.[22] Given all this, Köprülü's account of the Ottoman foundations, where he insisted on the presence of a lineage-based tribe as well as an ethnic stock and spoke against emphasizing the conversions, was very easy to read as nationalistic propaganda. And indeed his book is not free of blatant excesses.

On the other hand, Köprülü's version of events lacked the convenience of a singular "motive force." Shaped under the influence of the Durkheimian tradition in Turkish thought, Köprülü's account was distinctly akin to the new historiographic temperament of the *Annales,* the French historical journal, then only five years old.[23] Rather than dealing with politico-military incidents and presenting a succession of events, Köprülü explicitly stated that he intended to view the rise of the Ottoman state on the basis of the morphology of Anatolian Turkish society "and the evolution of its religious, legal, economic, and artistic institutions more than its political and military events."[24] Even though his aim was partially to depict early Ottoman history as a continuation of late-Seljuk Anatolia, he shunned a chronologically ordered narrative. In his review of Köprülü's book in the newly launched *Annales,* Lucien Fevbre noted approvingly the former's "aversion to one-sided explanations" and did not fail to add that "having gone beyond the stage of narrative history, [Köprülü] produced a solid work of explanation and synthesis."[25]

Written by a man who disdained deterministic single-factor explanations, however, Köprülü's account seemed to lack focus from the viewpoint of traditional history-writing. In his preface to the Turkish edition of his book in 1959, Köprülü remarked somewhat defensively that some "respected Orientalists who have been occupied with the problem of the origins of the Ottoman Empire, although good philologists [read Wittek?], have not been able to go beyond a narrow and simplistic framework when they dealt with historical subjects because they could not escape from the influence of the mentality of narrative history. . . . The frequent attempts to explain by a single cause, that is from one aspect, any historical process which has come into existence under the influence of many different factors is nothing but the neglect of the complexity, that is, the reality of life."[26] Köprülü's sociocultural portrait of the frontiers pointed to various factors that endowed the uc society with mobility and a potential for expansion and to various characteristics of the Ottomans that favored them in particular. The Kayı origins, for instance, were never assigned a causal or explanatory role, and the demographic push from the east was cited as only one of the elements that transformed frontier mobility into Ottoman expansion.

Whatever his historiographic sophistication, however, Köprülü was committed to an essentialist notion of nationhood even more strongly than the historians he opposed. If the Ottoman state was to be seen as a creation of Turks, these must be from the essence of Turkdom, not the newly Turkified. Thus he wrote: "Among the great men of the Ottoman state who won fame in the fourteenth century, and even the fifteenth century, there were very few Christian converts, like the family of Köse Mikhal for instance. Not only was the bureaucracy, which had been established according to Seljuk and Ilkhanid practices, composed entirely of Turkish elements, but those at the head of the government and army were almost invariably Turks. All the historical documents in our possession show this to be definitely the case."[27] Needless to say, this paragraph is not accompanied by any references, for how could it be? How does one show that the fourteenth-century bureaucrats were "entirely" Turkish? So few of them are known as individuals, and most of those appear in the historical record for the first time. Furthermore, we should note the gender-specific designation of the subject of the inquiry: "great men of the Ottoman state." However one chooses to characterize their ethnic origins, some of those great men, Köprülü failed to note, were born to great women who were not of Turkish birth, like Nilüfer Ḫātūn, the mother of Murād I.

As for lesser men and women, Köprülü seems to have been equally keen on maintaining the purity of as many as possible, absolving them of renegadism and probably also the Ottoman conquerors of forced conversion. Against the evidence, he argues: "According to Ottoman sources, Göynük, which was completely inhabited by Christians when Ibn Battuta passed through it, should have been Islamized toward the end of the same century, since Yildirim Bayezid had people brought from there and from Torbali to establish the Muslim quarter that he founded in Constantinople. Even if this report were true, it would be more correct to explain it by the establishment of a new Turkish element there than by a general conversion. Logically one cannot easily accept that the Muslim quarter in Constantinople was simply settled by Greeks who had recently become Muslims."[28]

Later on, he even drops the cautious "almost invariably" and states with absolute certainty that "the Ottoman state was founded exclusively by Turks in the fourteenth century." And then he finally lets the cat out of the bag when he argues, quite logically, that "just as the fact that a significant number of the rulers of the Byzantine Empire came from foreign elements is no proof that the Greeks lacked administrative ability, an analogous situation occurring in the Ottoman Empire cannot be used as proof that the Turks lacked administrative ability."[29]

The last point, namely, the "administrative ability" of a people, to be demonstrated to the "civilized world" in particular, was much more than a question of national pride, as was mentioned above. Such arguments resonated with one of the basic principles in the "new world order" between the two great wars: a people had a right to nationhood in a civilized world only if they could prove that they had in their historical experience what it takes to create a stable state and to govern in a civilized manner. That is one of the most important reasons why nation-states took up the construction of a past as avidly as they drew plans for industrialized modernity. New generations had to, as Mustafa Kemal Atatürk put it in a saying that is now inscribed on many public sites in Turkey, "be proud [of the nation's past achievements], work hard, and be confident [of the future]." Köprülü steered his own course clear of official history and of the so-called Turkish history thesis with its notorious, though fortunately short-lived, excesses like the "sun-language theory."[30] Naturally, however, he was a man of his times.

No perilous pitfall in logic seems to have trapped historians more than the genetic fallacy, perhaps because, by the nature of their profession, they are prone to evaluating the truth value of an assertion on the basis of its origins. It seems that the validity of Köprülü's account was suspect not necessarily because its contents were analyzed but merely because he was known to have indulged in nationalist polemics and to have given in to notions of ethnic purity. At any rate, Wittek's theory obtained general recognition in the international scholarly community writing in the western European languages, while Köprülü's ideas, if indeed considered, were relegated to the status of the best-possible account of a nationalist historiography, albeit with due respect paid to his stature as a scholar. His works on medieval Turkish literary and religious history were used as indispensable sources, but it was Wittek's "gaza thesis" that became the definitive account of the origins of the Ottoman state for a large part of the scholarly world and, with the chivalresque imagery that it conjured, entered many popular treatments.

Still, to present Wittek's thesis as the consensus of the whole field, as some of his critics tend to, would be to overlook the scholarly community in Turkey and to some extent also the Balkans, where the Köprülü-Gibbons controversy continued to be important.[31] In Turkey, Köprülü's tribalist-ethnicist views as well as his emphasis on the Turco-Muslim origins of the Ottoman administrative apparatus came to enjoy nearly the status of dogma and were eventually taken in a more chauvinistic direction as they were increasingly stripped of his demographic and sociological concerns.[32] And there always were some, in Turkey and elsewhere, who developed alternative views, as we shall see below. By and large, however, the terms of debate as they were developed from the First to the Second World War constituted the larger canvas within which the rise of the Ottoman state was depicted until recently; Wittek's depiction in particular was copied and recopied until it was reduced to a mere sketch or a textbook orthodoxy in a large part of the world, while the same fate overtook Köprülü in Turkey.

The opening of the Ottoman archives to scholars changed the course of Ottoman studies starting in the 1940s. Both the quantity and the quality of the archival materials, mostly hard data kept by a meticulous bureaucracy, coincided so well with the rising prestige of social and economic history worldwide that the question of Ottoman "origins," like questions of origins in general, started to look awfully dated, especially since it required all kinds of "drudgery" that a new historiography reacting to the nineteenth-century philological tradition felt it had better leave to old-fashioned historians.

There is one noteworthy exception to this generalization, however. In a book published in 1947, George G. Arnakis questioned the methodology and the conclusions of both Köprülü and Wittek.[33] In a review of that book, an eminent Byzantinist highlighted the main positions of these scholars while summarizing Arnakis's conclusions:

> Gibbons' celebrated conclusion that the Ottoman Empire was essentially a creation of a European rather than of an Asiatic people receives endorsement. Köprülü's opposite view that the Osmanlis were the very incarnation of every thing Moslem and Turkish is severely criticized as modern Turkish "ethnicism." . . . Wittek emphasizes Ghazi ideology rather than Turkish race, as Köprülü does; and indeed rejects the views of Houtsma . . . that the Osmanlis were part of the Kayı tribe of the Oghuzz branch of the Turks. Arnakis, however, believes that the *Iskendername* of Ahmedi breathes a heroic spirit rather than a historic one, and that the references to the Ghazis in his poem and in the Brusa inscription do not mean what Wittek says they

> mean. He emphasizes that the sources indicate no Moslem fanaticism in the military activities of the early Osmanlis: their goal, Arnakis maintains, was not the spread of Islam or the destruction of Christianity but simply plunder. He further points out . . . that the early Osmanlis made it easy for the Greeks to join them. . . . In sum, Arnakis believes that all the students of the problem of Ottoman foundations since Gibbons have gone astray in their emphasis upon the primarily Islamic or essentially Turkish character of the first Osmanlis; that local conditions in Bithynia must be intensively studied before one can arrive at a fair picture.[34]

This short passage, whatever its bias, succinctly encapsulates the different positions and issues involved. Methodologically, the central issue in studying the rise of the Ottoman state was whether one should focus one's attention on the local conditions in Bithynia or treat the early Ottomans as part of broader Islamic and Anatolian-Turkish traditions; the latter position would involve at least some use of fifteenth-century Ottoman sources which were dismissed by the former. Partially in tandem with one's position on that issue, one was then presumably led to put the emphasis either on Byzantine decay and the human resources that situation placed at the service of the early Ottomans or on the constructive capabilities of the Turco-Muslim heritage. It is difficult to see any but ideological reasons for treating these alternatives as mutually exclusive, but most of the scholars seem to have been keen on figuring out whether the Ottoman state was "essentially a creation of a European" or "of an Asiatic people" rather than on combining a narrow Bithynian viewpoint with the broader context of Turco-Islamic traditions. Wittek was somewhat more flexible than the others in that he attempted to mesh his account of the Ottomans as heirs to the gazi traditions with a portrait of Byzantine decay in Bithynia and with observations on defections of Byzantine subjects, but ultimately his singular reliance on "holy war ideology" did not leave much room for a serious consideration of the other factors.

In any case, there seems to be unanimity among these scholars in terms of their appreciation of the early Ottoman state, but the burning question was: whose achievement was it? Next to Köprülü's position cited above was Arnakis's assertion that with the conquest of Bursa, "the Osmanlis were now strengthened by the socially advanced townspeople. Making Brussa their capital, the Osmanlis . . . carried on reforms, and organized a model state. Their advance and rapid spread into Europe is largely due to the administrative experience and the civic traditions of the citizens of Brussa, Nicaea and Nicomedia."[35] Obviously then, Arnakis, like Gibbons, focused on Bithynia and on what he considered to be the "actions" of the early Ottomans rather than on the "fictions" of later generations, namely, the fifteenth-century chronicles. In terms of their specific conclusions, both of them emphasized the contributions of originally non-Islamic and non-Turkish elements to the rise of the Ottoman state, whereas Köprülü and Wittek stressed the role of Turco-Islamic traditions (understood more in a cultural than in an ethnic sense by the latter). In terms of their interpretation of the sources, Gibbons and Arnakis tended to dismiss Ottoman chronicles as later fabrications, whereas Köprülü and Wittek, though aware of their problematic nature, preferred to make use of them after applying what they considered to be rigorous means of textual analysis.

We can clearly identify two distinct lines of approach to early Ottoman history: the one followed by Gibbons and Arnakis and the other by Köprülü and Wittek. Many elements of the new critical discourse on the gaza thesis can be read as a rekindled interest, though not necessarily in the sense of a self-conscious intellectual legacy, in some arguments of the former approach.

These lines should not be drawn too rigidly, however. Some of the differences between Köprülü and Wittek have already been noted. It is also to be underlined that Gibbons's emphasis on the proselytizing zeal of the Ottomans in the early days and their loss of ideals in the empire's latter phase is to some extent paralleled by Wittek's views on the gaza. And this role assigned to religious motives by both Gibbons and Wittek is precisely what Arnakis, as well as the new critics of the gaza thesis, refused to see in the emergence of the Ottoman state.

THE SEARCH FOR ALTERNATIVES

Before moving on to the gaza thesis and its dismantling, we ought not to overlook some important contributions made to the study of that particular period in the meantime, if only to indicate that Wittek's thesis was not compelling for many scholars in the field.

Zeki Velidî Togan (1890–1970), a Turcologist who held the office of premier in the short-lived republic of Bashkiria before its incorporation into the Soviet Union (1922) and who then migrated to Turkey, brought quite an unusual perspective to Turkish history thanks to his background and training. In his magnum opus on the general history of the Turks, written while he was in prison on charges of pan-Turanianism, and in other studies, he often emphasized the importance of the Ilkhanid legacy as well as non-Oġuz, or eastern Turkish, elements as if he wanted to remind the western Turks, the heirs of the Ottoman tradition, of their non-Mediterranean cousins.[36] To the extent that the gaza ethos played a role, for instance, Togan argued that it was not the legacy of former Arab frontier traditions directly inherited by the Oġuz Turks who settled in Anatolia as their new homeland. It was rather brought to western Anatolia at the turn of the fourteenth century by those Muslim Turks who were forced to migrate there from eastern Europe since their lands were lost to Islamdom when Prince Nogay of the Chingisid Altunorda, a Muslim, was defeated (1299) by Toktagu Khān, a Zoroastrian.[37] In addition to this newly imported enthusiasm (supported by the Ilkhanids) for the (re)conquest of lands for Islam, the internal weakness of Byzantium, and the lack of "Islamic fanaticism" among the early Ottomans that facilitated the incorporation of quasi-Islamic Turks and Mongols as well as renegades from Christianity, Togan cited the location of Osman's tribe right near the major Byzantine-Ilkhanid trade route as the factors that made it natural for Turkish warriors to conceive of expanding their power and building a state.[38] The rest was good leadership, adoption of sound administrative practices (thanks primarily to the Ilkhanid legacy), support given to and received from aḫīs and dervishes, and a well-regulated colonization policy after crossing to Rumelia.

The significance of commerce was to be considered from another perspective by Mustafa Akdağ (1913–72), a Turkish historian who chose to focus on some references in the Ottoman chronicles concerning exchange between Osman's tribe and their Christian neighbors; from those, he developed a bold theory proposing the existence of a "Marmara-basin economy" that emerged as an integrated unit at the time of Ertoġrıl and Osman. The state that was created by them gave political expression to that economic reality and expanded along routes that linked the Marmara basin to other regional economies. This thesis never had a chance to gain any recognition, however, since it was soon demolished on the grounds of flimsy evidence and sloppy reasoning by a student of Köprülü, Halil İnalcık, who was to emerge as the leading Ottomanist of his generation and make his own contributions to various problems of early Ottoman history.[39] Even though Akdağ elaborated the same views in a later book,[40] with a yet stronger emphasis on commerce, symbiosis, and rosy relations between Turks and Byzantines or Balkan peoples, his views were not supported by any new evidence that responded to former criticisms; the book failed to have an impact on professional historians though it was widely read by the public. Considering that its author suffered imprisonment for his leftist views after the military intervention of 1971, the book is rather a curious reminder of the fact that certain significant strands of the nationalist discourse such as the purely positive assessment of the Turkish conquests cut across both sides of the political spectrum in Turkey.[41]

Speros Vryonis, a Greek-American (and a Byzantinist, as some reviewers noted, much to his resentment), published his monumental work on medieval Anatolia in 1971.[42] It covered the period that saw the rise of the Ottoman state but was not directly concerned with that specific phenomenon. Vryonis rather traced the broad currents of demographic movement, nomadization, and religious and cultural change in Asia Minor that, over four centuries, transformed what was a Hellenic/Greek Orthodox peninsula into a predominantly Islamic one dominated by a Turcophone political elite. In the shortest summary of the set of conclusions he reached at the end of his exhaustive research, he wrote that "the Turkish success ultimately was a product of the dynamics of Byzantine decline and Turkmen (nomadic) demographic pressure."[43] As for the role of frontier warriors in that process, whose absence in the book was noted by a reviewer, Vryonis commented that "the Wittek thesis was of interest and stimulus some two generations ago, but only as a tool to stimulate further discussion. To accept it as an established fact and then to apply it here and there to different areas and periods is erroneous methodologically."[44]

To Ernst Werner, a Marxist-Leninist medievalist of the former East Germany, the first two centuries of Ottoman history represented the framing of a feudal system through the subjugation of pre- and antifeudal elements.[45] Though his conceptual framework is dated and forced, Werner was quite astute in focusing on social conflicts within and around the growing polity in detail as the dynamic that shaped political developments. He explicitly criticized Turkish historiography for its chauvinistic tendencies, including the tendency to overlook conflicts in Turco-Muslim society in general and among its warriors in particular.[46] Since he made only scanty use of the sources in Islamic languages and clung to a rigid Marxist-Leninist position with a rather facile application of the notion of class struggle,[47] his views were not seriously considered in the guildlike mainstream of Ottoman studies, which, despite the considerable impact of quasi-Marxian materialism beginning in the 1960s, stood on the western side of the cold war divide. Although Werner identifies Köprülü as "Kommunistenhasser und extremer Nationalist,"[48] his methodological position has an obvious affinity with that of the latter, the only Ottomanist of the earlier generation to have a serious interest in sociological history. In his *Origins,* Köprülü had underlined the importance of "research on the *stratification* of various elements which constituted Anatolian Turkish society in the thirteenth and fourteenth centuries, their positions with respect to each other, their strengths and weaknesses, the causes of *conflict and solidarity* among them," but his agenda simply included too many other questions that he preferred to focus on.[49]

Whatever the merits of the insights they brought to the rise of the Ottoman state, these works had agendas that assigned higher priority to other matters. Thus, their comments on our specific theme remained by and large buried. Surveys (and syllabi?) of Ottoman, Islamic, and world history framed the activities of the state founders in terms of the gaza thesis. It should be obvious, however, that not all the scholars in the field were compelled by Wittek's gaza thesis even when it reigned supreme. Their works rather represent a continual, if not directly critical or widely influential, search for alternative explanations. Even if the gaza ethos was accepted to have played a role, there was an obvious urge to consider other factors, mostly social and economic, like trade, demographics, nomad-settled relations, as well as societal conflict, as the dynamics that produced an empire. In the beginning of the 1980s, İnalcık wrote a concise and masterly synthesis, to be discussed later, that brought many of these elements together with the gaza ethos.[50] It turned out to be not the last word on the subject, as one might have expected, but only the harbinger of a decade that saw a flurry of publications aiming to dismantle the gaza thesis altogether.

The Wittek Thesis and Its Critics

It is time now to go over the gaza thesis in more detail and then turn to its critics. As indicated above with respect to the methodological position he shared with Köprülü, Wittek could not have formulated his thesis without assuming some sort of diachronic continuum in the gazi traditions of Anatolia, and of medieval Islam in general, reaching the early Ottomans, as well as some level of synchronic communication and similarity between the gazis in Bithynia and elsewhere in Anatolia. That is precisely why he prefaced his account of the rise of the Ottomans with a survey of the gazi traditions in Anatolia starting with the Dānişmendids of the late eleventh and twelfth centuries. And that is also why he found the experiences of other emirates broadly contemporaneous with the Osmanlı relevant for an understanding of the uniquely successful case of the latter.

The political and military leadership of the frontiers always belonged to the gazis, according to Wittek. Since the late eleventh century, Anatolian frontier areas were dominated by gazis, whose independent, sporadic, and unruly activities did not always conform to the stability-oriented Realpolitik of the Seljuk administration. There were frequent clashes between Seljuk authorities and the gazis, whose most notable representatives were the Dānişmendids in the twelfth century. In the early thirteenth century, there was a rapprochement between the gazis and the Seljuks, but the Mongol invasions brought this situation to an end.

In the second half of the thirteenth century, the western Anatolian marches were swollen not only by new influxes of nomadic groups and their holy men pushed by the Mongol invasions but also by "prominent Selçuks seeking refuge, leaders from dispersed armies, old *gazis* whose rapprochement with Konya had come to an end." The chronicles of that period are therefore filled with accounts of central armies undertaking campaigns against unruly *ucāt*. Against the backdrop of the decay of Byzantine defenses in western Anatolia after the end of Lascarid rule from Nicaea, the revitalization of the marches from the Turkish side led to new political configurations, signified by the appearance of several small emirates. According to Wittek, nomadic Turks took part in the invasions, incursions, and emerging emirates, but they were subordinated to gazis, "those march-warriors who for generations had attacked and overrun the frontier . . . the leaders of the *gazis* became the princes of the emirates."[51] We have already seen that his detailed study of the Menteşe emirate led Wittek to attribute the formation of this polity to the successful piratical expeditions of the gazis joined by "the seafaring inhabitants of the coastal districts" and "a large number of Byzantine mariners."

Similar small states came into existence in other parts of western Anatolia. Among these, one was founded by Osman's followers, who, like other gazi formations, had "adapted themselves to the civilization of the country which they attacked," and this "made it all the easier for the *Akritai* [Byzantine border warriors] to join them in groups, and for forts and smaller towns to capitulate voluntarily." Also, these Ottomans "did everything to promote desertion among their adversaries. . . ."[52] Driven by the gaza ethos, which blended a search for booty or pasture, political opportunism, and a religious motivation, all these small begliks aspired to enlarge their territory and authority. Mostly due to circumstantial reasons, the Ottomans were the most successful chiefdom to accomplish this goal even though they were one of the least significant at first. Located at the very outskirts of the unstable frontier area, however, they were the closest group to one of the, defensively speaking, weakest points of Byzantium and enjoyed a comparative advantage in exploiting the gaza ethos relative to other emirates that were not as strategically located or had become more established. Their early successes, in turn, provided the Ottomans with fresh sources of warriors (including converts), facilitating further growth.

While Wittek's account clearly relied on an understanding of the gaza ethos that had many more nuances than merely a fervor for holy war, he was more categorical in his general statements, especially in drawing a distinction between the gazi and the "*hochislamisch*" tendencies. In a widely read article, he rather mechanistically applied his theory of an opposition between these two tendencies as the key to understanding Ottoman political developments from Bāyezīd I to Meḥmed II.[53] Such formulations and a general lack of concern with the details of his story led to a reductionist rendering of the whole gaza thesis that over time suffered what all accepted theses go through. It became a caricature of itself (an explanation by religious fanaticism) while enjoying wide recognition and recycling.[54]

The relative consensus around the gaza thesis prevailed for nearly half a century. Some specialists continued the search for alternative or supplementary explanations, as I have already shown, but there was no lively debate producing new research and ideas (except for the issue of the Kayı genealogy that occupied Wittek and Köprülü as well as some younger Turkish scholars for a while).[55] An undercurrent of dissatisfaction with that consensus and a revived interest in revisiting the problem of the Ottoman state's emergence were apparently building up, however, and they surfaced in the 1980s in the publications of an impressive number of scholars who, independently of each other, tackled Wittek's formulation.[56]

The main thrust of the critique was to underline certain actions of the early Ottomans that were now deemed contradictory to the spirit of holy war and to argue therefore that they cannot have been motivated by the gaza ethos. Rather, the critics of the gaza thesis argue, what once were plain political and/or material motives were adorned with higher ideals in later sources written by ideologues serving the Ottoman dynasty. Was it the weariness of a generation of scholars who lived through the Vietnam War, refusing to accept that "war for an ideal" or "to spread one's 'superior' values" could be anything more than rhetoric concocted by ideologues to legitimize actions "actually" fueled by ignoble motives? The more obvious weariness was with the idealistic assumptions of former generations of scholars steeped in philology, accompanied by the related and belated arrival of an interest among Ottomanists in the materialist end of the idealism-materialism debates.

It should also be noted that these discussions remained confined to Wittek. Köprülü's views were hardly discussed; Gibbons and Arnakis, hardly cited. Though it remains implicit, the position of the new critics in terms of the relationship of the early Ottomans to the rest of the frontier is in many ways a continuation of the Gibbons-Arnakis approach while the particular examination of the gaza thesis had already been elaborated by Arnakis.

Anthropological literature on tribes is the most obvious source of inspiration for Rudi Paul Lindner, who gave the most elaborate, systematic, and — by now — recognized critique of the gaza thesis. He is also the only one to develop an alternative theory. His basic argument rests on what he observes to be a contradiction between the "inclusive" nature of tribalism and the "exclusive" nature of the gaza ideology. Since he finds tribalism as it is defined by recent anthropological theory to be more representative of early Ottoman behavior and thus a likelier candidate as the motive force behind the emergence of the Ottoman state, he sets himself the task of disproving Wittek's gaza theory.

In Wittek's time, Lindner somewhat generously observes, tribes were assumed to be consanguineous groups basically closed to strangers. Only on the basis of such a definition could Wittek have attempted to argue that the first Ottomans must have had some other principle of organization than a tribal one since they could not produce a consistent genealogy. Recent anthropological studies, on the other hand, demonstrate that a tribe is "a political organism whose membership [is] defined by shared interests (and, in medieval Eurasia, subordination to a chief)."[57] Tribes are now seen as inclusive bodies whose members might attempt to fabricate a common genealogy only after the formation of the tribe. Therefore, Lindner argues, the discrepancies that Wittek detected in various genealogies produced by fifteenth-century Ottoman writers do not disprove the tribal roots of the Ottoman state, as Wittek believed. On the contrary, such discrepancies prove that later Ottoman writers were trying to impose a fictional consanguinity on the founders of their state, who actually were from various groups of Turks and Byzantines coming together under the chieftainship of Osman thanks to the inclusive nature of tribalism. But if an inclusive tribalism was indeed the dominant factor in the rise of the Ottoman state, Lindner further argues, then the gaza theory must be dismissed because gaza as "an exclusive or adversary ideology" would have excluded Byzantines from joining Turks to form a tribe. "If fervor for the Holy War played an important role in this frontier area, then our pool would clearly exclude Byzantines, for they would have become the detested enemy of the faithful."[58]

According to Lindner, Wittek's evidence for the gaza theory consists of the Bursa inscription of 1337 and Aḥmedī's history. Like Arnakis, Lindner feels that both of these sources can be interpreted to reflect a later ideology of the settled Ottoman state rather than the "real" ethos of the early Ottomans. He proposes to eschew such "later ideological statements" and base his argument on the early Ottomans' deeds. If they were indeed warriors animated by the gaza ideology, Lindner suggests, the early Ottomans would *not* have

1. recruited Byzantines into their ranks,
2. fought against other Muslim forces,
3. exerted no pressure to convert or persecute Christians,
4. displayed moderation and an "interest in conciliation and mutual adaptability," or
5. allowed freedom for heterodoxy and pre-Islamic cults.

Furthermore, according to Lindner, contemporaneous Byzantine chroniclers of "the stature of Pachymeres, Gregoras, and Cantacuzenes" would have recorded religious animosity as a factor in the Ottoman drive if the Ottomans were indeed driven by such animosity. Jennings raises the same point about Byzantine sources, which we shall take up in the next chapter, but for him too the most obvious failure of the gazi thesis is its incompatibility with the behavior of the early Ottomans vis-à-vis their Christian subjects and neighbors. Káldy-Nagy likewise finds incongruities between a spirit of holy war and what he observes to be a loose attachment of the early Ottomans to their Islamic faith, as can be discerned in the continuance of pre-Islamic practices such as the use of Turkic names, their wars with other Muslims, and lack of a zeal to convert. Needless to say, in terms of the sources that refer to Osman and his descendants as gazis, both Jennings and Káldy-Nagy feel that we are faced with later ideological adornments. Jennings, however, makes the additional argument that the "1337 inscription" was in fact produced much later during a repair, when the original building date of 1337 was maintained in a new formulation that included the reference to Orḫān and his father as gazis.

Even though the reopening of discussion on a theory that has enjoyed supremacy for nearly half a century is certainly to be welcomed, this line of argumentation against the gaza thesis contains many flaws. Most importantly, it is based on an essentialism that leads Wittek's critics to assume, even more rigidly than earlier Orientalists, the existence of a "true Islam" whose standards "true gazis" are then supposed to conform to. In this view, gazis are expected to be *orthodox* Muslims driven by religious zeal, relentlessly fighting against and forcibly converting infidels. Thus, as alien as they may deem Wittek's philological tradition and his philosophical idealism, all of these authors are firmly steeped in Orientalist perceptions of Islam which privilege the canonical as the truly Islamic and hold suspect anything that diverges from the canonical. In fact, they go further than earlier Orientalists, not only in assuming that there ought to be such a thing as a "true gaza spirit" to be defined without reference to any particular historical context but also in excluding those who engaged in uncanonical practices from the Muslim *umma* (the universal community of believers in Islam) altogether. Wittek and Köprülü at least recognized an intermediate category of heterodox Islam, in which they placed (not necessarily with analytical rigor as we shall see in later chapters) what they believed to be the uncanonical practices of Turco-Muslim tribes and warriors of the medieval Anatolian frontiers. The critics of the gaza thesis, on the other hand, are ready to take on more-inquisitorial roles and to pass sentences or moral judgments on the early Ottomans for not being Muslim enough.[59]

After mentioning the participation of Christian forces of Balkan vassals in Ottoman campaigns, even against Muslim foes, Jennings writes that "using Christian soldiers along with Muslim ones on campaign violates almost everyone's standard of a holy war, and leading Christian soldiers against Muslim ones is reprehensible." Or again, "it is hard to imagine how any Muslims who operated in those ways could be esteemed as gazis by Muslims who have any profound knowledge of their own faith."[60] But all of the later Ottoman authors, who were to some extent aware of these particular ways in which the early Ottomans operated, who are in fact the sources of much of the information used by Jennings, esteemed the builders of their state as gazis. Did they all lack "profound knowledge of their own faith"?

Among the "reasons for hypothesizing that Ertughrul and his sons were only loosely attached to Islam," Káldy-Nagy refers (among other things, which he treats less systematically) to the fact that all of the family members and associated warriors of the generations of Ertoğrıl and Osman have Turkic names.[61] Naming practices and changes in that sphere are certainly relevant for understanding the cultural orientation of the people involved, and the clear reversal of preference from Turkic to Arabic-Muslim names needs to be noted and understood, but it is not necessarily a criterion to gauge the depth of a person's "religious commitment" as Káldy-Nagy argues. There are many reasons why Mamluk rulers of Egypt, for instance, kept their Turkic names, and lack of religious commitment can hardly be one of them.[62]

In this respect, the most radical position is taken by Lindner, who is nearly ready to act like an Inquisitor and excommunicate the early Ottomans. Considering some examples of what he considers to be pre-Islamic beliefs and attitudes among the early Ottomans, for instance, he concludes that they may have been "crusaders for shamanism rather than for Islam." On another occasion, after citing some unorthodox beliefs or practices of early Ottomans to disprove once again the existence of "single-minded Muslim zeal," he decides to "leave aside the interesting possibility that Osman and his comrades were holy warriors in another just cause, that of shamanism."[63] But those early Ottomans, if they were crusaders of anything, must surely be allowed to have been crusaders of what *they* thought to be Islam. Some of their beliefs may have been contradictory to an assumed essence of Islam, but there is nothing we can do about the fact that the people of the marches, including the early Ottomans, chose to retain several of their "shamanistic" notions or, rather, to redefine them within a syncretistic understanding of Islam. A similar convergence of "heterodoxy" and gazi spirit is observed in many other frontier circumstances; it is noted, for instance, to have existed during the emergence of the Safavids as a political power as well.[64] This is the historical reality of the marches to be explained; it cannot be dismissed as a contradiction on the basis of an ahistorical definition of gaza as what it ought to have been.

The conduct of Geyikli Baba, for instance, a dervish of early Ottoman Bithynia, may have appeared un-Islamic to a hyperorthodox scholar but there is no doubt that Geyikli Baba considered himself a Muslim and was thus recognized by many others. Ṭaşköprīzāde, an eminent Sunni scholar of the sixteenth century, was probably much more conscious of the distinction between orthodoxy and heterodoxy than his fourteenth-century Ottoman forebears and much more stringent in the application of relevant criteria, but he does not question Geyikli Baba's belief when respectfully recording the latter's "miraculous deeds."[65] It is well known that many Sunni and 'Alevī Turks still believe in similar legends and tell them to their children as part of a religious upbringing; naturally, that does not render these parents "shamanist educators."

In fact, there is a serious problem with this use of "shamanism." First, in lumping together all that seems to be a "survival" from pre-Islamic Turkic beliefs under the category of shamanism, Lindner is simply following the precedent of Köprülü and other earlier Turcologists. But now that the comparative study of religions has advanced to a much more rigorous understanding of shamanism and particularly in the light of Lindner's own concern with discarding sedentary dispositions in dealing with nomads, it would be much more appropriate to take the early Ottomans' unorthodox beliefs and practices seriously. What does "ritual human sacrifice," assuming that some Ottomans indeed practiced it, as Vryonis and Lindner argue, or belief in the execution of posthumous deeds by holy figures have to do with shamanism?[66] Second, even if the early Ottoman practices contained some traces of shamanism, that would not make them shamanists, let alone warriors of shamanism. Lindner's comments on the "interesting possibility" of early Ottoman "shamanism" appear like a reformulation of Gibbons's thesis: that Osman was not a Muslim until a later stage of his career. That position naturally requires more evidence than pointing to some examples of lingering pre-Islamic practices.

Besides, there is an obvious contradiction in the line of argumentation followed by Wittek's critics. If the later chroniclers are characterized as ideologues who attempt to whitewash the pagan founders of the state from a Sunni point of view, how can one explain their inclusion of these "un-Islamic" legends in their narratives? 'Āşıḳpaşazāde (ca. 1400–90; hereafter abbreviated Apz), for instance, perhaps the best known of these chroniclers, does not merely record such incidents but tells us that he can personally assure us of their truth. If the deeds of the early Ottomans, because of their "pagan" characteristics, were contradictory to Apz's notion of Islam, why does he not suppress them or record them merely as traditions? On the contrary, he emphasizes his own belief in those legends. Was he a "shamanist" as well? In late-fifteenth-century Istanbul, where he wrote?

My point here is not to save the reputation of Osman and his family or to establish that they were "good Muslims" or even to make sure that they are recognized as Muslims from the very beginning of their political career. One may still construct an argument about the conversion of Osman in his later career, but that argument needs to be constructed rather than hinted at. I will refer to some evidence in chapter 3 that might in fact be used for such an argument, though I personally feel it would be farfetched. Nor do I wish to disregard the fact that some, perhaps most, of the early Ottoman practices may have been unorthodox, but this is no reason to maintain that their attachment to Islam must have been too loose or not sincere enough for them to be steeped in the gaza ethos. For what does the gaza ethos have to do with "correct Islam" and why should a warrior of the faith be expected to conform to it?

In this context, we should note that the observations of Lindner and others about the attitudes of the early Ottomans toward their religion or neighbors are not based on the discovery of new evidence. Wittek, and possibly all the writers on early Ottoman history, were aware of the conciliatory attitude and unorthodox practices among the early Ottomans as well as their struggles with other Muslim emirs. Except for Arnakis, however, they did not perceive these facts to be contradictory to the gazi spirit. As we have already seen, Arnakis had as early as 1947 raised both of the major points of objection to Wittek: that the Bursa inscription and Aḥmedī's chronicle could be dismissed as later ideology, and that there was a contradiction between the gaza spirit and the nonadversarial attitude of the early Ottomans toward their Byzantine neighbors and toward pre-Islamic cults.[67]

Why should the actions of the gazis be expected to be guided by religious animosity, fervor, and the upholding of "untarnished Islam," however? Wittek's description of the gazi milieux and their ethos was based on what he held to be historical facts and not on an a priori definition of gaza. Namely, it was not a canonical but a historical definition that took into consideration the descriptions by medieval Islamic authors, writing much earlier than the Ottoman chroniclers, of a particular social type called gazi and associated with the frontier regions of Islam.

The standard depiction of the gazi as a social type was derived from W. Barthold, the Russian Turcologist, whose work was closely followed in this regard by both Köprülü and Wittek.[68] According to Barthold's *Turkestan* (which quickly established itself as the classic treatment of the history of central Asia and eastern Iran between the seventh and thirteenth centuries), ever since the early reports in Islamic sources on the gazis of Khorasan from the tenth to eleventh centuries, we are faced with "restless elements" that "offered their services wherever a holy war was in progress and wherever booty might be expected."[69] Writing about an incident in which some "three hundred men who had been engaged in theft and robbery" were collected and executed by the ruler of Samarqand in the eleventh century, Barthold adds that these measures were "taken against that class of the population from which at another epoch the so-called 'volunteers' were drawn."[70]

The gazis appear as one manifestation of the still ambiguous social phenomenon of quasi-corporate male organizations in medieval Islamic history. Just like the *'ayyārūn* (lit., scoundrels), a word used by some medieval Muslim authors interchangeably with the word *ġāziyān,* the gazis represented potential troublemakers from the point of view of established states, which attempted with only partial success to channel the energies of these social forces toward targets other than the present order. Ġāziyān was the corporate name given to such associations (though the level of cohesion or organization is not precisely known) that functioned in the frontier areas obviously because there they would be able to undertake *ġhazwa* (raids) into the *dār al-ḥarb* (abode of war).[71] From the point of view of the central authorities, it was one way of keeping undesirable elements away from the regular flow of settled life, while it is only natural that in the religion-based worldview of the times such raiders would be ready to see and to present themselves as fighting for a religious cause. The gazis, then, were viewed by Barthold and by many Orientalists who relied on his work, not necessarily as the result of a compulsion to fight for religion, but as a socially unstable element finding itself a niche, a legitimation, and a chance for mobility through military activity in the frontier regions sanctioned and rendered meaningful within the framework of a higher cause.

Even then, such legitimization on the basis of religion was not necessarily suited to the ideals of the Islamic central states. Unorthodox, syncretistic, or even heretical ideas did find more-fertile ground in the unstable frontier areas, where the authority of central governments and their versions of Islam could hardly be enforced. Moreover, as Wittek often pointed out, a similar sociocultural situation pervaded the other side of the "border." In the Anatolian case, the gazis and the akritai had for centuries been living in closer proximity to each other, mentally as well as geographically, than to the central authorities.

To argue against this definition, one would need to reinterpret the sources that describe the activities of the gazis. The critics of the gazi thesis, on the other hand, assume that modern lexicographic definitions of gaza provide us with sufficient criteria to determine who was a gazi and who was not. "Fervor for the Holy War" (and this would be an incomplete definition even for a canonical work, as we shall see in the next chapter) is a sufficient definition for them in describing the ethos of a social phenomenon that manifested itself in as wide a geographic expanse as from Khorasan to the Balkans and as long a temporal stretch as from the tenth to at least the sixteenth century. This attitude is no less ahistorical than defining the bourgeoisie as "town dwellers" and then trying to determine anyone's relation to the bourgeoisie simply by studying his or her postal address.

In short, as defined by the critics of the gaza thesis, gazis are not historical entities but straw men relentlessly fighting for their lofty, untarnished ideals. It is not surprising that such men are to be found not as a real factor in early Ottoman history but simply as an ideological creation of later Ottoman historiography. The characteristics of social groups can be inferred not from a lexicographic definition of their titles, however, but from an interpretation of the sources describing their activities, relations to other social groups, and cultural characteristics as manifested in particular historical contexts.

It is to those sources that we shall next turn to see how gaza and related notions were conceptualized by those who called themselves gazi and their supporters. It is surprising that no one, among either those who accept or those who reject the role of the gaza ethos in the construction of the Ottoman Empire, has yet attempted to investigate the nature of that ethos as a historical phenomenon on the basis of a close analysis of the sources narrating the deeds of the gazis. That is precisely what I will attempt to do in the next chapter.

Before doing that, however, we should point out another major problem with the critique of the gaza thesis as it has been raised, namely, a confusion between a "motive force" and a "sufficient cause." Clearly, these are two different kinds of explanatory principles. Otherwise, all gazi principalities would be expected to form world empires. "If the ghazi spirit was so powerful among the Danishmendlis and Ottomans, why did this same zeal for the Holy War lead the Ottomans to success, while the Danishmendlis were somehow unable to defeat their enemies and even disappeared from power and influence in Anatolia after less than a century." Lindner asks: "if the ghazi spirit is to be the motive force that we have taken it to be, how could it lead to such discordant results?"[72] The question would have been valid only if the gazi spirit, or any other suggested motive force(s), had been presented as a sufficient cause to establish a world empire. However, Ottomanist scholars in search of the forces which propelled a small principality into a superpower, including Wittek, have always been eager to consider the specific circumstances which made the balance tip Osman's way, such as the peculiar advantage of the geographic location of his initial power base.

A further comment needs to be made in relation to "causality" and cultural history. Cultural or intellectual history does not necessarily entail implicit causal assumptions. Through the delineation of an ethos or ideology in the sources relating to a certain milieu or class, one can identify the nature of that class, its interests, demands, and relations to other social groups. This does not necessarily lead to the conclusion that the actions of the members of that class were "fueled" by their "ideas"; one merely understands them better through an examination of their ideas. In this approach, cultural history is only an epistemological path and not a causal statement. The failure to appreciate properly the cultural traditions of the frontier society stems from a mechanistic attitude to cultural history, or from confusing an epistemological itinerary with an ontological one.

Obviously the gaza thesis was much more flexible than its critics made it out to be. It could be incorporated, as İnalcık did in his article mentioned above, into a matrix of factors that included material ones even if Wittek himself seemed reluctant to do so. After an outline of the migrations of Turcoman tribes to western Anatolia that created a "great demographic potential and a heightened Holy War ideology," İnalcık writes that

> a thrust by this explosive frontier society . . . was accomplished in the following stages: 1) it began with the seasonal movements of the Turcoman nomadic groups into the Byzantine coastal plains; 2) it was intensified by the organization of small raiding groups under ghazi leaders, mostly of tribal origin, for booty raids or for employment as mercenaries; 3) it continued with the emergence of successful leaders capable of bringing together under their clientship local chiefs to conquer and then establish beyliks (principalities) . . . ; 4) with the involvement of these ghazi-beyliks, with their definite political and economic aims, in the regional struggle for supremacy in the Aegean and in the Balkans.

He still refers to gazi bands but calls them "ghazi-mercenary bands," for whom, due to "the generally rising prices of slaves . . . enslavement of the neighborhood 'infidels' became a most profitable business as well as a 'pious' act."[73] This was an account that tried to maintain a balance, or rather to argue for an interdependency, between the material and ideological factors whereby the "Holy War ideology, as much as the success of the actual raids, reinforced ties within the [gazi-mercenary] band to produce a cohesive social group centered around the leader."[74]

On that basis, we can proceed to our tour of the medieval Anatolian sources that have a direct bearing on the ethos of the frontier warriors and the early Ottomans.

CHAPTER 2

The Sources

There is not one incontrovertibly authentic written document from Osman's days as a beg.[1] And that is only appropriate for a chief who, when asked by a dervish for a document to confirm the granting of a village as freehold, is reported to have replied: "You ask me for a piece of paper as if I [knew how to] write. Here, I have a sword left from my forefathers. Let me give that to you. And I will also give you a cup. Let them both remain in your hands. And let them [who come after you] preserve these tokens. And if God Almighty endorses my bid for this service [of rulership], let my descendants observe that token and certify it." Relating this legend in the late fifteenth century, the chronicler Apz, himself a dervish, hastens to add that the sword is still in the hands of the holy man's offspring and that it is visited by every new ruler. We have, unfortunately, no extant sword that qualifies or any reliable records of its existence.[2]

The only pieces of writing that survive from the days of Osman are not on paper but on coins.[3] There is not much that one can infer from their terse formulae about the ideology of the early Ottomans. As insignificant as his polity may have been, Osman had obviously found the moment opportune to make the significant political statement of sovereignty that is implied in the striking of coins in one's own name. These findings should also put to rest the disbelief in Ertoğrıl as a real historical character since he is, at least on one of the coins, referred to as Osman's father. Otherwise, but for the fact that they were issued by a Muslim ruler, they do not reveal much about the political culture of the little beglik.

Yet we certainly do not need to wait until the time- and scholarship-worn inscription of 1337 for some glimpses into the self-image of the early Ottomans. A revealing piece of evidence on early Ottoman political culture is an endowment deed from 1324.[4] Two aspects of this document indicate that already by this early date, the budding beglik had been touched by the so-called higher Islamic, or Persianate, ruling traditions. The deed is composed in Persian, and the first appointee as the administrator of the endowment is identified as a manumitted eunuch of Orḫān's. Yet the true value of the document in this consideration of the history of notions concerning "war for the faith" lies in the fact that Orḫān, in whose name the deed is issued, and his recently deceased father, Osman, are both mentioned with their epithets: Şücāʿüddīn and Faḫrüddīn, respectively ("Champion of the Faith" and "Glory of the Faith"). These epithets prove well beyond doubt that the Ottomans had adopted Islamic nomenclature compatible with the rest of Anatolian Muslim society more than a decade before the Bursa inscription. It is also impossible that Orḫān would not be aware of the meaning of Şücāʿüddīn when his entourage included people who could produce a canonically impeccable endowment deed in Persian.

In this world of dizzying physical mobility—crisscrossed by overlapping networks of nomads and seminomads, raiders, volunteers on their way to join military adventurers, slaves of various backgrounds, wandering dervishes, monks and churchmen trying to keep in touch with their flock, displaced peasants and townspeople seeking refuge, disquieted souls seeking cure and consolation at sacred sites, Muslim schoolmen seeking patronage, and the inevitable risk-driven merchants of late medieval Eurasia—it is not at all surprising that information traveled. So did lore and ideas, fashions and codes, of course. The title that Orḫān had adopted, "the champion of the faith," was a highly popular one in western Anatolia among other begs of his generation; the Ottomans obviously were up-to-date on the frontier vogue.[5] It is simply impossible to consider that they would have been unaware of or untouched by cultural elements that the whole region was heavily immersed in. In fact, communication between the proto-Ottomans and their not-so-immediate neighbors can be established in the very earliest datable record of Osman's activities. Pachymeres (d. ca. 1310), the Byzantine chronicler, writes that Osman was joined by warriors from the Meander region, in addition to some from relatively nearby Paphlagonia, in his first confrontation with Byzantine imperial forces in 1301 (or 1302).[6]

Gaza and Gazis in the Frontier Narratives of Medieval Anatolia

The cultural life of the frontiers was clearly dominated by oral traditions, especially "historical" narratives that represented the frontier society's perceptions of its own ideals and achievements. Some written works were produced in the mini-courts of the principalities during the fourteenth century; these were not historical in nature but mostly translations or compilations in the Islamic religious sciences. Some begs undoubtedly commissioned such works in order to be comme il faut or to acquire prestige through courtly patronage. Building up their sphere of authority, some of the begs probably felt a practical need for having access to authoritative formulations of the tenets of Islam. There must also have been a pious concern with being correct or better informed about the faith one claimed to champion. As for non-religious learning, interest was displayed in the practical sciences of medicine and astronomy and in Persian literary classics. Many works in these categories were copied or recast in Turkish in the fourteenth century.[7]

From the evidence of extant sources, it seems that the people of the frontiers did not write their histories, with some exceptions to be discussed below, until the fifteenth century. They rather *told* what purported to be historical narratives woven around legendary warriors and dervishes. Two interrelated, sometimes even indistinguishable, types of narrative played a prominent role in formulating the historical consciousness of the people of the frontiers: warrior epics and hagiographies. If we are to understand the ideals and the motives of uc society, to grasp how they read meaning into their actions, how they conceptualized "war for the faith" and related notions, these are clearly the sources we must turn to. The following brief discussion of the sources, neither an encyclopedic survey nor an exhaustive analysis of a particular group, is meant only to highlight some of the relevant points in that regard.

Before turning to the narratives that claimed to portray the lives and deeds of frontier warriors of post-Mantzikert Anatolia, however, it must be noted that they were produced and told within milieux that were conscious of earlier layers of frontier traditions. The gests of various Arab warriors, deriving from early Islamic history or the ebb and flow of the Arabo-Byzantine frontiers, continued to be enjoyed by Muslim Anatolians even after the Turkish speakers gained predominance. These were not national epics but epics of a struggle between two religio-civilizational orientations, the Muslim side of which was dominated once by Arabic speakers and later by Turkish speakers. That earlier layer included the military exploits of Muḥammad, the Prophet, as embodied in works of *maġāzī* and tales of Ḥamza and 'Alī, the uncle and the son-in-law of the Prophet, respectively. Various other tales of Arab and Persian lore also enjoyed popularity, such as the *'Antarnāme* (the exploits of a Bedouin hero) and *Ebāmüslimnāme* (the life of Abū Muslim, who as a historical character played a central role in the transfer of power from the Umayyads to the Abbasids).[8] It is impossible to determine when Turkish renderings of such epics started to circulate, but over time translations appeared in writing. Thematic and narratological continuities indicate that some of the later epics simply reworked parts of the earlier ones for new contexts and audiences.

In fact, a keen consciousness of a continuum in the frontier traditions is evidenced by later works that explicitly refer to earlier ones. The *Dāniş-mendnāme,* for instance, which is set in immediate post-Mantzikert Anatolia and recorded first in the midthirteenth century, starts out by telling us of the abandonment of gaza activity since the glory days of Seyyid Baṭṭāl Gazi, a legendary Arab warrior, as recorded in legends about him, before it moves on to the story of the rekindling of the gaza spirit by Dānişmend Gazi. The story of Seyyid Baṭṭāl Gazi itself includes characters from the vita of Abū Muslim, such as the latter's comrade and brother-in-law Miżrāb, who also turns out to be Dānişmend's grandfather, thus appearing in all three narratives.[9] The *Ṣalṭuḳnāme,* which consists of lore compiled in the 1470s concerning the figure of a dervish-warrior, Şarı Ṣalṭuḳ, who seems to have lived in the thirteenth century, begins likewise with references to the earlier layers of the gaza traditions, in this case to both Seyyid Baṭṭāl Gazi and Dānişmend Gazi.[10]

The consciousness of the legacy of earlier gazis and the urge to situate later gazis within the framework of that legacy find a more poetic formulation in the image of 'Aşkar, the horse of Ḥamza, the uncle of the Prophet and the protagonist of a cycle of extremely popular narratives called *Ḥamzanāme.* This holy horse, who enjoys a miraculously long life, serves, after Ḥamza, both Seyyid Baṭṭāl Gazi and Şarı Ṣalṭuḳ. Around the beginning of the Şarı Ṣalṭuḳ narrative, he sees "his ancestor" Seyyid Baṭṭāl in a dream and is instructed as follows: "My dear [literally, "the corner of my liver"]! Go on and make your sortie [*ḫurūc*]. . . . Go to the bla-bla cave; there you will find 'Aşkar, the horse I used to ride. And also take the war equipment . . . all the arms of Lord Ḥamza are there."[11]

Later layers of gaza lore were aware not only of different stages in the long history of the "struggle for the faith" but also of its different geographical settings. Whereas Seyyid Baṭṭāl Gazi had been based in Malatya in eastern Anatolia, the scene of gaza had moved westward and northward under Melik Dānişmend, and even farther west and into the Balkans with Şarı Şalṭuḳ. And because what constituted the frontier was changing, the conditions of frontier warfare, life, and cultural activity at the time of the Arab conquerors must have been different from those of the Dānişmendids, which must have been different from those of the late-thirteenth-century frontier in western Anatolia. As frontier areas and powers changed, so did frontier culture. The earlier narratives that survived must have been constantly remolded, through oral retelling and transmission, before they came to be recast in writing.

The transmission of these narratives over time, place, milieux, and media presents many problems that have not yet been dealt with. The currently rather sharp boundaries that exist in Turkish studies between historical and literary-historical scholarship must be crossed in order to deal with some important questions that arise from the existence of this intricately interrelated body of narratives. No serious consideration, for instance, has yet been given to the scholarship on the interface between orality and literacy as developed by anthropologists and European medievalists. There are also more straightforward tasks, such as delineating the paths and mechanisms of transmission or analyzing and comparing different aspects of these narratives in terms of motifs, strategies, concepts, cosmology, geographic consciousness, degrees of "realism," casts of mythical beings (e.g., the witchlike *cāzū*), or topographies of legendary sites.

Even if the abovementioned legendary-historical and pseudohistorical narratives make up a reasonable body to be studied on its own, they were shaped within a cultural environment that produced various other kinds of works and recognized various other modes of expression. Ultimately, works dealing with the vitae of frontier warriors and dervishes need to be evaluated within the context of that larger cultural universe. It would be very important to know, for instance, when written works of *'aḳā'id* (articles of faith) arrived in frontier areas, or to examine the differences between the earlier and the later works of that kind. What appears to be the earliest such work from the neighborhood of the early Ottomans has a fascinating section on gaza, for instance.[12] In the emerging little "courts" of the emirs, literary and scholarly works were produced in the mode of courtly traditions. These works, their authors or translators, remind us that we must also consider the nature of the continued relationship between the frontier areas and the political centers, since a sharp, clean break can never be expected to have separated the two realms.

It would take us too far afield to deal with these problems here. Being aware of them, however, does not imply that we should consider the legendary vitae of warriors and dervishes irrelevant for an understanding of the cultural life of western Anatolia in the thirteenth and fourteenth centuries, an area that did not produce a large body of historical texts of its own. The gaza ethos, whatever lore it relied on, had permeated that part of the peninsula by the time of Osman's chieftaincy. Besides, the point in what follows is not to argue that Osman and his entourage built a state because they thought in a particular way but rather to demonstrate that certain attitudes that are seen to be contradictory to the gaza spirit by some modern scholars are very much a part of that spirit according to works produced to uphold the notion of gaza and to glorify the legacies of its various champions in Anatolian history.

It can be safely assumed that the people of the western Anatolian marches were exposed to at least some of the oral lore of earlier frontier struggles as embodied in the legends concerning Abū Muslim, Seyyid Baṭṭāl Gazi, and Melik Dānişmend. The center of the cult of Baṭṭāl Gazi, for instance, was his shrine "discovered" in the twelfth century near Eskişehir, not far from and connected to a main route to Sögüt, Osman's base of power around the end of the next century. We must also note, however, that we do not have access to that lore except in later written versions. This is also the case with the lore concerning post-Arab and post-Seljuk frontier heroes such as Ṣarı Ṣalṭuḳ and Umur Beg, as contained in the *Ṣalṭuḳnāme* and the *Düstūrnāme*. In each instance of recording, the particular circumstances of the moment must have determined, to some extent, the shape in which we now read those narratives. It seems that as long as the frontiers were "in operation" as true frontiers, no one cared to put their "history" into writing. Whenever the central states believed they had reined in the centrifugal energies of the marches, however (or when the frontiers were "closed," to put it in terms of the American experience), they were keen to patronize the recording of frontier lore, both appropriating and taming once-rival traditions.

The overarching theme in all these narratives is the services rendered by particular protagonists and their entourages in expanding the abode of Islam and/or gaining converts. Even in these idealizing depictions, however, the arsenal of the gazis goes well beyond weapons and exclusionistic zeal. The work of a gazi is not as simple as confronting the infidels with a choice between "Islam or the sword." Even though these works were produced to portray the achievements of gazis to audiences who had to be interested in correctness, that correctness obviously did not imply erasing all traces of latitudinarianism and of cooperation with the infidels.

The *Dānişmendnāme,* for instance, was first written down for 'İzzeddīn (Keykā'ūs II, d. 1279) of the Seljuks of Rūm, at a time of reconciliation between that branch of the ruling house and the subdued march warriors, who had once, especially when the Dānişmend family was at its prime, represented a serious challenge to Seljuk supremacy.[13] In the first half of the thirteenth century, however, the Seljuks of Rūm were consolidating their rule. A crucial part of that policy seems to have been pursuing centralization while gaining control over, but also support among, those elements that represented the frontier energies. While the policy failed in the long run, individual Seljuk figures, whether through personal qualities or prevailing circumstances, came indeed to be revered by Türkmen tribes and dervishes and to find a respectable place in the historical consciousness of the people of the frontiers. The two most noteworthy examples of such figures are 'Alā'eddīn Keyḳubād (r. 1220–37) and his grandson 'İzzeddīn; and it does not seem coincidental that the former patronized the cult of Seyyid Baṭṭāl Gazi (as well as the cults of a number of dervishes) and the latter was the one for whom the *Dānişmendnāme* was cast in writing.[14]

Despite its self-conscious religio-political correctness, however, the work is not free of elements that might be considered suspect from the point of view of orthodoxy, at least if it were to be rigidly conceived. Melik Dānişmend, for instance, the relentless warrior of the good cause, is not above bending rules as he forgives apostates who had not only reneged on their former affirmation of Islam but had even started raiding Muslims.[15] Even in this highly stylized and idealized depiction of gaza, then, the good name of a gazi is not diminished for engaging in Realpolitik.

As depicted in a later episode, the drawbacks of rigidity could be all too apparent to the Muslim warriors through its consequences. According to this account, the people of the town of Sisiya converted to Islam, but they converted "out of the fear of the sword." The governor whom Dānişmend left in charge of the town "was extremely devout, a solid [or, rigid] religious scholar, and made the people of Sisiya pray all five times every day *whether it was necessary or not.* If one of them were not to come to the mosque [to pray with the congregation at the regular hours], he would be reprimanded. The hypocrites remained helpless."[16] When the town was besieged by the infidels, however, the governor paid dearly for this attitude. He gathered an army of the townsmen ten thousand strong, but "there were only about two thousand Muslims, while the other eight thousand were hypocrites." The latter switched sides during the confrontation, and all the Muslims, including the governor, were killed. On the one hand, this is a story of treachery that prepares the ground for the unfolding of the gazis' inevitable revenge; it could be read as a lesson on the dangers of putting too much trust in converts. On the other hand, it can also serve as a lesson on the hazards of too much orthodoxy. The narrator seems to have wanted his audience not to miss that reading by inserting the phrase underlined above: praying five times a day is of course incumbent upon all adult Muslims according to Sunni orthodoxy.

The most important element of Melik Dānişmend's vita for our concerns here must be the hope of inclusion it offers to the Christians of Anatolia upon conversion to Islam. The same motif is central to the *Baṭṭālnāme,* where the best friend, the warrior companion, of Seyyid Baṭṭāl Gazi happens to be his former foe on the Byzantine side.[17] And if the *Baṭṭālnāme* provides a matrix for the joint ventures of an Arab and a Greek warrior, the *Dānişmendnāme* goes further in that its warrior heroes come from different sides not only of religious and ethnic but also of gender boundaries. Melik Dānişmend is joined in the beginning of the narrative by Artuḫı (an Armenian?) and Artuḫı's beloved Efromiya (a Greek?), who recognize the military as well as religious and moral superiority of Melik Dānişmend and convert. The two are so quickly absorbed into the whirlwind of gaza that they do not even find time to change their names as they fight alongside the melik for the rest of his exploits. One of the most celebrated gaza narratives thus presents its audience with an eloquent surprise, namely, the seemingly incongruous image of a woman named Efromiya, even after she has become Muslim, leading raids on horseback or engaging in chivalric one-to-one combat in the name of Islam. In one of their first joint ventures, for instance, all three heroes take their ablutions, pray, and dine together, and Efromiya stands guard while the other two sleep. This does not prevent her, however, from being the first to ride into the field the next day and challenge the enemy, led by her own father, to send somebody for combat. That infidel "made three attacks but could not succeed. It was Efromiya's turn. Grabbing her lance, she attacked the infidel; he collapsed, then stood up again in order to attack Efromiya, but she struck such a blow with the sword that his head dropped on the ground." Thereupon, twenty infidels attack her at once, but "Efromiya severed the heads of all twenty."[18] In all this and similar activities for the rest of the book, there is no mention of her covering herself or staying away from the company of males who are not of her immediate family, which would include Melik Dānişmend and even, for a while, Artuḫı, since they are married scandalously late in the narrative.

In the highly idealized world of the *Dānişmendnāme,* cooperation and inclusion are predicated on conversion. Some other gazi epics, however, display a readiness to be more flexible. Stuck in the middle of the cycle of narratives that make up the *Book of Dede Korkut* is a story that is set in the northeastern Anatolian marches, around the Byzantine kingdom of Trebizond.[19] The narrative starts out with Kan Turalı, "a dare-devil young man," looking for a bride who "before I reach the bloody infidels' land must already have got there and brought me back some heads." (The quest for power often goes hand in hand with desire as represented in the quest for the beloved in these narratives.) After this tough talk, however, he falls for the daughter of the *tekvur* (Byzantine lord or ruler) of Trebizond and works diligently to defeat three mighty beasts to win her hand. When he duly destroys those monsters, the tekvur says: "By God, the moment my eye saw this young man my soul loved him." Yet he goes back on his word and with six hundred of his men attacks the two lovers feasting in the "borderland." The young couple fight off the enemy but then turn against each other since Kan Turalı has difficulty accepting the fact that his life is saved by a woman. The hot-headed young man soon gives up, however, when she shoots an arrow that sends "the lice in his hair scuttling down to his feet." All Kan Turalı can do now is to claim, somewhat disingenuously, that he was "testing" her. Then they embrace, give "each other their sweet mouths and kiss," and finally gallop to their wedding banquet, which is enlivened by Dede Korkut's music and stories recounting "the adventures of the gallant fighters of the Faith."

If there is any real hero in this story, it is not Kan Turalı, whose hot-headed male warrior ethos is noticeably mocked, but Princess Saljan, and nowhere is it stated explicitly that she converted to Islam. As for her love of the gallant gazi, it has, at least in the beginning, nothing to do with who he is or what he represents; we read (and the audiences of the numerous oral renderings must have heard) that when she saw him, "she went weak at the knees, her cat miaowed, she slavered like a sick calf . . .

[and] said, 'If only God Most High would put mercy into my father's heart, if only he would fix a bride-price and give me to this man!' "

Behind the cheerleading for gaza, the story of Kan Turalı contains an object lesson on the complex realities of relations with the infidels in a frontier environment and provides some entertainment at the expense of zealous warriors. This may have been particularly timely in the midfourteenth century when the son of an Akkoyunlu chief named Turalı married the daughter of Emperor Alexios III Comnenos of Trebizond.[20] The two powers had been locked in a struggle that the Akkoyunlu saw in a religious coloring, but this did not render such a union impossible, and it led to reciprocal visits to the respective realms and further intermarriages. It would be too simplistic, and unfair to the subtlety of Dede Korkut or whoever the storyteller might be, to see this narrative as merely a distorted rendering of "real" events surrounding this or another particular marriage. But an ancient epic seems to have been customized to address late medieval Anatolian realities, to assign them meaning within a flexible understanding of the gaza ideology. If gaza were to be understood as zealously as it was by Kan Turalı at the beginning of the story, the narrator seems to suggest, one is bound to go through many surprises; but as the warrior attunes himself to the realities, he still ends up a winner, and so does his side.

The *Düstūrnāme,* completed in 1465, takes us much closer to the Ottomans in both time and geography. Embedded in a largely unoriginal history of Islamic states, its core is an original epic that relates, with much more historical specificity than the works so far mentioned, the exploits of Aydınoğlu Umur Beg (d. 1348).[21] The House of Aydın went through various phases of cooperation and competition with that of Osman until Umur Beg's descendants were subdued and their lands annexed in 1425. The Ottomans of the next generation could be generous in recognizing his achievements and might even benefit from patronizing Umur Beg's cult, which continued strong among the sailors of the Aegean for many centuries. Much harassed by European navies until both channels of the Dardanelles and the Bosphorus were secured, the Ottoman state was busily engaged in building a navy under Meḥmed the Conqueror.[22] The *Düstūrnāme* was commissioned by Maḥmūd Paşa (d. 1474), Meḥmed's longest-serving grand vezir, and it must have undergone some changes, perhaps making it more conformable to political and/or religious orthodoxy, in the hands of its compiler/editor, Enverī. Yet Enverī's own source for the epic, possibly an oral rendering of the story of Umur Beg's deeds originally told by one of his fellow-mariner gazis, is full of surprises. The internecine struggle between two gazi leaders, Umur and Sasa, is recorded without inhibition: Sasa Beg is on one page praised as a gazi who led pioneering raids into the Aegean region but is blamed on the next for having cooperated with the Christians against Umur Beg.[23]

If this example were to be dismissed because ultimately it condemns Sasa Beg's cooperation with the Christians (but the title of gazi is not taken away from him), we can note the further incident in the *Düstūrnāme* of the favors shown to Umur Beg by the baroness of Bodonitsa.[24] In fact, such help (and love?) offered by Byzantine women who are incited in their dreams to fall for warriors of Islam seems to have been a fantasy of the gazis, and such narratives may well have served to attract adventuresome young men into the armies or to keep them there. A similar legend is related in an Ottoman chronicle about Gazi Raḥmān, one of Osman's fellow warriors, and a Byzantine woman who allegedly helped the Ottomans take possession of the Aydos fortress.[25]

Even more striking is the nature of the relationship between the "usurper" emperor Kantakouzenos (1341–55) and Aydınoğlu Umur Beg as it is reported again in the *Düstūrnāme*. After a meeting where the emperor asks the gazi not to destroy his empire and the latter tells the Byzantine ruler not to be sad, our source reports: "They talked, wished each other well, and became brothers."[26] So serious is Umur Beg about this brotherhood that he turns down Kantakouzenos's offer of his daughter's hand as if marrying her would constitute incest: "The tekvur is my brother, his daughter my daughter; our religion does not permit this sort of thing."[27] He does not budge even later when the beautiful princess practically throws herself at his feet and says: "take me, and let me be your slave."[28] He hides his face in his hands to conceal his sorrow, but a gazi must observe a code of conduct; he cannot do certain things once a brotherly relationship is established even if that brother is the ruler of the infidels.

My intention here is not to provide more evidence of cooperation between Anatolian Muslim warriors and Byzantines, the prevalence of which is beyond doubt. The point is rather to show that the literature produced by or among the gazis to glorify their deeds did not find it contradictory to present their gazi protagonists in cooperation with Christians. If such was the gazi mentality, why should we define it to have been otherwise?

We should not, on the other hand, assume that because the gazis were able to embrace the infidels, they would proudly have all such embraces announced and recorded. Their lack of inhibition regarding cooperation with the infidels was certainly not boundless and should not be romanticized. There were times when the gazis would sooner forget any alliances they may have made with their Christian neighbors. Orḫān's wedding to the daughter of a local Bithynian ruler, traditionally dated to ca. 1299, is merrily reported in Ottoman chronicles, but there is total silence concerning his marriage with the daughter of Kantakouzenos (the princess Umur Beg had turned down). Orḫān's marriage was part of a relatively protracted period of cooperation between the Ottomans and the Kantakouzenos faction in the Byzantine Empire that turned out to be a turning point in Ottoman expansion toward southeastern Europe; and that whole period represents a lacuna in Ottoman histories, which prefer to present a very different scenario of the early military achievements in Thrace, as we shall see below. The *Düstūrnāme,* on the other hand, chronicling the story of a long defunct polity, is not inhibited in dealing with the pact between Kantakouzenos and the House of Aydın.[29]

It is not always easy to distinguish between these warrior epics and hagiographies of holy men, just as it is at times difficult to differentiate a warrior from a dervish or vice versa. These difficulties are particularly manifest in the vita of Ṣarı Ṣalṭuḳ, who seems to have crossed the line between the two vocations with particular ease.

The *Ṣalṭuḳnāme* was compiled by Ebū'l-ḫayr-i Rūmī, who traveled extensively to collect oral traditions concerning Ṣarı Ṣalṭuḳ, a legendary figure of the thirteenth century, on behalf of Prince Cem (d. 1495). Completed ca. 1480, the book doubtlessly contains a good deal of earlier material. This work is even more "pagan" than the other epics so far mentioned in terms of the presence of various elements of pre-Islamic lore; there is even a brief episode with a flying prayer-rug. Even more importantly, there are numerous instances where Ṣalṭuḳ gains converts among Byzantines by a display of empathy toward their Christian culture. He participates in numerous battles slaying infidels, but he can also stand by the altar in the Church of Hagia Sophia, when Constantinople is still Byzantine of course, and recite the Bible with such emotion that the Orthodox congregation dissolves into tears.

These holy figures are in fact trained for such cross-cultural exercises. Both Melik Dānişmend and Ṣalṭuḳ, according to their hagiographers, were taught in their youth the "four books and seventy-two languages."[30] And what is the main purpose of Ṣalṭuḳ's activities? To gain converts, to expand the hold of Islam over ever-more hearts and lands. Like the Europeans in the New World who "insinuate[d] themselves into the preexisting political, religious, even psychic, structures of the natives . . . to turn those structures to their advantage," the Muslim conquerors [of not just Asia Minor] were well aware that if one wanted to achieve victory over a rival or alternative system of meanings and values, one needed to enter into that system, turn it into "a manipulable fiction," and thus subvert and appropriate it.[31] Empathy, conciliation, and improvisation can be seen in some measure as a proselytizer's tools of trade. We should be cautious, however, about reducing the ideological rivalry and exchange to semiotic gamesmanship in the service of power. Positivist cynicism may prevent us from seeing that exchange with and absorption of other truths may have been the main concern of many actors involved who might still believe in the superiority of their own side and wish to achieve its supremacy, though not necessarily in an exclusivistic sense.

Obviously, then, the people of the marches did not see a contradiction between striving to expand their faith and engaging in conciliatory (not necessarily insincere) gestures toward members of the other faith. One insight gained from the hagiographies of dervishes like Ṣarı Ṣalṭuḳ is that an atmosphere of "tolerance" and symbiosis (of some departure from orthodoxy), or "improvisation" in Greenblatt's vocabulary, does not preclude a desire to gain converts.[32] In fact, is it not more intelligent to be conciliatory, whenever possible, in gaining the hearts and minds of others? Why deny this insight to the people of the marches, who had been faced for centuries with the dilemma of "the other faith"? Very probably, they were acutely aware of the wonders syncretism could work, and that is precisely the insight reflected in these hagiographies, which, like the warrior epics, operate on the basis of a dualism of us against them while recognizing that the boundaries of those two spheres are constantly being redrawn. For the self-confident proselytizer, after all, the world is not divided into "us" and "them" but into "us" and "those who are not yet us" or "those who may someday be among us."

Why should we suppose that the gazis or dervishes would wish to repel the Byzantine peasants when they could appeal to them? At any rate, the *Ṣalṭuḳnāme* provides ample proof that a call for conversion coexisted with latitudinarian attitudes or gestures. Not that such syncretism was mischievously planned by a secret organization of gazis and dervishes who held a conference and decided that this would be the better "tactic." No one ever theorized it, either. It appears to have been a shared insight deriving from the cumulative experiences gained through the fusion of Islamic elements with pre-Islamic beliefs of the Turks on the one hand and Anatolian Christianity on the other.

In fact, to expect the call for conversion from representatives of "untarnished Islam" rather than from other elements would be to misread Islamic history on the basis of an ahistorical assumption. It was rarely if ever the ulema and the courtiers in Baghdad or Konya who set themselves the task of actively gaining converts. It was rather the largely unorthodox dervishes of the marches in southwestern Asia and southeastern Europe who did so. A comparison between the hagiographies stemming from different Anatolian orders reveals that the antinomian orders are almost the only ones whose self-portrayal in their own hagiographies reflects a proselytizing mentality, whereas the literature of the orthodox orders does not seem as concerned with conversions.[33]

We should recognize here that it is in fact extremely difficult, if not impossible, to distinguish orthodoxy and heterodoxy in those regions or among those segments of the population that were not dominated by such structures of authority as could define and enforce a "correct" set of beliefs and practices in the mode of learned Islam. For one thing, central states themselves are concerned with orthodoxy or engaged in correcting others in varying degrees. Recognition of limits to authority in a particular administrative structure, pragmatism, and custom and tradition, which can be as imposing as orthodoxy, are some of the major determinants of state behavior in this regard. Looking at the heightened concern of governments with imposing orthodoxy from the turn of the sixteenth century, one can appreciate how little need the Turco-Muslim polities of western Asia felt to be rigorously correct until the rise of the (Sunni) Ottoman–(Shi'i) Safavid rivalry. There was even less room for learned definitions and scholarly rigor among those circles that were physically and/or socioculturally on the margins of institutionalized Islam, though they may have been more sincere in their faith and more aggressive in its promotion.

The best illustration of these blurred boundaries comes from a hagiography produced in a milieu that is of particular relevance for the early Ottomans. *Menāḳıbü'l-ḳudsiye,* written in 1358/59 by Elvān Çelebi, relates episodes in the life of Baba Ilyās, the leader of a Türkmen tribal movement against Seljuk authority that was suppressed after a series of bloody confrontations in 1240–41, and of some of his descendants and disciples.[34] Like the *Düstūrnāme,* it is relatively less legendary; that is, it is somewhat more precise with respect to the historicity of its protagonists as well as the sites and dates of the events that mark their activities compared to the epic cycle of the Baṭṭālnāme, Dānişmendnāme, and Ṣalṭuḳnāme narratives. The author himself is a great-grandson of Baba

Ilyās, who was of the Vefā'ī order but whose followers came to be better known as Baba'īs.

The relations of Osman's political community with its neighbors in both the immediate environment of Bithynia and the broader context of western Anatolian frontiers will be dealt with in the next chapter, but we must note here that the few dervishes whose presence can be ascertained in early-fourteenth-century Bithynia and who had some connection to Osman and Orḫān were of these Vefā'ī-Baba'ī circles. One of the key characters of Osman's early alliance, Ede Bali, is in fact mentioned by name as a disciple of Baba Ilyās or of one of his descendants.

Elvān Çelebi presents the Baba'īs as extremely successful proselytizers. Not only did they guide their flock among Türkmen tribes, but they also were able to gain hearts and minds among pagan Mongols as well as Christian and Jewish Anatolians. When writing of the passing away of his father, 'Āşıḳ Paşa, Elvān Çelebi cannot find a better image than "Armenians, Jews, and Christians" crying and asking, "where is our sheikh?"[35] Were all these mourners converts?[36] Maybe. Perhaps Elvān Çelebi does not make it explicit in order to emphasize their backgrounds. But possibly he wishes to indicate that 'Āşıḳ Paşa's influence had spread over all non-Muslims. This was certainly not impossible. Ḥācī Bektaş, a disciple of Baba Ilyās, was revered as Saint Charalambos by some Christians; and Elvān Çelebi himself was to be identified by a sixteenth-century German traveler, presumably on the basis of reports he heard from local Christians around Çelebi's shrine, as a friend of Saint George.[37]

Strikingly, such saint-sharing by Muslims and Christians was not limited to dervishly figures but could even include holy warriors, namely, gazis. The Greek inhabitants of Gianitsa (Ottoman: Yenice Vardar) down to this century displayed reverence for "Gazi Baba," that is, Evrenos Gazi, who conquered the area from his base in that township, where his mausoleum is situated.[38] And when 'Abdülḥamīd II's (r. 1876–1909) agents went to Söğüt in the late nineteenth century in the process of reviving the legacy of the "founding fathers" who hailed from that sleepy little town, they were surprised that some of the local Christians venerated Ertoğrıl's tomb.[39]

To go back to the Baba'īs and the *Menāḳibü'l-ḳudsiye,* it is clear that at least some of the Baba'ī figures were engaged in proselytization that was both militant and open to syncretism — a combination with proven appeal to Türkmen nomads. But what kind of an Islam were they spreading? Now, Baba Ilyās is best known for his political role as the leader of a

Türkmen tribal revolt. Perhaps struck by the indubitable and militant Shi'ism of Türkmen tribes in Safavid-contested Anatolia of the sixteenth century and of one giant post-Baba'ī order that crystallized around the legacy of Ḥācī Bektaş, a disciple of Baba Ilyās, many scholars have attributed extremist Shi'i views also to Baba'īs and all sorts of other dervishes and their followers among the tribesfolk in the thirteenth and fourteenth centuries. From the point of view of Ottoman central authorities in the sixteenth century, Safavid-inspired Shi'ism converged with Türkmen tribes and the Bektāşī order, but teleologically inclined modern scholarship has written its religious history backward from this. Various elements of the earlier tribal beliefs have been identified as heterodox—be they the so-called survivals of shamanism, the alleged influences of *bāṭinī* esotericism, or 'Alīd sympathies—and that heterodoxy then seen to be packaged within an extremist Shi'ism.[40] Köprülü wrote, for instance, that "the Islam of these Türkmen . . . was a syncrétisme resulting from the mixture of the old pagan traditions of the early Turks, a simple and popular form of extremist Shi'ism—with a veneer of Sufism—and certain local customs."[41] The most recent student of the movement is ready to cast doubt on the Shi'ism of the Baba'īs but reiterates the views on bāṭinī influences, extremism, and heterodoxy.[42] A revisionist view has attempted to turn this all around and has argued that the Baba'īs, as well as various other figures of Anatolian history who were portrayed as Shi'is by Köprülü and Gölpınarlı, were "actually" orthodox and Sunni.[43]

Elvān Çelebi's family hagiography provides evidence in both directions. There are, on the one hand, motifs that fall beyond the purview of Sunni orthodoxy and are part of the later 'Alevī / Shi'i worldview. On the other hand, one of Baba Ilyās's sons is named 'Ömer and a disciple 'Oṣmān, names that a Shi'i cannot be expected to honor.[44] The alleged adoption of Shi'ism by one of the western Anatolian principalities is also suspect. There is indeed a treaty signed "in the name of Muḥammad, 'Alī, Zeynel'abidīn, Ḥasan, and Ḥüseyin" by Aydınoğlu Ḥıżır Beg in 1349. But the House of Aydın could hardly have been Shi'i with one of its princes named 'Oṣmān (Ḥıżır Beg's uncle) and with strong links to the Mevlevī order.[45] Perhaps Ḥıżır Beg represented a particular case within the family like Oljaitu of the Ilkhanids, but even then more evidence is needed than a list of names that are perhaps more significant in the Shi'i tradition but are certainly also revered by Sunnis.

Turkish nationalist-secularist ideology and Orientalist images of the warlike but tolerant Inner Asian nomad have led to the depiction of nonsectarianism as a national trait among Turks in the Muslim orbit. But

Sultan Selīm and Shah Ismāʿīl should be sufficient proof that Turks are as capable of sectarianism as anyone else. The latter's Türkmen followers may look wildly antinomian from an orthodox Sunni point of view, but they demonstrate that nomadic tribesfolk are not above turning to violence for their own "correct" path. To the extent that nonsectarianism applies to earlier Turco-Muslim polities, it ought to be seen as a product of historical circumstances that made such sectarianism meaningless or pragmatically undesirable until the sixteenth century.

The religious picture of Anatolia in the thirteenth and fourteenth centuries appears much more complex than the neat categorizations of a simple Sunni / Shi'i dichotomy would allow. In this context, even if one were able to identify some particular item of faith as heterodox, this would not necessarily imply "Shi'i" as it is usually assumed; questions of orthodoxy and heterodoxy, even if they are meaningful, should not be formulated along the lines of a Sunni / Shi'i sectarianism. On the other hand, it seems equally misleading to see "heterodoxy" in any act or sign of belief which runs counter to the established norms of a learned orthodoxy. No such orthodoxy was yet established from the point of view of our protagonists, at least not with any clear-cut boundaries for them to stay within or to step outside. Maybe the religious history of Anatolian and Balkan Muslims living in the frontier areas of the period from the eleventh to the fifteenth centuries should be conceptualized in part in terms of a "metadoxy," a state of being beyond doxies, a combination of being doxy-naive and not being doxy-minded, as well as the absence of a state that was interested in rigorously defining and strictly enforcing an orthodoxy. None of the frontier powers seem to have had that kind of an interest. It was much later that a debate emerged among Ottoman scholars and statesmen with respect to the correctness of some of the practices of their ancestors.

Wherever they stood with respect to the "right" kind of religiosity, warrior chieftains of the principalities neighboring Bithynia were not ridden with self-doubt as to what they stood for. A cursory glance at the epigraphic and titulary evidence left from these emirates reveals that they had heartily adopted the championship of the faith and related principles like gaza. Already settled in western Anatolia in the 1270s, a beg of the Germiyan family was called Ḥüsāmeddīn, or "Sword of the Faith." Another member of the same family fell captive to the Mamluks in the Battle of Elbistan (eastern Anatolia) in 1277; he was called Şihābeddīn (Flame of the Faith) Gazi.[46] Muẓaffereddīn Yavlaḳ Arslan (Victor-of-the-Faith Fearsome Lion, d. 1291) of the Çobanoğlu family in Kastamonu is addressed as *naṣīrü'l-ġuzāt* (helper of the gazis) in a book completed in 1285–86 and dedicated to him.[47] One of the gazis he "helped" as the beg of the begs of the uc may well have been Osman Beg, who was based in the vicinity; in any case, a fellow warrior of Osman's in his first recorded battle was one of Yavlaḳ Arslan's sons.[48] In Kütahya, the House of Germiyan's eventual seat of power where they played the role of suzerain over the other principalities for a while, an inscription from 1314 informs us that a medrese was built by an Umur Beg who bore the epithet Mübārizeddīn, the "Combatant of the Faith."[49] The same epithet was donned by Aydınoğlu Meḥmed Beg, who had been sent to the Aegean region as a commander in the Germiyan forces. After falling out with Sasa Beg, a fellow warrior who was the actual conqueror of Birgi, Meḥmed Beg took over that town, where he established his own dominion and built a mosque in 1312. The inscription of that mosque identifies him as a gazi in the path of God (*el-ġāzī fī sebīlillāh*).[50] When Mevlānā Celāleddīn Rūmī's grandson, 'Ārif Çelebi, traveled from Konya to the frontier regions to establish his spiritual authority between 1312 and 1319, he referred to the same beg as the lord of the gazis. To the north of Bithynia, a certain Ġāzī Çelebi ruled Sinop until his death in 1322, when his daughter replaced him.[51]

These self-styled champions of the faith may have left a good deal to be desired in terms of conforming to the standards of some of the faithful: an enraged 'Ārif Çelebi, the Mevlevī, released his extraordinary powers to blow away the tents in the camp of the Germiyanid beg, who busied himself with slaves while the Koran was being recited.[52] Ibn Baṭṭūṭa, the Moroccan traveler, was scandalized by the higher respect shown to a Jewish physician than to Muslim scholars in Aydınoğlu's court in Birgi.[53] Still, the learned men evidently did not consider that the begs ought to be stripped of their titles for such suspect behavior. After all, the title of gazi had appeared in far stranger places than next to the name of Aydınoğlu Meḥmed Beg or the 1337 inscription in allegedly preideological Ottoman Bursa. Melik Muġīṣeddīn (Succorer of the Faith) Ṭoġrılşāh (d. 1225), "son of the Seljuk Kilij Arslan II, who largely built the awesome walls of Bayburt in 1213 and . . . who had the misfortune of being prisoner and sort of vassal of first a Cilician Armenian king and then a Trapezuntine emperor, and whose son was baptised to marry a Georgian queen, evidently allowed (or even sponsored) the building of a surviving Orthodox church within his new citadel on whose walls he is still proclaimed a gazi."[54]

None of these sources is directly related to the Ottomans. Neither the gazi lore nor the hagiographies mention Osman in any way that might be construed as direct historical evidence. The studies of the emirates begin to shed light on specific events of Ottoman history only during Orḫān's reign. Could we, then, neglect these sources and focus our attention exclusively on hard evidence about Osman and about Bithynia during his lifetime?

To answer this question affirmatively, we would have to assume that some of the nomadic groups in Anatolia, at least the one led by Osman, had none or only negligible cultural attachments and similarities to the rest of Anatolian-Turkish frontier society. There is no justification for such an assumption. The proto-Ottoman nomads may have been uncouth members of a crude milieu; to argue for the relevance of their Turco-Muslim identity does not necessarily entail their commitment to "lofty ideals" or their grounding in "untarnished Islam." Still, it can reasonably be assumed that they had heard of the legendary exploits of Seyyid Baṭṭāl Gazi or of Melik Dānişmend or that similar elements of the uc culture had touched them. Leaving aside "culture," did no news reach them about the exploits of the Menteşe warriors, for instance, about the Aegean adventures of the House of Aydın, or about the fabulous booty amassed by Ġāzī Çelebi of Sinop? Did they not hear that Aydınoğlu Umur Beg's ship was named "Ġāzī"?

Or were none of these groups gazis either, because they, too, collaborated with the Byzantines or other Christian powers when such action looked desirable? Whatever our definition of gaza, it is obvious from the way these neighbors of Osman projected themselves in their titulature and inscriptions that they considered themselves, or at least thought they had a believable claim to being, gazis. Given that the Ottoman beglik engaged in competition with its Turco-Muslim as well as Byzantine neighbors from the outset, it is not surprising that the earliest document from that beglik should reflect its chief's claim to being the "champion of the faith." Even in the absence of written evidence, it can hardly be imagined that Osman and his warriors, as soon as they came out into the political arena with a bid for regional power, would be unaware of the language and code of the frontiers or that they would not couch their claims within those terms.

Whether the early Ottomans belonged in that category or not, there clearly were warriors in Anatolia, as in many other regions of the medieval Islamic world, who claimed to be gazis fighting in the name of Islam. In the next chapter, we shall look at them more closely as a part of the historical reality of medieval Anatolia, as social types in a particular historical context. Here we must continue with our exploration of what gaza meant. What kind of a struggle did those warriors and their supporters imagine they were involved in?

With respect to gaza, the first thing to be noted is that it is not synonymous with *jihad* even though all the scholars mentioned in the previous chapter use the two terms interchangeably or use one English term, "holy war," for both as if there were no appreciable difference. But there clearly was such a difference in both the popular imagination and in canonical works.[55] Whether one takes the position of a learned Muslim or a narrator of frontier lore, who may not have had a rigorous training (and his audience, I presume), these terms are not to be collapsed into one. The word "jihad" is rarely used in the frontier narratives analyzed above or in the early Ottoman chronicles to be analyzed below; the sources clearly maintained a distinction.

Recent studies have pointed out that jihad should not be understood as incessant warfare to expand the abode of Islam or a mentality that recognizes a permanent state of war.[56] The assumption of perpetual hostility between the abode of Islam and the abode of war (which could better be translated as the abode of infidelity) and thus of a duty upon all Muslims to undertake incessant warfare upon non-Muslim lands is not valid. Such a view would be nothing more than a crude caricature of both the learned/centralist circles' notion and that of the frontier milieux. Accommodation was not necessarily outside the pale of Islamic "international law." It cannot be said that the frontier (and its conception of gaza or jihad) was inherently more or less accommodationist than the central powers; conflict arose between the two on this matter because the needs of warfare and accommodation did not always coincide in the two loci of decision making. By and large, however, the central powers were accommodationist more for historical reasons than for a priori ethical-political principles differing from those of the frontier.

Furthermore, jihad is defined by most canonical sources as a war undertaken when the world of Islam or the peace of the umma is threatened. There is thus a defensive quality to it, which became more pronounced during the nineteenth century when colonialist European encroachments were met with movements in the name not of gaza but of jihad. Still, the discussion about jihad as an offensive or defensive war overlooks the fact that, at least in terms of military logic, it is not always easy to distinguish between the two. What about a "preemptive strike"? Is it offensive or defensive? Or, how should one deal with the dictum that "the best defense is offense"? Can offense be seen as a defensive strategy?[57] In a world where any self-respecting polity of some scale could make claims to "world rule," does it make sense to expect people to operate with the concepts of defense and aggression as defined in a world of nation-states in "eternal" homelands with "inviolable" boundaries? Therefore, in the context of medieval Anatolian frontiers, a discussion of jihad as an offensive or defensive undertaking would be to some extent academic.

Nevertheless, a difference between jihad and gaza was maintained whereby the latter term implied irregular raiding activity whose ultimate goal was (or at least the warriors and their supporters could imagine that it was) the expansion of the power of Islam. Gaza, after all, had the original sense only of a "predatory raid" or "excursion into foreign territory."[58] It is not at all certain when the word acquired an exclusively religious connotation or whether this semantic transformation was complete by the fourteenth century. Even then, gaza was a lesser category than jihad. Canonical works describe it as a lesser *farż* (religious duty); that is, contributing to it was not incumbent upon everyone in the Muslim community, as was the case with jihad. The recently discovered codebook of fourteenth-century western Anatolia reveals that the same understanding prevailed in that environment.[59]

The much more striking point that emerges from that codebook, however, is that gaza, even when defined legalistically, did not preclude certain practices that some modern scholars prohibit to the warriors of the faith. While delineating the rules for the distribution of the pot deriving from gaza, this treatise with no inhibitions mentions the "share of the infidels" in case the latter have contributed to the acquisition of booty.

Naturally, the day-to-day business of the frontiers could not be expected to conform to most standards laid down in such codebooks even if the codes themselves were well known and had some pragmatism built into them. In fact, that must be the reason why works like this were produced; who would need codebooks if all the codes were internalized and applied? The actual behavior of the gaza-minded must be a combination of canonical codes that they were familiar with (not necessarily accurately, and primarily through oral transmission), emulation of examples known to them personally or through gazi lore, and various other considerations arising from the particular circumstances of the moment as well as shared norms of conduct such as honor and glory. These different elements may have contradicted one another at times, and a successful leader would probably be the one who would find the most appropriate resolution to such conflicts without ending up in failure or giving rise to questions of illegitimacy vis-à-vis his authority.

It is difficult to imagine any ideological complex without potentially and, at times, actually conflicting norms. Is there not always a tension between principles of "individual freedoms" and "law and order," for instance, in modern societies imbued with the ethos of democracy? Medieval societies likewise upheld values that could turn against one another but could also be balanced, at least temporarily or among certain segments of the population, through the enforcement of some authoritative resolution, complicated negotiations between different interests, some consensus on priorities, or similar means. Even if it may have been a major force in the ideological matrix of medieval western Asian and eastern European frontier regions, the "championing of one's faith" could never function as the sole concern of historical actors in that stage or as a single-minded zeal.

This is as true for non-Muslims as it is for Muslims. In fact, significant parallels can be found in the nature of the concerns and code of behavior displayed by the warriors of the two sides, as evidenced in, for instance, the Byzantine legend of Digenis Akritas, the borderland warrior, which allows us a glimpse into the frontier ethos of the "other side." One very important reason for such parallels is, as many scholars have pointed out, the fact that the sociocultural formations on both sides developed their traditions during many centuries of close contact and intensive exchange, which does not preclude the role of violence.[60] The role of shifting boundaries, loyalties, and identities should also be underlined here. At any given moment, some of the populace on either side of the frontier, warriors and others, would have been recent arrivals—converts, slaves, or recently subjugated people—who were steeped in the cultural traditions of the other side but were now in a position to contribute, voluntarily or forcibly, to this one. Given all this, it is not surprising that a student of Byzantine cultural life finds in her inspiring study of the Digenis Akritas legend a "measure of understanding" intensified by "the long existence of the frontier zone. . . . [T]he frontier Byzantine differed from the rest. For, as has already been observed by other scholars, the Byzantine-Arab [or Byzantine-Turkish] frontier regions were different in character from the territories behind them, developing specific cultural, social, economic traits."[61]

Like the Muslim gazi epics, the tale of the Byzantine frontier lord presents a dualistic universe of "us" and "them" defined in religious terms. However, the line between the two warring worlds is more remarkable for the ease with which one can cross it than for its rigidity. And Digenis Akritas is certainly not ashamed that his father was once a Muslim, who, like the Trebizondine princess in the story of Kan Turalı, switched sides not out of piety but love, and that his grandparents were Paulician heretics.[62] Indeed, the very name of the hero, Digenis (Two-Blooded), is a constant reminder of his background, just like the names of Artuḫı and Efromiya in the *Dānişmendnāme*. Rather than suppressing the inclusivism of the political communities they glorify, both the Christian and the Muslim holy warrior epics thus underline the possibility of inclusion and the fluidity of identities in those frontier conditions.

The motif of the protagonist's mixed origins in these rich texts can certainly not be reduced to a "sign" of ethnic mixture. The ambiguity of the hero's origins might well serve as a metaphor for all kinds of social ambiguities other than or in addition to an ethnic one, which has been the sole focus in literalist readings of historicist folklore.[63] That the soiled and the sacred, the two faces of what lies beyond the normal, are related to one another must be obvious to readers of Mary Douglas, the anthropologist, or of *La dame aux camélias*, the novel; hence the attributes of impurity and ambiguity can express sacredness embodied in a Digenis or in Dānişmend's companions. While the preceding interpretation of the frontier legends is not meant to provide the only or the most privileged reading, I would still maintain that the selection of ethnic fluidity as a meaningful and popular metaphor for social ambiguity in medieval Anatolia cannot have been totally arbitrary.

In addition to the plasticity of identities in frontier environments, we must note the possibility of cooperative ventures by people of different identities at any given moment even if those identities may be seen to be engaged in a conflict in a larger setting. In fact, contrary to modern scholars' arguments as to the incompatibility of the gaza spirit and cooperation with or toleration of infidels, the congruity of these two allegedly disharmonious attitudes appears to be a topos in frontier literature which reveals an essential point concerning the gaza spirit: it is, among other things, an attempt to gain hearts and minds; it is always possible that the pure-hearted infidel will join your fold. He or she is not necessarily an enemy to the bitter end.

Numerous examples of such collaboration—real or metaphorical or both—occur in gaza narratives. I have already mentioned the case of Köse Miḫal and Osman as well as the one of Umur Beg and Kantakouzenos. Wittek, too, explicitly noted the possibility of cooperative undertakings, such as the one between a certain Nicetas the Greek and a Saladinus ca. 1278 on the Caria coast.[64] Even in *ġazavātnāmes* produced much more self-consciously and knowledgeably in later orthodox environments, to develop a friendly relation with an infidel was not frowned upon. In the gests of Ḫayreddīn Paşa (Barbarossa), grand admiral of Süleymān the Magnificent, for instance, the gazi seaman captures a large number of Christian ships and their captains, including the renowned Captain Ferando. When he sees that the brave infidel is wounded, the pasha orders that "a building in the palace complex [of Algiers] be vacated and reserved for Ferando and that surgeons visit him and serve him all day" until he is cured.[65]

A late-seventeenth-century novella of the Mediterranean corsairs shows how exigencies could render the transition from Christian-Muslim cooperation to the championing of Muslim faith abrupt yet relatively unproblematic.[66] The author tells us that he and some other Muslims were captured by Christian corsairs while traveling from Alexandria to Istanbul. In a most surprising narrative twist, the warden of the corsair ship turns out to be the protagonist of the story; he delivers the Muslims from captivity and leads them, along with some of his "infidel" shipmates, to glorious and gainful adventures on the seas. As a group, the Christian sailors, including the warden, are referred to as "dirty infidels"; the world is divided into "us" and "them" in a confrontational dualism based on religious identity. Yet this does not preclude the possibility of friendship and cooperation with individuals from "the other world." It is always possible that those individuals will eventually join you and fight for the same cause, just as the warden declares himself Muslim more than halfway through the novella. And the author has no qualms about using the word gaza for the joint undertakings of the Christian and (freed) Muslim shipmates, including himself, under the chieftainship of the warden-captain as gaza even before the latter's conversion.

This is only to be expected from proselytizing faiths, and is not surprising among Muslims, who did not need to be theologians to know one of the basic tenets of their faith, namely, that all human beings are born Muslim since it is the natural religion. (Only thus could the *ḳul* system flourish to the extent that it did. Through this system, thousands of non-Muslims from the fourteenth to the seventeenth century were enslaved or recruited, converted to Islam, and trained to function as ḳuls, or servants, of the House of Osman in the military and administrative cadres of the Ottoman state, including the highest positions. You could indeed trust these ex-infidels because once shown the true path of Islam, which accords with the innermost nature, the *fiṭra,* of every human being, they would follow it in accordance with their natural tendency.)

It would be wrong to see only cold-blooded calculation toward future gains in those acts of cooperation. As implied by Barbarossa's gests, there must indeed have been those who appreciated the valor or scruples or skills or connections or humor or beauty or plain human warmth of others even if they were on the wrong side. Even the literature that was produced after the total and brutal rupture which followed the intense violence of the Anatolian war between Greeks and Turks in this century had room for complex relationships of hostility and affection, repression and solidarity, between the two peoples.[67]

One should, on the other hand, not forget that they fought bloody wars after all. Complex relations developed, symbiosis and cooperation were possible, but over the long run people's behavior was, at least in part, shaped by or attuned to an either/or struggle. The two sides of the frontier had over the centuries molded overlapping planes of social and cultural interaction and lived, in certain respects, in more proximity to one another than to certain elements within their "own" societies. The frontier was a "veritable melting pot of religions, races, and cultures."[68] But in countering this kind of nonexclusivist vision to the nationalistic exclusivist depiction of medieval Anatolia,[69] one should not get carried away and forget that there were indeed two sides that fought one another on the basis of identification with this or that side. In an article that successfully delineates the biases of sources written from the point of view of sedentary peoples, Keith Hopwood, for instance, seems to nearly suggest that our perception of a pattern of conflict between the two peoples and their "lifestyles" derives solely from the misperceptions and skewed reportage of urban-biased historians of Rome, Byzantium, etc.: "the conflict between pastoralist and sedentary farmer is a construct of a settled civilization and . . . in many places accommodation between nomad and farmer is mutually profitable."[70] Accommodation and symbiosis were possible and occurred much more often than historians have so far recognized; identities changed, inclusivism was common, and heterogeneity was not frowned upon. Still, hostilities and exclusions were, or could be, part of the same environment, and one should be careful not to romanticize, whatever the weight of inclusivism in frontier realities or narratives.

Beyond inclusivism, a "code of honour serves in Digenes as a kind of lingua franca for the frontier peoples" as it does in the earliest recorded narratives about Osman.[71] In these traditions, which portray him as a gazi, Osman enjoyed friendly relations with his Christian neighbor, the lord of Bilecik, until the latter plotted against him. In another version, the rupture occurred because the Christian lord treated Osman with arrogance. If the gazi identity mandated indiscriminate warfare against the infidel, Osman would not have needed an excuse to attack the Christians; but it is only when they act dishonorably that this gazi takes action against his Byzantine neighbors. Osman was thus driven to undertake military action not because of any automatic compulsion to finish off the unbelievers but because of a breach of confidence or etiquette.

It is also noteworthy that, to take the most legendary, the most "Osmannāme"-like, early sections in those chronicles, his hostility seems to be directed primarily toward the "Tatars" rather than toward Bithynian Christians, just as Digenis's main enemies apparently are the "apelatai" rather than the Muslims.[72] And this higher hostility did reappear at least once more, at the time of Timur's invasion. According to the contemporary historian Ibn 'Arabshāh, who knew both Timurid and Ottoman traditions from within, Bāyezīd asked Timur to "not leave the Tatars in this country, for they are material for wickedness and crime. . . . and they are more harmful to the Muslims and their countries than the Christians themselves."[73]

Recognizing the role of honor and etiquette enables us to understand that being a gazi means that one fights not necessarily for a particular set of beliefs but for one's side, which defines itself through its upholding, perhaps ignorantly, of a religious identity that claims, perhaps inaccurately, to be based on a set of beliefs and rituals. Once one has chosen a side, it goes without saying that one's side has the right beliefs; when one is fighting, one is not necessarily, and probably not very often, thinking of one's belief system. To the extent that system has permeated one's values and practices (and whether these are orthodox or not is not always a meaningful question), one is embedded in it anyway. The rest can be a question of honor (one does not want to let one's side down in that category) or worldly gain (why should it not be your side that enjoys the bounty of God?) or a combination of these and many other considerations.

Whether championing one's faith or protecting one's honor, or both, a frontier warrior or even a dervish could, without contradicting himself, seek and enjoy material benefits so long as he had his priorities straight. Had gaza been the kind of puritanical struggle implied in a literal reading of the notion of holy war, it would also conceivably conflict with the pursuit, display, and positive evaluation of wealth. But in the Anatolian-Muslim frontier narratives, as in the story of Digenis, where "honour is conceived of as going hand in hand with wealth/nobility" and "wealth/nobility is an ingredient of both male and female honour,"[74] material prosperity is not frowned upon.

In the codebook mentioned above, gaza is in fact listed as the most desirable means, but as one means, of "gaining one's livelihood."[75] The need to share gaza booty with cooperating infidels is mentioned in the same source in conjunction with their military services as well as with their assistance in locating the hidden goods of other infidels.[76] And the gazi narratives are full of joy and pride with respect to the booty amassed as a result of the raids, whether they are conducted in all-Muslim armies or not. Some bragging about or ostentatious display of the booty could even be commendable since evidently it might encourage others to join the good fight. It might also be one way of demonstrating the successes bestowed on the warriors of Islam and of discouraging the infidels, who would thus confront what seems to have been the strongest practical argument for the supremacy of Islam: if the Muslim faith did not represent the correct path, would God have allowed Muslims to succeed like this?[77]

Neither warriors nor schoolmen and dervishes upholding the gaza ideal apparently saw anything wrong in being explicit about the material dimension of warfare. There is an account, for instance, of a strikingly explicit bargaining episode between Orḫān Gazi and his manumitted slave Lala Şahin Paşa, who says he would fulfill a particular military assignment only if all the booty were left to him. Orḫān accepts Şahin's terms but then regrets his decision, and when the ex-slave commander turns out to be successful, reneges on his promise. In the court of law, however, Tāceddīn-i Kürdī, notwithstanding the fact that he is related to Orḫān, enforces the earlier deal that had been struck. The mid-sixteenth-century scholar Ṭaşköprīzāde, who relates the possibly apocryphal anecdote, may have intended primarily to moralize about the responsibilities of jurists and to remind his readers of the superiority of law over even the highest secular authority.[78] What interests us here, however, is the fact that he relates the incident without any hint of disapproval vis-à-vis the bargain itself. He does not seem to have felt that the reputation of Orḫān or that of Lala Şahin as gazis is at stake.

It was not unbecoming even for a dervish to savor material returns from gaza. Apz, the dervish-chronicler of the fifteenth century who accompanied many exploits among the warriors of the faith and personally engaged in some of the fighting, boasts of the slaves and other objects that fell to his lot. Moreover, it is not only wealth derived from the pursuit of gaza that one could enjoy with an easy conscience. Ottoman chronicles relate that another prominent figure in the Bithynian frontier at the time of Osman was a certain Sheikh Ede Bali, who "displayed many miraculous deeds and was the pivot of the people's faith. He was known as a dervish, but dervishness was in his esoteric being. He had plenty of worldly belongings and livestock."[79] This rancher-dervish may have been a fictive character, but the fictionalizing chroniclers of the early Ottoman gaza exploits had so much respect for the character that they made him the father-in-law of Osman Gazi.

Thus another pair of seemingly contradictory values could peacefully coexist in the frontier: on the one hand, living one's life according to high ideals that may demand self-sacrifice; and on the other, the pursuit of wealth and glory. As long as one knew when and where to give priority to the right drive, and as long as one knew how to dispose of wealth (through charity, hospitality, gift giving, appropriate ostentatious display, etc.), wealth was not just acceptable but even incumbent upon anyone who wanted to achieve prominence and good repute as a champion of the faith.

In order to enjoy one's riches without embarrassment, however, one had to be clear about one's priorities. Ede Bali, for instance, was rich but "his guesthouse would never be vacant."[80] On the other hand, even charitable distribution could be suspect if accompanied by the wrong kind of secondary motives. Some were sharp enough to note, for instance, that generosity could be a morally hollow gesture, a means to a self-serving end. Such a perception led to rivalry between two community leaders in Arab Malatya, the ultimate frontier town at the time of the Byzantine-Arab struggles: " 'Abd-al-Wahhāb . . . wrote to Abu-Ja'far stating that he ['Abd-al-Wahhāb] gave food to the people, but al-Ḥasan distributed many times more, his aim being to contend with him for superiority in beneficence."[81] The traveler Ibn Baṭṭūṭa cherished the competitive hospitality that he observed in Anatolia in the 1330s, but one can only imagine that some host manqué might have read similarly ulterior motives into the beneficence of those who snatched the guest.

If even charity could be equivocal, pursuit of material returns most certainly could be. There were times when the appetite for bounty looked excessive and the zeal for the faith wanting. Only a few days before the conquest of Constantinople, for instance, the ultimate goal of Muslim gazis for centuries, Aḳşemseddīn, the Sufi mentor of Meḥmed II, was obviously frustrated by the failed attempts to conclude the protracted siege and wrote a letter to the sultan which reveals how piercing leaders of gaza could be in conceptualizing their ventures. "You know well," the dervish writes of the Ottoman soldiers, "that fewer than a few among them are ready to sacrifice their lives for the sake of God, but as soon as they see booty they are ready to walk into fire for the sake of this world."[82]

We have seen, however, that as long as one could maintain a balance between the two concerns, which must have been easier when gaza brought quick and plentiful returns, one need not be shy about the appeal of bounty. Engaged in battle and plunder on his way from Delhi to Kashmir, Timur was invited by his commanders to rest and not take the risk of being personally involved in physical confrontation. He is reported to have replied "that the War for the Faith had two supreme advantages. One was that it gave the warrior eternal merit, a guarantee of Paradise immediately in the world to come. The other was that it also gained for the warrior the treasures of the present world. As Timur hoped to enjoy both advantages, so he intended to justify his claims to them."[83] We may be skeptical about the sincerity of Timur or any other individual or even the majority of those engaged in gaza, but as an ideological construct it clearly recognized the role of the pursuit of riches as a legitimate incentive among the warriors. It all depended on how one went about acquiring it and how one disposed of it.

Among the different ways of bringing potentially contradictory goals to some modus vivendi is the distinction made between the short and the long terms. Thus you may in the short term compromise so that you gain allies and are stronger in the long term, or you may for the moment have to fight against a coreligionist in order to gain the victory for your faith in the long run. There is no reason to assume that gazis or their supporters would be unable to order and legitimize their affairs on the basis of such elementary prioritizing and strategizing.

If read in this light, the violent struggles between Muslim principalities do not necessarily contradict their self-identification with the gaza ethos. If those other fellows were foolish or misguided enough to block your way, the way of the true gazi, surely you would want to eliminate such obstacles for the sake of continuing your mission. Thus it is not at all surprising to observe that Muslim sources, at least ostensibly upholding the ideals of gaza, deal with intra-Muslim conflicts without inhibition.[84] Ibn ʿArabshāh, for instance, the Arab scholar-historian who spent many years in the Ottoman realm in the early fifteenth century, calls Bāyezīd I a "stalwart champion of the faith" and on the same page recounts the fact that that sultan "subdued the whole kingdom of Karaman" and those of Menteşe and Saruḫān and other Muslim emirates before telling us that he also subdued "all the realms of the Christians from the borders of the Balkan mountains to the kingdoms of Erzinjan."[85] The historian obviously does not see any contradiction here, nor does he expect his readers to do so. That gazi states could turn some of their aggressive energies to each other should indeed be expected because competitions can be particularly bitter among those with shared values.[86]

To summarize, the culture of Anatolian Muslim frontier society allowed the coexistence of religious syncretism and militancy, adventurism and idealism. In this, one side of the frontier simply paralleled the other, and the Anatolian frontier experience of Muslims and Christians as a whole paralleled the Iberian one. The Ottomans had social and cultural ties to the rest of the *ucāt* so that they, too, shared its ethos. Naturally, none of this proves that the rise of the Ottoman state was due to that ethos. The main argument up to this point has been the impossibility of reconstructing the nature of frontier culture without considering its own products and that such an analysis will contradict some modern expectations of the gazis. The cultural character of the frontier warriors, tribes, and holy men can be discussed only on the basis of the sources emanating from that milieu, and the cultural life of the early Ottomans cannot be expected to be distinct from that broader framework.

Before turning specifically to Ottoman sources, we ought to consider briefly the argument based on the observation that "gaza" does not appear in the pertinent Byzantine sources. It is indeed the case that Moravcsik's survey of Turkish onomastics and vocabulary in Byzantine sources reveals no mention of the words "gaza" or "gazi" with respect to the early Ottomans, but the same sources fail to mention these words altogether. In other words, Byzantine authors are stingy with the title of "gazi" not merely with respect to Osman and Orḫān but even when referring to several other warlords who were incontestably steeped in the gaza ideology, such as the Aydınoğlu family.[87]

Clearly, then, this is a point the sources were ignorant of or chose to remain silent about. Or perhaps Byzantine authors, like some modern ones, had a conception of nomads that had no room for cumbersome ideological trappings. At any rate, in the case of Kantakouzenos, who is writing in the 1360s, well after the alleged importation of the gaza ideology ca. 1337, the reasons of the oversight can be conjectured. His failure to mention the gaza implies not that he was unaware of it but probably that he preferred to underplay the Islamic aspect of the Ottomans with whom he chose to ally himself several times and whose ruler was, after all, his son-in-law. And on one occasion when a Byzantine source does in fact attribute a Turkish attack to a sense of antagonism, Lindner is merely dismissive: "What Acropolites terms irreconcilable hatred was in fact nomadic necessity."[88]

One of the rare Byzantine sources to relay firsthand observations on early Ottoman cultural life is the captivity memoir of Gregory Palamas (d. 1359), a Byzantine theologian and mystic. Here further evidence can be found for Ottoman moderation,[89] but this needs to be contextualized. Palamas was a captive in Ottoman Bithynia in 1354. If earlier in the reign of Orḫān the Ottomans adopted a policy of zeal following an influx of religious scholars from the East, ought we not to expect to find signs of zeal rather than moderation in Palamas's account of Ottoman discourse? Palamas participates in at least two debates—once in the sultan's court with some "*xiónai*" and once, due to his own curiosity, with a schoolman.[90] It is exactly in those circles that one would expect zealot representatives of the concept of gaza to dominate if, as argued, gaza as fervor for the extinction of the infidels became a *state* ideology after the middle of Orḫān's reign through importation by learned courtiers or men of religion. In the court of the beg who called himself "the champion of the faith" on a document of 1324, and "gazi, son of gazi," on an inscription of 1337, Palamas rather entered a discussion where his opponents ended their comments by saying that "the time will come when we will be in accord with each other."

Had Palamas come to the court of Orḫān's grandson in the 1390s, he might have been baffled to observe an even more eclectic religious culture, since there he would in all likelihood have met Ellisaeus, a Jewish philosopher, and his pupil Plethon, who was later to be persecuted by Byzantine authorities as an advocate of pagan Hellenism.[91] The influence of foreigners, non-Muslims, and representatives of unorthodox Islam is visible in the Ottoman court for quite some time, at least until the earlier part of Süleymān the Magnificent's reign. Thereafter orthodoxy took hold much more strongly, but even then the inclusivism of the Ottoman elite was never fully abandoned, while its dimensions and nature kept changing. Some of the Polish and Hungarian refugees of 1848 converted and rose to the rank of pasha in the Ottoman administration.

The Chronicles of the House of Osman and Their Flavor: Onion or Garlic?

Given the preceding discussion, we can see that the Ottomans never became gazis if the ahistorical definition analyzed above is to be applied, but it is obvious that, at least beginning sometime in the fourteenth century, they considered not only their forefathers to be gazis but also themselves. And the concept of gaza never disappeared from the ideology of the Ottoman state or of its Turco-Muslim subjects; the leader of the Turkish forces fighting against the Allied occupation and the Greek invasion in 1919–22 was popularly called Gazi Mustafa Kemal. Did Ottoman behavior not change over time? It certainly did, with respect to religious orthodoxy, conduct in warfare, treatment of non-Muslims, and all sorts of important matters. It would thus seem inappropriate to conceptualize gaza by assuming, like Wittek and his critics, that it was one and the same notion of "war for the faith" from its earliest emergence (in the dating, causes, and consequences of which Wittek and his critics would disagree) to the end of the empire (when it was finally abandoned, with disastrous consequences for the Ottoman state according to Wittek). Another way of looking at it would be to observe that the conception of gaza underwent transformation in Ottoman thought. Even this formulation is misleading, however, because it might be read as a linear evolution from a unified core concept. A much more appropriate understanding of gaza and of the whole legacy of warfare and conquest in medieval Anatolia has to be based on the realization that they were contested and constructed by different historical agents in different ways.

As reflected in its oral and written lore, hagiographies and epics, the Turco-Muslim society of medieval Anatolia evidently put a high premium on the championship of gaza—a complex notion and code of conduct that cannot be reduced to a relentless zeal on the part of ideologically correct Muslims. It would also be simplistic to assume that being a gazi meant the same thing(s) to everyone or that its meaning(s) did not change over time. Any aspiring individual could don the title of gazi, since there does not seem to have been a formalization of the kind that would define the French chevaliers or the Ottoman *sipāhīs* (prebendal cavalry), but to be called a gazi by others implied recognized achievements often accompanied by entitlements.[92] As symbolic capital that could turn a title into (political and economic) entitlement, the championship of the faith naturally constituted a contested resource. Competition raged not only over present spoils and possibilities but also, more and more as the champions of the faith kept achieving, over past achievements. That is, gazis, gazi-dervishes, and their followers or clients laid competitive claim to the glorious deeds of the past in the name of themselves, their kin, their patron, or their solidarity group. That a particular area or town, for instance, had once been gained for one's side would be obvious, but who exactly captured its fortress or the hearts of its inhabitants? Even if the immediate hero of a military or spiritual conquest was known, one could ask whether he or she was acting under a higher authority. In some cases, the answers were clear. But in others, there were apparently several conflicting reports or enough obscurities for differing claims to be advanced. Worse yet, the situation may be unclear even when it happens, since different participants may have differing notions of their contribution. To some extent, the discrepancies in the historical sources written down during the Ottoman era can be read as traces of such competition for the appropriation of past accomplishments.

As some of the small gazi-mercenary bands or Sufi orders expanded their sphere of influence, they also enlarged their claims over the past at the expense of those who were now diminished. This contest over the appropriation of the symbolic capital embedded in public recognition as a gazi implied that the meaning of gaza might also be construed differently by different people or parties according to their backgrounds and needs. Particularly as the nature of the polities changed dramatically with the establishment of sedentary bureaucratic practices and principles, some aspects of the earlier conceptions of gaza looked increasingly primitive and possibly also dangerous if any other sociopolitical forces claimed to represent it.

The dervishes who were in control of the Seyyid (Baṭṭāl) Gazi shrine in the mid-sixteenth century, for instance, were unacceptable to the Ottoman state, which now was conscious of its role as the defender of Sunni orthodoxy.[93] Clearly, neither the military-administrative nor the religio-scholarly branches of the state would want to give the impression or even think to themselves that they had abandoned the gaza spirit, but they could and did charge the dervishes of the Seyyid Gazi shrine with deviation from purity of the faith. The latter, on the other hand, could claim that they were there because of certain privileges that had been given to their spiritual forebears by earlier and purer gazis. This should not necessarily be read as the preservation of an Ur ideology from which the increasingly sedentary and bureaucratic Ottoman power apparatus diverged. It is more likely that both groups had redefined themselves since the thirteenth century and that both had refashioned the legacy of Seyyid Gazi and the meaning of gaza from their own perspectives. The seventeenth-century dervishes of the Seyyid Gazi shrine were Shi'i Bektaşīs, for instance, but there is no such evidence for those of the thirteenth century. In any case, when Pīr Sulṭān Abdāl (fl. second half of sixteenth century?), arguably the best-known voice of *ḳızılbaş* anti-

Ottomanism, wrote of the imminent arrival of the Safavid shah to deliver the Türkmen tribes from the hands of the House of Osman, he described the forces of the shah as the "real gazis."[94] It cannot be taken for granted, however, that the gazi-dervishes who gathered around the cult of Seyyid Gazi or the tribal populations that switched their allegiance to the Safavids represented the original and "real" gaza ethos while the Ottomans degenerated it. Obviously at least two different modes existed in the sixteenth century, but both of them were, in different ways and degrees, variants of the earlier spirit(s). The mutations were configured during the tension-ridden process of Ottoman state building, which does not seem to have been accompanied by a concern with history-writing in its first century.

There are no known historical accounts of Ottoman exploits by the Ottomans before the fifteenth century. But this must be seen as part of a broader phenomenon: the blooming of a literate historical imagination among the representatives of post-Seljuk frontier energies had to await the fifteenth century.

The earliest written rendering of an Anatolian Turkish narrative of a "historical" nature seems to have been the *Dāniṣmendnāme,* composed in 1245, but no copies are known of that original version. The earliest extant works written in Anatolian in Turkish on any topic are, in addition to the mystical poetry of Yūnus Emre, a few thirteenth-century poems by a couple of lesser-known poets such as Dehhānī and some verses penned as curious experiments by Sulṭān Veled, Rūmī's son, at the turn of the fourteenth century. The rest of that century saw primarily translations of romances or ethical and medical works (mostly from Persian) as well as works of Islamic law and rites (mostly from Arabic). There were also original works produced in Anatolian Turkish, such as 'Āşıḳ Paşa's mystical masterpiece, the *Ġarībnāme,* in which the author felt compelled to defend his use of Turkish, but few of these can be considered historical in nature. If it were not for Gülşehrī's brief vita of Aḫī Evren and the *Menāḳibü'l-ḳudsiyye,* one would not be able to point to any works written in Turkish before the fifteenth century dealing with contemporary historical events and circumstances.[95] Even in Persian and Arabic, not much historical writing (even including hagiographies and epics) was undertaken in post-Seljuk Rūm in the fourteenth century.[96] But clearly, events were told and cast into oral narratives, which seem to have awaited the Timurid shock to be rendered into writing.[97]

A versified chronicle of the Ottomans appended to an Alexander romance by Aḥmedī, who had an earlier attachment to the House of Germiyan, is the oldest account we have of early Ottoman history. It was written, as we have it, for Prince Süleymān, who was one of the competitors for reestablishing the integrity of the Ottoman realm after his father had lost the Battle of Ankara in 1402. Timur, the victor, quickly left Anatolia with his eyes set on other goals but not before dividing the domain that Osman and his descendants had been consolidating for over a century. Many beg families were given back their former territories that had been annexed by an increasingly dominant Ottoman state in the latter part of the fourteenth century. Timur even divided what might be called the "core lands" of the Ottoman family among Bāyezīd's sons. Ottoman historical consciousness was probably moving toward literary expression already under Bāyezīd, when the polity started to outgrow its frontier identity and to acquire, much more systematically and self-consciously than before, modes of governing and ideologies associated with the nonfrontier civilization. The earliest redaction of Aḥmedī's chronicle seems to have been written before the 1396 Battle of Nicopolis (Niğbolu).[98] It may be around those years that his brother, Ḥamzavī, composed a collection of tales of Ḥamza from the existing lore about that hero of Islam, the uncle of the Prophet.[99]

Whatever the precise dating of these early attempts turns out to be, there can be no doubt that historical writing came into its own among Turcophone Anatolians in the fifteenth century. In addition to the sizable body of literature on the Ottomans themselves, to which we shall turn our attention shortly, many "classics" of the long adventure that saw Muslims settle in and then overpower Asia Minor—the vitae of Şarı Ṣalṭuḳ and Ḥācī Bektaş, the gests of Seyyid Baṭṭāl Gazi and Gazi Umur Beg—were written down in this century. The history of the Seljuks was rendered into Turkish for the first time by Yazıcızāde, who appended to his largely translated work some original material on the principalities and the Oġuz traditions.[100] He even referred to the main epic of the Oġuz people, the tales of Dede Korkut, which also was given its written version at around the same time, in a separate book that included ancient Inner Asian lore along with the somewhat more "historical" gaza adventures of the Türkmen in northeastern Anatolia.[101] All of these works were written under different circumstances of course; not all were produced for the Ottomans or even in the Ottoman realm. The Akkoyunlu dynasty, too, the main rivals of the Ottomans in the east between the heyday of the Karamanids and the rise of the Safavids, had their story written down under Uzun Ḥasan (r. 1466–78).[102] More-focused studies of patronage and composition are needed to assess the meanings and interrelationships of these works. It should be clear, however, that the impressive historiographic output of the Ottomans in the fifteenth century must be seen in the larger context of transformations in the historical consciousness of Turco-Muslim Anatolians.

These transformations were undoubtedly related to the maturing identification of Turks, "real" or newly made, with the history and geography of the region as it was refashioned in the late medieval era. There were also claims to be made, rivalries to be sorted out, and hegemonies to be confirmed and legitimized. All this must also be related, on the one hand, to the transition from oral to written culture in certain circles and, on the other, to a series of complex ideological experiments in response to unprecedented political problems starting with an identity and confidence crisis following the Timurid debacle. Numerous signs point to the emergence of a new historical consciousness among the Ottomans as the dust began to settle after Timur's violent intrusion and the ensuing internecine wars among Bāyezīd's sons. There was not only a heightened awareness of the need to understand what went well and what went wrong before Timur but also the fact that his descendants continued to treat the Ottomans as vassals, forcing the latter to represent themselves in a new mode.

It may not have been necessary for Murād I (r. 1362–89) and Bāyezīd I (r. 1389–1402) to account for the way they eliminated their rival siblings, but by the time Meḥmed I reached the throne in 1413, the rules of the game had changed. At least two written accounts were produced to teleologically chronicle the internecine strife among Bāyezīd's sons as an ultimately felicitous tale that ended with the fairest conclusion, the victory of the best prince of course. One of these two accounts remains anonymous; it is known to us not as an independent work but as one embedded in later works.[103] The other one, like Aḥmedī's work, is a distinctly historical chapter in a larger text of a legendary nature, a *Ḫalīlnāme,* written in 1414 by 'Abdü'l-vaṣī Çelebi.[104] Yet the ultimate manifestation of Ottoman historical consciousness in that post-Timurid juncture may well be that Meḥmed I spent some of his precious resources to build a mosque in Söğüt, the small and by then politically insignificant town where Ertoġrıl was believed to have settled down.[105] The legitimacy of the Ottoman enterprise was ultimately based on its own adventure, its own dedication to gaza generation after generation since Ertoġrıl.

The new historiographic output was not necessarily produced directly under the patronage of the House of Osman; nor was it uncritical of the Ottoman enterprise. In trying to understand the Timurid rupture, some authors, even if they were loyal to the reemerging Ottoman state, were apparently ready to question certain developments, especially what they apparently felt to be departures from the "purity" of the earlier generations. The two major ingredients of the later fifteenth-century output were in all likelihood composed in the years following the Battle of Ankara. A certain Yaḫşi Faḳīh, the son of Orḫān's imam, sat down to write his memoirs in those years. His ***menāḳib*** (tales), too, survive only embedded in a later work (the chronicle of Apz). Another collection of early Ottoman and related historical traditions was composed by 1422; it constitutes the common source of Apz, Uruç, and several anonymous chronicles that came into being in the latter decades of the same century. Those later chronicles constitute the largest body of historical information, and misinformation, about early Ottoman history; their proper evaluation is one of the most important tasks for historians of Ottoman state building.

Other historical works, relatively independent of this set of interrelated chronicles, were produced in the same century. Yazıcızāde's history of the Seljuks, written in the 1430s, also contained a short account of Osman's begship and, even more importantly, a major and influential attempt to use Oğuzid political traditions to legitimize Ottoman rule. In this version, Ertoğrıl descends from the glorious Kayı branch of the children of Oğuz Ḫān. Şükrullāh, who wrote his universal history in Persian in 1457, seconded that. A grand vezir of Meḥmed II, Karamānī Meḥmed Paşa (d. 1481), composed another example of this relatively more "establishment" view of the Ottoman adventure in Arabic. To these must be added another relatively independent set of works: annalistic calendars (***taḳvīm***) that were apparently produced by a variety of Anatolian astrologers and/or dervishes, only some of whom were connected to the Ottomans.[106]

While the Timurids were receding into distant memory in the second part of the century, more-immediate concerns, about various elements of Meḥmed's imperial project, emerged and were incorporated in later chronicles that include a critical voice (Apz, Uruç, and the anonymous ones mentioned above). The three decades from the conquest of Constantinople to the victories of Kilia-Akkirman in 1484 witnessed the most intensive phase in the development of the Ottoman political technology that we now call the classical Ottoman system. The best-known aspect of this process has been described as the graduation from a frontier principality to an empire, with accompanying changes in the institutional and ideological spheres. Like any major political transformation, this process was not free of strain and strife. Some of the losers appeared as soon as the day after the grand conquest, when Çandarlı Ḫalīl, grandson of the scion of this vezirial dynasty, was arrested and soon executed. His rivals did not end up as winners either. Two prominent frontier warlords, leaders of the anti-Çandarlı party, were also executed in a couple of years. There was obviously much resentment, from various corners, toward Meḥmed II's systematic pursuit of an "imperial project," starting with the establishment of Constantinople as the new capital.[107] Much of that resentment found expression in the chronicles and coalesced with the critique against the earlier centralization-cum-imperialization drive attributed to Bāyezīd I. But the most sweeping transformation and the broadest-based uproar came toward the end of Meḥmed's reign when he confiscated more than a thousand villages that were held, as freehold or endowment, by descendants of early colonizers, mostly dervishes. We shall deal with Meḥmed's imperial policy and its losers again in the next chapter, but here it must be noted that the most substantive body of early Ottoman historical output — the chronicles of the House of Osman — was produced by those who lived through that era. Most of these authors were evidently dervishes or close enough to the gazi-dervish milieux to have been touched, either personally or through their patrons, by those policies.

When Bāyezīd II replaced his father in 1481, he faced not only the challenge of his younger brother but also the fury of the uprooted. Bāyezīd made no compromises with his brother, whom he forced into tragic exile and, allegedly, arranged to be poisoned, but he was forced to appease the losers of Meḥmed's confiscation drive by rerecognizing their entitlements to earlier privileges. After the elimination of Cem's challenge and the reprivatization of lands, Bāyezīd undertook a campaign into the realm of the infidels and also proved himself not wanting in the spirit of gaza. It was upon his return from that campaign in 1484 that he ordered the recording of what thus far had been mostly oral traditions about the founding fathers. Most of the critical chronicles were published after that juncture, in a context that was ready to hear those voices, when Bāyezīd was searching for the right dose of appeasement after his father's harsh centralism, and still hoping to tame cults that had not yet become fully anti-Ottoman by patronizing them (e.g., Hācī Bektaş).

All of these works and the rising number of hagiographic works, which included their own version of the history of the conquests, must be read with another aspect of fifteenth-century ideological developments in the Ottoman world in mind. From the early fifteenth to the early sixteenth century, the House of Osman and the order of Ḥācī

Bektaş achieved supremacy in their respective spheres while also developing a historical vision of themselves that confirmed, explained, and legitimized that supremacy. In other words, two organizations laid a claim to the energies that had made possible what was by then a clear victory of Islam over Eastern Christendom: the Ottoman state and the Bektāşī order. These two by no means monopolized all former accomplishments but were able to present themselves in paramount position with respect to the other forces. The two large institutional umbrellas seem to have started this adventure in some harmony and cooperation but ended up as the two opposing poles of Ottoman religio-political culture; in the sixteenth century, the Bektāşī order emerged as the main representative of anti-Ottomanism and as the rallying point for various religious and religio-political movements that found themselves on the wrong side of the dogma battles.

It is neither possible nor desirable to present an exhaustive survey of early Ottoman historiography here.[108] My purpose is basically to deal with selected problems in order to assess the usefulness of fifteenth-century Ottoman historical consciousness, shaped in large part by the ideological and political currents mentioned above, for understanding earlier Ottoman realities. From the brief sketch just given, it should be clear that by the time the major chronicles (of Apz and others) were composed, there were many different layers of oral and written historical traditions. To envision them only as layers of a linear progression would be misleading, however, since they also included competing or at least mutually incompatible accounts representing different politico-ideological positions. Since Gibbons, a strand of scholarship has tended to lump these sources into a relatively undifferentiated mass of unreliable information, while another strand, dominant in Turkey, has simply followed the old line of raiding them and the calendars for raw data.[109]

Lindner, for instance, is all too ready to treat the fifteenth-century chroniclers as a homogeneous block: court historians. "To the eye of a medieval historian their smooth, clean surface shines with the light of Einhard's life of Charlemagne. . . . To be a chronicler at court was also to be an amanuensis, of course." The only reliable information in these "court chronicles" about the Ottoman past, according to Lindner, is provided by "the incongruous, the unexpected statement," which may reveal "an older tradition truer to past life than to present ideology. . . . It took the entire fifteenth century for the Ottoman orthodoxy to emerge. . . . Passages which conflict with that orthodoxy should *a fortiori* reflect an earlier memory."[110]

In this version, then, Ottoman historiography, if not all Ottoman cultural history, is reduced to the evolution of "state ideology." The early Ottomans adopted "tribalism," which possibly converged with shamanism parading as Islam. Then came learned Muslims from the East, who convinced the rulers of the suitability of orthodox Islam and of the gaza ideology, thus erasing the memories of the "tribalist" past. By the end of the fifteenth century, court histories were commissioned to glorify the founders of the state as gazis (who they never were).[111] Due to accidents or sloppy editing, however, some remnants of earlier and truer memories crept into these accounts. And those are the only parts of late-fifteenth-century chronicles that can be assumed to reflect early Ottoman realities.

The specific image Lindner chooses for Ottoman historiography is that of an onion. The core of the onion in his account is Osman's "tribalism." Layer upon layer has accumulated to conceal this core so that by the end of the fifteenth century, we are faced with a fully ripened onion. Accidents, mistakes, and crudities give us glimpses of the earlier, deeper layers, however. Such an accident, for instance, was Apz's illness as a very young man that confined him to the home of Yaḫşi Faḳīh, the son of Orḫān's imam. Apz states that during that sojourn at Yaḫşi Faḳīh's house, he saw some menāḳib written by the latter; these tales he incorporated into his history.

For a long time, it was believed that the traditions Apz received from Yaḫşi Faḳīh must be sought in those passages of his chronicle that are common to other chronicles. V. L. Ménage, whose exemplary studies are the building blocks of all discussion on early Ottoman historiography, has demonstrated, however, that Yaḫşi Faḳīh's menāḳib must rather be traced to the sections that are unique to Apz.[112] On this basis, Lindner argues that those unique passages in Apz "represent a layer of the Ottoman historiographical onion considerably closer to the core than the other versions."[113] Apz is believed to have had accidental access to some information. When he later sat down to produce his chronicle for the court, that information was included within his chronicle through his simple-mindedness or oversight. "Not contaminated by Apz's preferences," those passages are closer to truth because they are earlier.

It is not necessarily the case, however, that the closer in time a source is to certain historical events, the more reliable it is, particularly if a policy of ideological purification is believed to have started in between that source and those events. If a significant ideological shift occurred during Orḫān's reign with the intention of sanitizing the reality about his ancestors, the chieftain's imam would be the least trustworthy source for recovering that reality. If the attempt at ideological purification was so successful as to obliterate all alternative accounts, later sources would not be any more useful of course. But to establish such a dominance, one first has to assume the existence of competing views and trace their interrelations. There is no room for such an analysis in the schema of a unidirectional, step-by-step development of ideology that does not take into consideration the complexity of early Ottoman social structure and the tensions within it.

Moreover, to liken Apz to Einhard is unjustified and problematic because the former is not a court historian. Though he does sing the praises of many achievements of the Ottoman enterprise, his chronicle is also informed by a critical streak that he shares, in varying degrees, with Uruç and the anonymous chroniclers. Taken altogether and treated systematically, Apz's criticisms consistently reflect the worldview of a certain milieu which, particularly after the conquest of Constantinople and the adoption of the imperial project, stood outside and in some opposition to the Ottoman court, or at least the dominant centralist position upheld by most sultans and statesmen of the classical age.

Apz's personal and ideological connections to the gazi milieu have long ago been identified.[114] It may well have been true that Apz decided to publish his chronicle due to Bāyezīd's demand after 1484 to have the deeds of his ancestors collected and told. This does not predicate either an ideological homogeneity or an official character in the chronicles. Apz and the writers of the anonymous chronicles may have modified the final versions of their books to some extent to protect themselves from possible danger; they were also probably influenced to a significant extent by the official ideology emerging throughout the fifteenth century. Such compliances and convergences do not undermine their distinct position, however. The specific criticisms in these chronicles consistently reflect the views of the frontier warriors as opposed to the emerging central state. Compare the accounts of the establishment of the ***pençik*** system (whereby the Treasury's right to one-fifth of the gaza booty was extended to include slaves), the objections to Bāyezīd I's lifestyle, the murdering of Ḥācī İlbegi, the application of a new monetary system by Çandarlı Ḫalīl Paşa, and the policies of Meḥmed the Conqueror in terms of property rights and rents after the conquest of Constantinople. All of these cannot be dismissed as slips or as a mere show of righteousness.

And why should it be thought accidental that Apz had access to Yaḫşi Faḳīh's chronicle and decided to rely on these traditions in his own book? Does he not openly state his source rather than try to conceal it?

In fact this passage and many others interspersed in his chronicle that tell us of his friends and acquaintances who often serve him as oral sources provide the reader with many precious clues about Apz's social network.

Growing up in a village of Amasya during the turbulent years of the Interregnum (1402–13) when a century's worth of Ottoman acquisitions seemed to be up for grabs, Apz apparently had a knack for being where the action was. In his teens, he tagged along with the army of Prince Meḥmed, the eventual winner. The young dervish found himself on the winning side probably for no other reason than that they were both based in the same area. While the forces of the future sultan were proceeding to what proved to be the final showdown with the only other surviving contender to the throne in 1413, however, Apz fell ill on the way and had to stay behind.

Whatever disappointment this turn of fate led to must have been alleviated by the fact that he thus became a guest of an old man by the name of Yaḫşi Faḳīh. Why would the young dervish stay in the house of the *faḳīh*? But then, isn't it only to be expected that Yaḫşi Faḳīh, the son of Orḫān's imam and a man of letters, would know of the family of ʿĀşıḳ Paşa and Elvān Çelebi, Apz's great-grandfather and grandfather, respectively? There is every reason to assume Apz felt comfortable in the sociocultural milieu he was born into. He chose to include Yaḫşi Faḳīh's menāḳib in his chronicle not merely because he happened to have access to them (in that sense, it is true that our own access to the faḳīh's narrative is partly due to an accident) but also because they made sense to him. The menāḳib he inherited from the faḳīh were skillfully woven into Apz's later fifteenth-century compilation because he wished to do so. A quick look at some of the later developments in his life will help us understand his preferences and his own approach to gaza.

Back again in his (overbearingly?) revered ancestors' community in Mecidözü, Amasya, a young man in his twenties with no irresistible calling for a studious intellectual or mystical vocation if we are to judge by his later career and chronicle, Apz was offered an exciting adventure by Miḫaloğlu Meḥmed Beg in 1422. The warrior-lord from the illustrious line of Osman's companion Miḫal had just been released from imprisonment in Tokat, where he had been confined due to his earlier alliance with the wrong prince. On his way to join Murād II's campaign against Muṣṭafā (the Imposter), the renowned beg of the marches visited the monastery and offered to take along his young namesake, Apz Meḥmed, from another illustrious family of those legendary days. Here we already have a telling case of gazi-dervish "networking." The young dervish seems to have taken to this opportunity like Marlow in Conrad's *Heart of Darkness* but with none of the latter's gloom. (Nor is Miḫaloğlu, the warrior, a Kurtz.) Like others of the gazi-dervish milieu as reflected in their literature, Apz appears to have been free of concern for any dark recesses in his soul; rather, he cheerfully undertook his journey to participate in this saga played out around the theme of spreading the light of Islam, which also promised material gain and a good time.[115]

In his new life, he came into contact with various other gazis and dervishes, who also make up most of the oral sources he cites in his history, and participated in many raids and campaigns, which he relates with relish. A difference can be noted in this regard between Apz and Neşrī, who wrote only slightly later but from a different perspective as a man from a different social and educational background. A member of the ulema, whose oral sources and thus presumably social connections are mostly from the ulema, Neşrī aimed at bringing together different Ottoman historiographic traditions that flowed more or less independently of each other up to his time, as has been demonstrated by the meticulous source criticism of Ménage. Neşrī had in front of him one set of traditions running through Apz (including YF)[116] and the anonymous chronicles (including the "common source" and the anonymous account of the Interregnum), a second set tying together Aḥmedī, Şükrullāh, Ḳaramanī Meḥmed Paşa, and some other samples of "courtly" historiography, and a third set reflected in the annalistic calendars. Until Neşrī, we can talk of at least three different historiographic rings that were bound to each other but kept their distinct identity. (If one were to consider the historical arguments of hagiographic works, a curious example of which will be analyzed at the end of this chapter, one could identify even further traditions; however, these did not figure in the eventual synthesis reached by the Ottoman establishment after Neşrī). And within each one of these sets, say between Apz and the anonymous chronicles, *systematic* differences can be found that provide the specific character of each work. To maintain Lindner's alimentary imagery, "garlic" is a more apt metaphor for certain aspects of early Ottoman historiography than "onion" because it recognizes a plurality of voices without assigning any of them, even the earliest, the monopoly over a "core reality." Or rather, like many Mediterranean dishes, both garlic and onion can be appropriate in the reconstruction of Ottoman historiography since there is also room for a layered approach in understanding the interrelationships of some of the texts that, in part, display a linear development.

A good example of the mixed flavor is provided by Wittek's masterly comparison of Apz's and Neşrī's respective treatments of a particular gazi legend: the taking of the Aydos castle.[117] So close are the two passages that the one in Neşrī at first appears like a verbatim borrowing from Apz. A minute comparison and analysis of seemingly minor discrepancies reveals, however, that Apz's version of the tale bristles with an insider's understanding of the gazi mentality, at least of its early-fifteenth-century version, which he cannot but have grown deeply familiar with since he participated in so many gaza undertakings in the entourage of renowned gazis. In this account, all the images and nuances convey authenticity. Neşrī's version, on the other hand, reveals a predictable lack of appreciation of such traditions. In Wittek's words, "Apz's story commends itself as a genuine document of the earliest Ottoman times by the lack of any anachronism."[118] Although Apz was transmitting a tradition he had obtained from another source, possibly Yaḫşi Faḳīh, he was able to capture the mentality of his source while Neşrī was not. This difference occurred, not because he was closer in time to the events than Neşrī, who wrote only a decade or so after Apz, but clearly because they were from two different social worlds.

We are not dealing with different stages of a unidirectional development here but with alternative (though somewhat overlapping) ways of looking at the past, and present. There is no more telling example of the differences between these two historians than the way they conclude the tale about the Aydos castle. Apz boldly announces: "Hey friends, of everything in this story which I have written down, by God, I have obtained full knowledge. From this knowledge I wrote. Do not think I wrote out of [my own] imagination." Neşrī of the ulema, on the other hand, totally omits this self-confident assertion and cautiously remarks: "But He knows best."

Ottoman historical writing of the fifteenth century can be neither taken for granted nor dismissed in terms of its relevance for understanding the historical reality of the earlier century; a critical reading based on systematic suspicion can uncover significant truths underneath the seeming distortions. The problem is a wholesale, undifferentiated characterization of the Ottoman chronicles. Different versions need to be understood on their own terms; without looking for a one-to-one-correspondence between textual variations and ideological orientations, one can still search for patterns identifying distinct traditions before determining their value.

A good example of systematic doubt is shown by Lindner himself when he deals with the way Osman came to power. On the basis of a comparison of different Ottoman sources, he concludes that Osman was elected to office in keeping with tribal traditions, which is crucial to his theory. Why, then, dismiss other traditions without reasoned argument? He asserts, for instance, that the story concerning the institution of the market tax (*bāc*) for the first time upon Osman's capture of Karacahisar is "anachronistic" without any argument. There does not seem to be any obvious reason to dismiss this tradition offhand, deriving from Yaḫşi Faḳīh in all likelihood, other than the fact that Lindner wants to attribute any ulema influence on the Ottoman polity to a later period. Particularly if one were to accept Lindner's own argument that the Ottomans captured Karacahisar from the Germiyanids and not from the Byzantines, it is reasonable to assume that Osman was merely faced with the continuation of a local tax. If the Germiyanid rulers of Karacahisar exacted bāc, the same source of income would naturally be offered to the city's new ruler.

Several other traditions about the capture of Karacahisar provide further evidence for Lindner's argument that that city was taken not from the infidels but from the Germiyanids. It is there that Osman is suddenly bombarded with choices he has to make in relation to established Islamic administrative practices as opposed to the loose conditions of the ucāt. It is in Karacahisar, we read in the YF-Apz narrative, that the *ḫuṭbe* (Friday sermon) was read for the first time in Osman's name, that a kadi (judge) and a *subaşı* (police prefect) were appointed, and that bāc was applied, upon the demand of those who came from "Germiyan and other provinces."[119] Whether all this indeed happened in Karacahisar cannot be ascertained, but after capturing a few towns like it, Osman was probably approached by several sheikhs, faḳīhs, kadis, priests, and scribes who confronted him with such matters and offered their services.

Many other examples can be cited of scholars systematically analyzing specific historical traditions in the fifteenth-century chronicles and delineating meaningful patterns that have some bearing on early Ottoman realities and/or ideological developments. In addition to Wittek's study of the Aydos castle legend and İnalcık's analyses of the chroniclers' criticisms of Meḥmed II's policy after the conquest of Constantinople, one can note Irène Beldiceanu-Steinherr's treatment of the first conquests in Thrace, to be discussed below. Ménage's comparison of the different versions of the "dream" that led to the foundation of the state in Ottoman legend, Zachariadou's comparison of Byzantine and Ottoman accounts of Orḫān's alliance with Kantakouzenos, and Lefort and Foss's explorations of the chronicles on the basis of Bithynian archeology are other examples.[120] The detailed analyses of Yerasimos, who compares the different versions of the Ottoman genealogy and of the legends about Hagia Sophia, also succeed in shedding significant light on the ideological programs of different chroniclers.[121]

THE CASE OF OSMAN AND HIS UNCLE

While the Ottoman chronicle tradition should be treated with extreme caution, we cannot forget that it contains some of the precious few things we have on early Ottoman history. Rather than dismissing it, we ought to venture boldly into the wrinkled space of its textual intricacies, compare variants in detail, focus on choice of stories, words, and even spelling if promising, and try to ascertain what if anything these may reveal of early Ottoman realities. This is a road filled with traps and there are bound to be dead ends and wrong paths taken. And most of what one cay say in the end will remain hypothetical. But isn't giving up on this task even less rewarding?

Take the fascinating case of Osman's competition with his uncle Dündar, for instance. It is related by Neşrī, but missing in all of the known earlier chronicles, that after Ertoġrıl's death, some wanted Osman and others Dündar to be the new beg. Realizing that Osman had strong support, the uncle gave up and accepted his nephew's chieftainship.[122] The reconciliation seems to have been superficial because in a later episode we read that Osman, annoyed by the patronizing attitude of the (Christian) lord of Bilecik, wanted to seize him, but Dündar argued that they already had enough enemies and could not afford to make any more. Osman interpreted this response, Neşrī writes, as his uncle's wish to undermine the young man's political bid (literally, his "coming out," *ḫurūc*). So he shot his uncle down with an arrow and killed him.[123]

Where does Neşrī get these pieces of information about Osman and Dündar which are not to be found in any of the earlier sources known to us? Could he have made them up? To make the post-Meḥmed II practice of fratricide seem more palatable? This is not impossible, but a much more likely explanation is that Neşrī had access to some early traditions which the chroniclers chose to edit out of their texts.[124] Besides, why would Neşrī, if he were fictionalizing to legitimize fratricide, not have Osman kill his brother Gündüz, especially in the episode when the two disagree, just like Osman and Dündar, on the course of action to be taken vis-à-vis their neighbors? Furthermore, writing slightly later than Neşrī and using his chronicle, Ibn Kemāl relates not only Neşrī's version of this story but also another one with the same ending.[125]

There were clearly "Osman and Dündar" stories that did not make it into the texts of Apz, Uruç, and the anonymous chroniclers. Whether the stories were true or not, it is not surprising that the narrators of those particular texts would choose to censor episodes concerning dynastic strife resolved through murder in the family (deflected parricide?). To sustain the logic of their argument, or the moral of their tale, Apz, Uruç, and the compilers of the anonymous chronicles would simply need to omit Dündar's case, because their narratives are structured around a rupture in the moral uprightness of the Ottoman enterprise in the reign of Bāyezīd I (1389–1402): all evil deviations from the purity and sincerity of early frontier years are to be located after that juncture, all those nasty developments toward the construction of an imperial political system and its ideology. The case is the same with fratricide, which the anonymous chroniclers and Uruç explicitly cite as an evil that was not practiced, so they claim, in the early generations. Just after reporting Orḫān's peaceful agreement with his brother 'Alā'eddīn upon their father's death, these sources add: "brothers consulted each other then; they did not kill one another."[126]

Curiously, this passage is omitted in the YF-Apz narrative, which also omits reports, found in some other chronicles, about the murder of Ḥācī İlbegi, to be discussed below. It is unlikely that Yaḫşi Faḳīh had not heard these gruesome stories, whether they were true or not. He may have found them unbelievable or chosen not to write them down, or perhaps Apz excluded such passages from his edition.[127] It must have been Apz's choice, for instance, to omit the antifratricide editorial recorded in the anonymous chronicles and Uruç, because it is presumably from the common source. Did Apz omit this passage because he knew better, namely, because he had read about Osman and Dündar in the menāḳib of Yaḫşi Faḳīh? In any case, the anonymous chroniclers and Uruç are in general more consistent in erasing all memory of familial strife in the early generations before Bāyezīd. They also omit the passage, related by Apz and preserved by Neşrī, of Osman's disagreement with his brother Gündüz. Uruç is in fact so cautious that he makes Osman's two brothers die before Ertoġrıl's demise, that is, before Osman has any political claims, so that he cannot be imputed.[128] In the anonymous texts, the brothers are named but nothing is said of their deaths.

As for Dündar, he is mentioned before Neşrī only in Bayatlı Maḥmūd-oġlı Ḥasan's *Cāmi Cem-Āyīn*.[129] Bayatlı writes that Ertoġrıl's father had four sons: two of them took their clans eastward when their father drowned in the Euphrates; the other two, Ertoġrıl and Dündar, came to

Anatolia. Dündar is not mentioned again in this work, which leaves some room for speculation but no more than that. How could that vile deed be imputed to the glorious founding father in a work written for Prince Cem, the loser of a violent struggle for the throne and the prime target of fratricidal designs entertained by the victorious brother? Apz, Uruç, and the authors of the anonymous chronicles as well as Aḥmedī assign only three sons to Ertoġrıl's father; none of them is named Dündar. (Şükrullāh and Ḳaramanlı Meḥmed simply do not refer to any brother of Ertoġrıl.)

Is it coincidental that the policy defended by Dündar is the very one Ertoġrıl is claimed in some sources to have maintained during his chieftainship? A pattern emerges here that must be related to conscious editorial adjustments. In the narratives that have traces of disagreement within the family, very strongly in Neşrī and faintly in Apz, the political orientation of the little principality or tribe changes dramatically with Osman: under Ertoġrıl, coexistence with the Christian neighbors and tension with the House of Germiyan; under Osman, continued strife with the House of Germiyan but the main thrust of the raids eventually turning against Christian neighbors. In the chronicles that erase Dündar, the anonymous ones and Uruç in particular, gaza activity starts already under Ertoġrıl only to be intensified under Osman—no change of policy, no conflict, no rivalry.

Thus, it may well be worthwhile to look for consistency in the editorial policies of these texts. They do not seem to be haphazard aggregations of data that are somehow lumped together because the compiler happened to have access to them. The compilers chose what to include and exclude, and there is a certain logic to those choices because there is a moral or an argument of the tale that changes according to the editor.

There is an episode concerning Osman's disagreement with family members also in the vita of Ḥācī Bektaş, the earliest version of which seems to have been composed in the fifteenth century.[130] Here, Dündar and Gündüz are collapsed into one character. Gündüz appears as Osman's uncle, who becomes the beg of the district of Sulṭānöñi upon Ertoġrıl's death. He arrests his nephew in the name of the Seljuk sultan because Osman, after coming of age, undertakes raids against Bithynian Christians despite the sultan's ban on raiding activity due to a treaty with Byzantium.[131] On the way to prison, Osman is received by Ḥācī Bektaş and given the good news of future rulership. Later he is released and appointed beg of the same district. Gündüz is not mentioned again. There is an echo here of a historical tradition concerning familial conflict and of the same policy differences between the two generations mentioned above, but no murder.

If Osman had an uncle, then, and a violent conflict with him due to incompatible ambitions and differences of policy, this was by and large suppressed in the known examples of early Ottoman historiography. Until the grand synthesis of Neşrī, only the author of the Ḥācī Bektaş stories mentions a brother who survived Ertoġrıl. He also describes a policy difference between the uncle and the nephew that leads to tension, but it is apparently resolved without any violence by Osman against family members. Why should he need to resort to murder if he already had the blessings of Ḥācī Bektaş, the Superveli? Some other sources, from the second half of the fifteenth century, when fratricide was codified but still opposed in some vocal circles along with several other imperial policies, not only erase all memories of friction within the family in the early generations, even the presence of an uncle or potentially rival brothers, but also explicitly absolve Osman of such "evil" action.

For Neşrī and Ibn Kemāl, fratricide was not an absolute evil any more but an accepted part of political life for its perceived relative merit over the alternative of protracted civil war and/or fragmentation. These two historians therefore not only were uninhibited about recording Osman's murder of his own uncle but also knew better than to editorialize against fratricide when they wrote about Orḫān and 'Alā'eddīn. Ibn Kemāl in fact attributes to Osman the same reasoning that is advanced in Meḥmed II's code to legitimize the legislation of fratricide: "saying that damage to an individual is preferable to damage to the public, he shot and killed . . . his uncle Dündar, who entertained ambitions to chieftainship."[132] In short, the stubborn old man got what he deserved; why should one fuss about it?

Given all this, one is tempted to conclude that the later authors may well be telling a truth that is suppressed by earlier authors due to their narrative priorities. With respect to the historicity of Dündar, there seems to be further confirmation in a piece of "hard" evidence found in the archives. In the land survey of the district of Ḫüdāvendigār (including Söğüt) from A.H. 928/A.D. 1521, a plot is identified as land once held and then endowed by a certain Dündar Beg.[133] There is certainly room for caution here since no information is given about this person other than his name and title. But then, the plot of land happens to be in the village of Köprühisar, in the vicinity of which, Neşrī specifically points out, Osman's uncle was buried.

Obviously, later sources cannot be treated as mere derivatives. A careful scrutiny of how a later compiler edits, what he or she chooses to maintain, omit, or change of the material available to him or her, reveals a good deal about the literary, political, and ideological proclivities of the editor and hopefully glimpses of the sources at the editor's disposal. Furthermore, later sources may provide information from earlier ones now lost to us. It is clear that Neşrī (d. ca. 1520), Leunclavius (1533?–93), Müneccimbaşı (d. 1702), to take a few examples from different periods, had access to works that we have not yet been able to locate or to as yet unidentified manuscript versions of works we know from other, variant copies. Until the recent discovery of the *Menāḳibü'l-ḳudsiyye,* containing the stories of Baba Ilyās and his descendants, Uruç was our only source for some fascinating information on the Baba'ī Revolt, which took place more than two centuries before he wrote. Neşrī may have read Dündar's story in some written source which may or may not eventually be discovered. Or perhaps he heard it told by a raconteur. In either case, his account of it two centuries after the fact seems to relate a reliable report about a crucial incident in Osman's political career.[134]

Clearly, the task of the historian is not as easy as using the early or tardy appearance of sources as the criterion of their reliability. Nor is there a clear-cut single path of ideological evolution whereby the meaning of these rich texts can be ascertained by wholesale characterizations.

GAZA: AN IDEOLOGY OF SCHOOLMEN?

The dismissal of the chroniclers' tradition creates yet another serious problem. Those who refuse to assign the gaza principle any role in early Ottoman history write it off as a later ideological construct, but even so the question remains: whose construct is it? Lindner, again the most systematic of the critics of the gaza thesis, confronts this question and claims that the gaza ideology that is reflected in the 1337 inscription is due to the Muslim scholars who "began to gather in the Ottoman domains" in the reign of Orḫān. "In the earliest days the most visible representatives of Islam were dervishes, but soon thereafter more orthodox figures emigrated from the east in order to serve, and be served by, the Ottomans . . . to the secure revenues accruing from the settled administration of the Ottoman future they added the gift of an orthodox heroic past. . . . The gaza became a useful convention for interpreting, to orthodox and sedentary audiences, the formative years of the dynasty."[135] No doubt an influx of Muslim schoolmen to Ottoman domains occurred during the rule of Orḫān, or even as early as that of Osman, as the traditions concerning the conquest of Karacahisar imply. However, no sources link these schoolmen specifically to the gaza ideology, though undoubtedly they were well aware of the concept and upheld their own version of it.

On the contrary, one exceptionally poignant line of criticism encountered in early Ottoman chronicles representing the gazi point of view is the one raised against the *dānişmends* (schoolmen) and the ulema who came to the Ottoman domains from the cultural centers. These sources accuse such groups of introducing many novelties and leading the rulers astray from their original path. The tenor of this criticism is nowhere as sharp as in the anonymous chronicles and, to a lesser extent, in Apz's text, namely, in the sources that can be the most closely associated with the gazi-dervish milieu. If the Muslim schoolmen coming from the east were the innovators and propagators of the gaza ideology, why are the books reflecting that gaza ideology vehemently critical of them? The truth of the matter is that the more orthodox figures who emigrated from the east were rivals of the dervishes, who were "the most visible representatives of Islam" and of the struggle for the faith, as these were understood in the early years of the Ottomans. Furthermore, it would be unfair to another, often neglected, social group to restrict the representatives of religious life in early Ottoman history to the dervishes. Looking at fifteenth- and sixteenth-century land surveys conducted in the areas of early Ottoman conquests, which meticulously record the grants and endowments made by the previous generations, it is clear that a large group of faḳīhs, apparently not as sophisticated as the ulema in terms of their educational background and administrative expertise, enjoyed the support of early Ottoman chiefs and warriors in return for religio-juridical services.[136] This group, too, would obviously have much to lose with the ascendancy of the medrese-trained scholar-bureaucrats, the ulema.

The ties of the dervishes to the gazi milieu are attested to in the hagiographies and the gazi lore analyzed above; copious evidence of the ties of both dervishes (naturally, of some orders) and faḳīhs to the early Ottoman chiefs and warriors can be found in the land surveys. No wonder that the most lively and sympathetic accounts of early Ottoman gaza traditions were maintained among the later representatives of these milieux. The anonymous chronicles and the YF-Apz narrative are imbued with a nostalgia for those early years when their ruler, as these sources would have it, had not yet been seduced by the ulema and the courtiers into adopting the habits of sedentary, bureaucratic states.

Two aspects of this criticism must be emphasized: it represents a consistent argument against the development of a centralized administrative apparatus, and there is a certain logic to the distribution of the critical passages in different chronicles.[137] One of the most important lines of censure is directed against the Çandarlı family, of ulema background, that nearly monopolized the top juridical and administrative offices in the Ottoman state from the midfourteenth to the midfifteenth century. While Çandarlıs bear the brunt of the chroniclers' attacks, the rest of the ulema is not spared; not even the Ottoman family remains untouched. A few passages need to be cited to gauge the tenor of that critique, raised by authors who champion the cause of gaza, against particular developments in the Ottoman enterprise as brought about by the schoolmen who came from the cultural centers:

> At that time [the reign of Murād I (1362–89)] . . . the rulers [pādishāh][138] were not greedy. Whatever came into their hands they gave away again, and they did not know what a treasury was. But when [Çandarlı] Hayreddin Pasha came to the Gate [of government] greedy scholars became the companions of the rulers. They began by displaying piety and then went on to issue rulings. "He who is a ruler must have a treasury," they said. . . . Whatever oppression and corruption there is in this country is due to scholars. . . . [They] commit adultery and pederasty, lend money on interest, and make no difference between permitted and forbidden. . . . Until Vulkoglu's daughter came to him, Yıldırım Khan did not know what drinking parties were. He did not drink and held no carouses. In the times of Osmān, Orkhān Ghazi, and Murād, wine was not drunk. At that time there were ulema who made their words effective. At that time the Sultans were ashamed before the ulema. . . . When the Persians and the Karamanlis became the companions of the princes of the house of Osmān, these princes commited all kinds of sins. . . . Until then nothing was known of keeping account books. The practice of accumulating money and storing it in a treasury comes from them. . . . When [Çandarlı] 'Alī Pasha . . . became vizier, sin and wickedness increased. . . . The house of Osmān was a sturdy people, but these outsiders came to them and introduced all kinds of tricks.[139]

In short, members of the Çandarlı family, along with other schoolmen, are blamed for the introduction of such "evil" practices as the establishment of a treasury and of regular bookkeeping procedures since they "had no thought of the end and did not remember that they would have to leave it all behind them." The institutionalization spearheaded by the Çandarlı, then, is presented as a denial of the profound truth that informed and guided the founding fathers of the frontiers: the world's transitoriness. One could legitimately enjoy the bounty of booty, as we saw above, but only if one knew where and when to give of one's self to higher principles. Such sacrifices were made by the earlier generations, the chroniclers imply, because worldly accumulation was not their main concern; they knew they were merely mortal human beings.[140] This juxtaposition serves to explain the major problem of early Ottoman historical consciousness: Bāyezīd's defeat to Timur. Having been steered by cunning ulema toward a new political orientation that abandoned the frontier spirit, he could not maintain the realm of his ancestors, the glorious gazis.

The chroniclers were clear about the fact that the conflict of political orientations was not a matter only of abstract principles. The structures and practices introduced by the schoolmen are also decried in terms of their concretely negative effects on those good old frontier folk. Çandarlı 'Alī Paşa, for instance, "gathered pretty boys around himself and called them pages [*içoğlan*]. When he had misused them for a while, he let them go and gave them posts. Before that time there were the old-timers who were the heads of families; these held all the posts; they were not sent away and not dismissed, and their positions were not given to others."[141] Some of the "old-timer" gazi and beg families were thus being reduced to dismissable appointees as a centralized state started to take shape; but they had started to lose ground against the centralizing orientation already in the former generation.

Among the nefarious innovations of Ḳara Ḫalīl, the patriarch of the Çandarlı family, was a tax that was clearly aimed at skimming the gaza booty of the frontier warriors. The idea for this tax is said to have come from a certain Ḳara Rüstem, a "Karamanian Turk," namely, an outsider to the world of the frontiers, who was one of those who "filled the world with all kinds of cunning tricks." The only "cunning trick" that is reported about this Rüstem is that he suggests to Çandarlı Ḳara Ḫalīl, who was serving as the *ḳāḍī'asker* (judge of the affairs of the military-administrative class) at the time, that one-fifth (*ḫums*) of the slaves captured in the raids, like other kinds of booty, ought to be taken by the state treasury. Çandarlı finds the suggestion sound in terms of the religious law and relays the message to Murād I, who adopts this *iḥdāṣ* (novelty). That, of course, is the beginning of a new army under the direct control of the House of Osman, *yeñi çeri* (Janissary), that was evidently staffed at first through this tax called pençik (one-fifth).

The tax is obviously exacted from the gazis and possibly as a punishment for their independent actions in Rumelia when the Gelibolu link was severed. It is significant that Ḳara Rüstem is appointed to collect the tax in Gelibolu, the transit port of the massive war booty from Rumelia into Anatolia. Naturally, he cannot have functioned as a *pençik emīni* (supervisor of the "fifth") there between 1366 and 1376, when that port city was lost to the Ottomans. It is almost certain, therefore, that Rüstem oversaw the collection of that levy only after the recapture of that city in 1376/77, when Murād I reasserted his power over the gazis in Rumelia, who seem to have followed a semiautonomous course of action during the previous decade, as we shall discuss later. At any rate, the tax was imposed on the gazis by the bureaucratic central state guided by scholars emigrating from the east, and it is clearly the resentment of the gazi circles that we find reflected in the chronicles.

It is certainly sometime during the fourteenth century that the sedentary administrative traditions of classical Islam began to enjoy influence and then gain ascendancy in the Ottoman state. Islamic and Anatolian cultural history shows us, however, that gaza had never been a consistently dominant political value for sedentary Islamic states; in fact, the raiders of the frontiers were shunned and even degraded (as *ʿayyārūn*, "scoundrels," for instance) by the learned schoolmen and courtiers, representatives of classical Islamic traditions. How can we suppose that migrants from this milieu brought the gaza ideology to the Ottoman domains? Furthermore, the recorded actions of these schoolmen contradicted the interests of the frontier warriors and drew criticism from the spokesmen of the latter group.

This is not to say that the Muslim schoolmen opposed the gaza ideology. How could they at a time when the Ottoman family were enlisting the gazis of other principalities (especially renowned figures of the Karasi emirate, who held the area right across the channel from Gelibolu) for an even more vigorous expansion in the Balkans? The imported or appropriated gazis from other principalities who became affiliated with the Osmanlı enterprise during Orḫān's reign must have bolstered the gaza ethos at that time.

The medrese-educated intellectuals serving the Ottomans did not oppose the gaza ideology but interpreted it differently; they gave it an orthodox coloring somewhat removed from the frontier traditions. In their version of Ottoman history, which retains a fascination with the quaint charm of the early Ottomans' naivety but omits most of the blatantly critical passages, the natural conclusion of earlier successes is the centralized Ottoman state with its sophisticated administrative apparatus. The thread binding the narratives written in the gazi-dervish-faḳīh mode, on the other hand, is the increasing alienation of the Ottoman ruler from the world of the earlier and egalitarian frontier society in favor of a sultanic rule. It is hard not to recognize the underlying sense of moral decline, or the waning of *ʿaṣabiyya* (group solidarity), as Ibn Khaldūn would have said, in the anonymous chronicles and in Apz.[142] The family of Osman, the center of these narratives (which are, after all, called Chronicles of the House of Osman), retains its purity up to a certain point — for three generations, to be exact — namely, until Bāyezīd I. Notably, cooperating with Christian Bithynians does not tarnish this purity, but their fall from the innocent world of struggle and solidarity is marked by the influx of the ulema.

Ménage summarizes the nature of the latter's resented influence: "in the good old days honest *ghazis* were not pestered by the central government; there was no *penjik* (= *khums,* one of the basic prescriptions of Islam) to tax private enterprise; there were no laws compelling the surrender of an earlier sound currency for a debased new one; and there were no nasty *ic-oghlans* (everyone knows how *they* won favor) coming out of the Palace to lord it over free-born Turks."[143] Obviously, all these practices were typical of or acceptable within the sedentary states of classical Islam, but they contradicted the norms and demands of frontier warriors. Hence, these criticisms are to be found not in Şükrullāh or Ibn Kemāl but in the anonymous chronicles and Apz. The sources that are critical of this transformation in Ottoman political life cannot possibly be classified as court chronicles; nor can the championing of the gaza principle in early Ottoman history be presented as a construct of orthodox schoolmen.

ALTÈRHISTOIRE IN THE FIFTEENTH CENTURY: THE VITA OF SEYYİD ʿALĪ SULṬĀN AND TALES OF ḪĀCĪ İLBEGİ

The best sampler of the garlic flavor must be the differing accounts of the gazis' achievements in different "historical" narratives. That is, some of the sources leave no doubt that they present us with alternative accounts that cannot be treated as different layers of one tradition. For example, even the harshest of the anonymous chronicles seems tame when compared to one particular source that, ironically, has no direct criticism to make of the House of Osman. The challenge to Ottoman historiography here is through an unabashed "*altèrhistoire*" that distributes the credit for the conquest of Thrace, one of the most glorious feats of the fourteenth-century gazis of western Asia Minor, in a shockingly different manner from all the other known chronicles.

A detailed analysis of the Vita of Seyyid ʿAlī Sulṭān, an enigmatic source among the fifteenth-century flurry of frontier narratives, would be inappropriate here.[144] Given the fact that it seems to be trying to defend one of its protagonists against defamation and his followers against loss of some of their rights, it was most likely written during Meḥmed II's expropriation drive or soon afterward when the names and rights of the losers were being restored by Meḥmed's son.

The most curious aspect of this work is its radical departure from the accepted story line of the conquest of Thrace. Here, too, the House of Osman is the royal family, and in fact the Ottoman ruler is a higher political authority than the protagonists, but the role of the other gazis is much grander than in any of the chronicles of the House of Osman. The real heroes of the work are Seyyid ʿAlī Sulṭān, also called Ḳızıl Deli, and his companions, who leave their home in Khorasan for the land of Rūm after the appearance of the Prophet to Seyyid ʿAlī in a dream. Seyyid ʿAlī and company are perfect combinations of warrior and dervish; their military role is more pronounced than that of many other holy figures who represent a similar combination, even more than Sarı Ṣalṭuḳ. The work was clearly produced after the Ḳızıl Deli cult (near Dimetoka, now Dhidhimoteichon, in Greek Thrace) had been incorporated into the Bektaşiyye, because our protagonists pay a homage-visit to Ḥācī Bektaş as soon as they arrive in Rūm. Once the latter blesses them and assigns them to specific ranks (i.e., formats the Khorasanian raw material into a Rūmī configuration), they join the Ottoman sultan, who happens to be on the Anatolian side of the Dardanelles pondering ways of sending his forces across the channel into Rumelia.[145]

Süleymān Paşa, an Ottoman prince who is the champion of the earliest conquests in Thrace according to Ottoman historiography, is among the forces that successfully undertake the crossing, but he is not the leader. His death, a major story in Ottoman chronicles, is reported here without much significance attached to it; nor does it imply anything in terms of the future of the venture. More strikingly, it is not followed by the replacement of Süleymān Paşa by his brother, later Murād I, as in the other chronicles, which thus convey an image of a *seamless* Ottoman leadership in the Thracian conquests.[146]

Emīr Sulṭān, another major figure of the Ottoman chronicles and the son-in-law of Bāyezīd I, appears in this vita but in a much lesser capacity.[147] He comes to Anatolia in the company of Seyyid ʿAlī and is appointed the standard-bearer of the latter's army by Ḥācī Bektaş. While moving from victory to victory in Thrace, the conquerors fall upon a town where they cannot find any water to perform their ablutions. Emīr

Sulṭān, seemingly unhappy with his rank or the amount of recognition he is getting, hastens to strike his stick on the ground, and a spring emerges. One might expect the other gazi-dervishes to be pleased with this performance, but peer recognition should not be taken for granted among this competitive lot despite their mystical-heroic vocation. Seyyid 'Alī first reprimands Emīr Sulṭān for his "hastiness" (*tizlik*) (i.e., for showing off) when there are so many others with power and then bumps him off with a lethal glance. After burying the deceased next to the water source he had discovered, the dervish-conquerors move on to new adventures.[148]

It has been proposed by Irène Beldiceanu-Steinherr that Seyyid 'Alī (alias Ḳızıl Deli) may well be Ḥācī İlbegi, the leading figure among the Karasi warriors who joined the Ottoman forces upon the incorporation of their principality by Orḫān Beg, which occurred in several stages beginning in the 1330s.[149] While Ottoman historiography has by and large represented the inclusion of the Karasi gazis as a fraternal integration of like-minded warriors who were happy to serve the struggle for the faith under Ottoman leadership, there are several indications that the relationship was not so smooth. The Karasi, after all, not only were the only ones to adopt the title of khan in that frontier environment but also must have had no mean claim to the championship of gaza, since they derived their descent from Dānişmend Gazi. Additionally, some of the Karasi warriors incorporated by the Ottomans, namely Ḥācī İlbegi and company, apparently also had claims to a Seljuk lineage.[150] Whether such claims were ever accepted by their neighbors or even their own subjects is not clear, but it hints at the nature of the Karasi self-image.

Given all this, it is not surprising to find laconic but distinct traces of discord between these warriors and the Ottoman ruler. Some of the anonymous chronicles, after reporting the pro-Ottoman version of the victory of 1371 against Serbian forces by the Meriç (Maritsa) River, relate a variant in which it is a superhuman effort by İlbegi that defeats the Serbs while the Ottoman army is still asleep. Some of these chronicles also relate that İlbegi was executed under the orders of Murād I, and by a ḳul to boot, while most of the chronicles prefer to omit the former's demise altogether. Whatever the precise nature of his death, it is curious that later Ottoman cadastral surveys include no freehold or endowment in the name of a conqueror like İlbegi. It may well be a pro-Ottoman counterattack on his reputation that created another version of İlbegi's biography in which he is a Cain-like figure who murders his own brother because the latter gave the family lands to Orḫān. The people of Bergama hate İlbegi so much, however, that they capture him and cede the town to Orḫān anyway; İlbegi dies after two painful years in prison.[151]

Like the Osman and Dündar stories mentioned above, a body of tales of Ḥācī İlbegi was obviously in circulation, and it may be related to the construction of the Ḳızıl Deli cult.[152] From my point of view here, it does not matter at all whether İlbegi indeed did all that is attributed to him, whether he was executed or not, or whether he is to be identified with Seyyid ʿAlī, which seems highly probable. It is certain that there once were variant accounts of his life and deeds that are not reconcilable with one another. The general thrust of these stories and the incidents reported in the hagiography of Ḳızıl Deli, whether the two are related or not, indicate that the credit for some of the major gaza feats in Thrace was contested by the Ottomans and other warriors. It may be more important to note this variance than to discover who was right. We shall turn to the history of these events again in the next chapter, but whatever their relationship to historical reality, that very conflict over the appropriation of the past, both immediate and remote, was clearly a part of early Ottoman realities and must once have resonated with meaning to actual tensions.

It is not surprising that variant accounts of the capture of Thrace represent a major line of tension in our sources about early Ottoman history. The transplantation of the frontier energies and of gazi activity across the channel, along with the ensuing conquests of Thracian towns leading into the Balkans, constitutes one of the most significant successes of the Anatolian gazis, and it can be argued that it ultimately sealed the fate of Byzantium or at least confirmed Turco-Muslim presence in southeastern Europe. As we shall discuss in the next chapter, the few decades after the crossing into Rumelia were particularly tension-ridden. During this period, the emerging Ottoman state, like so many others that had sprung up in similar conditions, faced the abyss of fragmentation. The House of Osman proved much more successful, however, than any of its forerunners or competitors in establishing its supremacy over its former gazi allies and neighbors, who were gradually but systematically rendered into commanders and fief-holders and their actions and duties regulated by the dictates of a centralized sultanic state. It is not surprising that if history remembers them, it is basically through their services to the development of the Ottoman state.

CHAPTER 3

The Ottomans

The Construction of the Ottoman State

Ekme bağ bağlanırsın
Ekme ekin eğlenirsin
Çek deveyi güt koyunu
Bir gün olur beğlenirsin

Do not cultivate a vineyard, you'll be bound.
Do not cultivate grains, you'll be ground.
Pull the camel, herd the sheep.
A day will come, you'll be crowned.

The poem was recorded by an ethnographer in the earlier part of this century among the seminomads who survived in the hills of the Bithynian Olympus where Osman's tribe once roamed. Maybe the thirteenth-century tribesfolk did not know this particular quatrain, but its lesson was certainly not lost on them. While they roamed rather than settling down to agriculture, "a day came," and a certain Osman, who seems to have been a leading member of the tribe's leading house (or rather, tent), imagined that he could carve a body politic under his leadership, that he could be Osman Beg. He decided to seize that opportune moment and never looked back.

Determining the auspicious "day" to assert one's will over a tribe in such a way as to make explicit its political nature was a matter of sensing the opportune moment and seizing it.[1] As implied by the term used in premodern Islamic sources for the making of a political bid, *ḫurūc* (coming out), the earlier history of the bidder is often obscure. There must have been many "closet begs" at any given moment waiting for their opportunity to come out; many brave men must have thought their moment had come to be begs and failed. When a "sortie" is not successful, it is of course no more than an assault or revolt, and the word *ḫurūc* is commonly used in that sense as well, which gives a good indication of the problem of legitimacy involved in such a claim. But a very rigorous test of verifiability was built into any claim of this sort: you would succeed only if your bid had divine sanction; if you succeeded, you could claim to have divine sanction and thus legitimacy—an argument a bit circular perhaps, but not sloppy.

This transformation, the assertion of a political will by the proto-Ottomans, seems to have occurred in Osman's generation, as will be discussed below. It is impossible to say anything with certainty about the earlier history of that tribe and the process whereby it started to play the role that it did.

Once it did initiate its political bid, the small tribe of Osman entered into competition with various Turco-Muslim and Christian rivals in the area. The tribe was eventually able to establish its hegemony, but it was no foregone conclusion that there would be one power as the ultimate winner and that it would be the House of Osman. Even if by the end of the thirteenth century it could be expected—and that is highly doubtful—that the Turco-Muslim forces would consume the Byzantine Empire, there was no reason to assume that all of it would fall into the hands of one dynasty. And even if that were to be expected, there was no reason to assume that it would be accomplished by the Ottomans. Why were *they* able to harness the frontier dynamism and the gaza ethos, as well as the mixed cultural heritage they all shared to some extent, more successfully than the rival polities? Or rather, what were the factors that enabled the Ottomans to eventually do better than the other statelings and even the Seljuk state?

Insofar as the gaza ethos played a role, it must be remembered that the Ottomans were not the only ones who could claim to be fighting in the path of God. A similar point can be made about "tribalism" or any other notion, concept, ethos, principle, ideology, or institution that one can neither show nor logically expect to be uniquely Ottoman. In other words, the investigation of the rise of Ottoman power must always proceed comparatively.

Furthermore, the question must be continually reformulated with respect to the different stages in the development of Ottoman power.

The empire was not built by 1337, the year the Bursa inscription went up, which has been pegged as marking the supersession of tribalism by the gaza ideology. Even if a phenomenon like inclusivist tribalism looms large in the earliest Ottoman success, how are we to explain the rest of Ottoman state building? The question of the "cause(s) of Ottoman success" cannot be expected to yield a unitary answer for the whole period one needs to consider. It must be raised and reraised in, say, 1300 or 1330 or 1360 or 1410. The answers in each case might differ, at least in terms of the emphases one needs to place on different factors.

An ideological commitment to gaza was in all likelihood common to all these periods, but its character and intensity kept changing, just as inclusivism was never fully abandoned by the Ottomans but was constantly redefined. It may be more significant that in all these phases there were warriors who wanted to see and present themselves as representatives of that ideological complex of heroism, honor, and striving in the name of Islam. As we shall analyze in this chapter, however, their standing within the principality and their relationship to the House of Osman also kept changing, as did those of other social forces like the dervishes. The social and political configuration as a whole kept changing while power, shared and contested in varying degrees at any given moment, was gradually concentrated in the hands of an administration serving a dynasty. This chapter will focus on the general dynamics of that change and its important phases in order to understand the rise of the Ottoman state as a process rather than as a mechanical relationship between a particular cause and an outcome.

Many scholars have noted that the location of Osman's beglik provided it with a unique advantage, which will be reconsidered below, in the earlier stages of its development. But it was not just a matter of the circumstances in which the Ottomans happened to find themselves. They also acted upon those circumstances in certain ways and forged their destiny. In this respect, the Ottoman practice of unigeniture, for instance—of keeping their territories intact in each succession under the full control of a single heir—stands out as a significant difference from the other principalities, which allowed for fragmentation by recognizing the rights of the different heirs according to Turco-Mongol tradition.

This was just one of the means whereby the Ottomans pursued a centralizing logic and protected the expanding realm under their grip from fragmentation much more consistently than any other polity that existed in those four frontier centuries of Anatolia. The other, and much more complicated, story is of the way the Ottoman state builders manipulated, often with success, a constantly shifting matrix of alliances and tensions with other sociopolitical forces. This was a process consisting of a series of carefully selected exclusions as well as inclusions, improvisations as well as continuities. To put it comparatively, the earlier or contemporaneous Turco-Mongol and Turco-Muslim polities in the region were unable to resolve the tensions between centrifugal and centripetal tendencies as effectively as did the Ottomans.

All the principalities were heirs to the political culture of Seljuk Anatolia, which Köprülü deems so important in Ottoman state building, but the Ottomans were much more experimental in reshaping it to need, much more creative in their bricolage of different traditions, be they Turkic, Islamic, or Byzantine. A comparison made by a historian of art between the architecture of the early Ottomans and that of their longest-lasting rivals, the Karamanids, can also be read in terms of its relevance to the political plane:

> The Ottoman architect delved into the basic principles of architecture and concentrated his energies on problems of space, form and structure. The Karamanid architect, on the other hand, was unable to graduate from the frame of medieval Seljuk architecture . . . and looked for monumentality in surface plasticity. And this attitude prevented Karamanid architecture from going any further than being a continuation of Seljuk architecture, or further than preserving a tradition instead of creating something original as the culmination of a conscious development.[2]

This chapter attempts to retrace some of the significant steps in the path of Ottoman state building. As a narrative, it is a highly selective one that does not aim to cover all the events in early Ottoman history that even this author happens to know. My goal is rather to follow the trajectory of the Ottomans' centralizing thrust, which supplemented the expansion but was carried out at the expense, whenever necessary, of the forces that were included in the expansionary process. Along the way, I will point to their selective use of several strategies to bring about or dissolve a network of alliances to consolidate and expand power while maintaining dynastic control over it. While this process kept producing tensions, the Ottoman success was in overcoming those tensions, real or potential conflicts, and eventually developing a vision of a centralized state, shaping it according to circumstances, and maintaining their drive toward it.

Strategizing for Alliances and Conflicts: The Early Beglik

The Ottoman historical tradition maintains, with some exceptions, that the tribe that later represented the core of Osman's earliest base of power came to Asia Minor in his grandfather's generation in the wake of the Chingisid conquests in central Asia. This makes chronological and historical sense, but otherwise the details of their story, including the identity of the grandfather, are too mythological to be taken for granted.[3] Most importantly, it is also unclear when and how they ended up in Bithynia, at the very edge of Turco-Muslim Anatolia. This is important because it could tell us what, if any, ties they had to any political structures in the established centers and what their status was in that march environment, surrounded by Christians, by other Turkish and "Tatar" tribes, and, toward the northeast, east, and south, by some begliks recognized by Seljuk and/or Ilkhanid authority.

That they hailed from the Kayı branch of the Oğuz confederacy seems to be a creative "rediscovery" in the genealogical concoction of the fifteenth century. It is missing not only in Aḥmedī but also, and more importantly, in the YF-Apz narrative, which gives its own version of an elaborate genealogical family tree going back to Noah. If there was a particularly significant claim to Kayı lineage, it is hard to imagine that Yaḫşi Faḳīh would not have heard of it. This in fact does not contradict Yazıcızāde, who gives the earliest written reference to the Kayı in the 1430s but also adds that the traditions of the Oğuz, presumably including the "true lineage" of Ertoğrıl's tribe, had been all but forgotten in his day.[4] So they had to be re-remembered. Şükrullāh, writing somewhat later, tells us that it took a trip to the Karakoyunlu court in 1449, where he was sent as the Ottoman ambassador, to learn about the Ottoman family's descent from Oğuz and Kayı.[5] And despite Köprülü's disclaimer to the effect that Kayı lineage was not particularly prestigious and hence not worth forgery, the political stakes are obvious in both cases. At least Yazıcızāde thought that "so long as there are descendants of Kayı, rulership belongs to nobody else"; and Şükrullāh was presented with this evidence as proof of kinship between the Ottomans and the Karakoyunlu at a time when the two states were considering alliance against the Akkoyunlu.

On the other hand, despite the skepticism surrounding the historicity of some of the names that appear in later chronicles as key characters in the late thirteenth century, especially Osman's father, Ertoğrıl, and father-in-law, Ede Bali, there is sufficient evidence to take these traditions seriously. Ede Bali's case will be considered below; as for Ertoğrıl, we have already noted the coin on which Osman struck his father's name. There seem to be good reasons to consider the historicity of even Ertoğrıl's brother Dündar, as we discussed in the last chapter. The more important question is, what kinds of activities did Ertoğrıl, Dündar, and their tribe engage in other than nomadic pastoralism?

With respect to this issue, the Ottoman sources clearly diverge. While some of the chronicles attribute gaza raids and some military success to Ertoğrıl, others portray that generation as militarily and politically inactive, at least after they came to Bithynia. The YF-Apz narrative, for instance, states that at the time of Ertoğrıl, after the tribe moved to Bithynia, "there was no fighting and warfare, they just moved between the summer and winter pastures."[6] About Şamşa Çavuş, who came to the region with Ertoğrıl, we read that "he got along with the infidels of Mudurnu."[7] The story of the conflict between Osman and his uncle (analyzed in the previous chapter) also suggests a change in the policy of the tribe. It seems from all this that a public and competitive political bid was not made until Osman. The circumstances that propelled the tribe to active participation in the political life of the frontiers, and thus ultimately to historical record, may well have come about in the 1290s as Togan suggests.[8]

At least so much is certain: the tribe enjoyed a fundamental upswing in the level of its military success and visible political claims under Osman's leadership so that it was the name of Osman and not that of any of his forefathers which ultimately defined the polity. We do not know by what name the tribe was known before his "coming out"; according to a nineteenth-century tradition, which smacks of invention, Ertoğrıl's tribe may have had the impersonal and rather lackluster name of Karakeçili (Of the Black Goat).[9] Whatever Ertoğrıl and his "Karakeçili" may have accomplished, they were not visible enough to appear in the sources of the literate cultures around them. But as Osmanlı (namely, "those who follow Osman"), the tribe and the polity went a long way.

If there is any point at which it would make sense to replace secular notions of heroism (*alp*-hood in medieval Turkic cultures) with gaza, this would be the time. But even before that, it seems improbable that Ertoğrıl's generation would be unfamiliar with the notion of gaza. In any case, the main rivalry of Ertoğrıl seems to have been with the House of Germiyan, and it continued into the early part of Osman's beglik. We have already seen that being a gazi was never understood to involve indiscriminate warfare against infidels and that it could involve warfare against coreligionists. If a unique passage in the Oxford Anonymous manuscript is accurate, Ertoġrıl's tribe was given pastureland around Söğüt when the neighboring area that later ended up as the land of Germiyan was still part of "the abode of war," namely, before the Kütahya area was conquered and the House of Germiyan had been settled in the western Phrygian uc.[10] Thus, Ertoġrıl's tribe may have seen its earlier freedom of movement threatened by the arrival of the relatively more powerful Germiyan and resented it. It is well known that the Germiyan played the role of an "elder brother" in those frontier areas until at least the early fourteenth century. Tensions between Osman's tribe and the House of Germiyan must also be due to the fact that the latter served the Seljuks in the suppression of the 1239–41 revolt led by the Baba'ī dervishes, many of whom, such as Ede Bali, fled to Bithynia, where they eventually forged close ties with the proto-Ottomans.

Still another mystery surrounds the early years and identity of Osman. In the earliest Byzantine sources referring to him, his name is spelled with a τ as Atouman or Atman. Considering that the Arabic name 'Uthmān and its Turkish variant 'Os̱mān are regularly rendered with a θ or τθ or σ in the Greek sources, some scholars have concluded that the founder of the Ottoman beglik did have a Turkish name at first, perhaps At(a)man, and that it was later changed to 'Os̱mān.[11] Curiously, one of the earliest Arabic sources to mention his name, the geographical work of al-'Umarī from the 1330s, also spells it with a ط in one of two occurrences (but "correctly" in another mention).[12] And there is an echo of this "other name" in a later Turkish source, the hagiography of Ḥācī Bektaş Velī, written in the fifteenth century.[13]

One does not need to revive Gibbons's theory of Osman's conversion to Islam from paganism to consider this name change possible and relevant. Turkish names were, as they are now, commonly given to children born Muslim, and this practice, though diminished, did not disappear within the Ottoman family very quickly; the name of Ertoġrıl was given to the eldest son of Bāyezīd I ca. 1376 and that of Oġuz to a son of Prince Cem in the second half of the fifteenth century. Orḫān's imam, to choose an example from the class of religious functionaries, called his son Yaḫşi. Namely, being born with a Turkish name certainly did not imply being born non-Muslim.[14] If Osman was called Atman, however, and adopted a similar but more prestigious Arabic name later on, this could point to an important turning point in the self-identity or political ideology of the early Ottomans, probably an intensification of their claims to representing the struggle for the faith sometime after the ḫurūc of Ertoġrıl's son.

The fragmentary nature of Bithynia's political landscape at the time can hardly be exaggerated. The dynamics of political life in the area seem to have been shaped by units as small as villages, small towns, nomadic tribes (with no sizable confederative articulation), and dervish or monastic religious communities and attached estates. These small units fashioned their political destinies mostly within the matrix of local dynamics, usually with minimal and sporadic intervention by the authorities of established political centers. Many decisions and preparations concerning war and peace, alliance and conflict, were apparently made locally by the leaders of those communities. Even the long siege of Bursa, one of the most important towns in Bithynia, was suffered by its inhabitants with no significant involvement on the part of the imperial government in Constantinople.[15]

This political wilderness is one of the important reasons why the notion of "frontiers" is applicable to western Anatolia at this time. However, the area was not free from all interference by the larger authorities in political centers. Not only did they have real muscle, which they occasionally used in these regions, but perhaps more importantly they also maintained significant control over mechanisms of legitimation that were part of the political language of the frontiers. Thus, the autonomy of small frontier powers should not be exaggerated. Whatever their levels of physical and/or mental distance, the Byzantines and the Mongols, and even the Seljuks, maintained some authority over the frontiers. Even if that authority was not able to have its representatives there all the time, even if it was obliged to comply with some cases of fait accompli, it was needed at least as a referent to provide some credibility to one's claims.

With respect to the Turco-Muslim side of the western Anatolian frontier in the final decades of the thirteenth century, one can speak of multiple layers of authority: (1) the Mongol ilkhanate and its governors, (2) the Seljuk sultanate, (3) the Mamluk sultanate (mostly in the south and the southwest), (4) occasional Seljuk princes who were physically present in the frontiers but whose eyes were set on the sultanate after establishing a power base for themselves, (5) begs of the uc, who were appointees of or at least nominally approved by the Mongols or the Seljuks, (6) begs of tribes, who may also have been begs of the uc as defined in the previous category, (7) holy figures with a following, and (8) upstarts who aspired to, and some of whom did, become begs. Given the complexity and fluidity of the frontier regions, it would be a mistake to present the "Turco-Muslim side" as a self-enclosed entity, or a "national team," as it were. The Byzantine emperor, too, was not without direct influence among both Muslims and Christians if we consider the case of 'Alī Amourios (to be discussed below) or the presence of various local Christian lords and communities of monks. Not all of the powers representing the established political centers of the region were present with the same force at any given moment; it is not only their capability but also their interest that ebbed and flowed. The relations between these layers kept changing as claims and ambitions clashed or coincided to shuffle different powers into allied or hostile camps.

Osman apparently displayed considerable political acumen in that environment where alliances could and did cut across religious, ethnic, and tribal lines; symbiotic relations developed between nomadic and settled communities. The YF-Apz narrative relates stories of Osman's neighborly relations with the Christian chiefs of towns and villages, and there is no reason to assume that these were fictionalized in the fifteenth century. When he hears his brother propose that they ought to burn and destroy the area around them, Osman is said to have replied: "If we destroy these areas, our own town of Karacahisar cannot prosper. What needs to be done is to maintain *müdārā* (feigned) friendship with our neighbors." It is also related that Osman's tribe, on its way to summer pastures, deposited some of their belongings for safekeeping at the fortress of Bilecik and on their return sent its tekvur, as a token of their appreciation, "cheese and buttercream in animal skins as well as fine carpets and kilims." The nature of these gift items also illustrates the nature of the symbiosis that could develop between the pastoralists and the agriculturalists or townsmen due to the different items produced by each. Commercial exchange was another facet of this symbiosis; soon after taking charge of his first urban possession, Osman is said to have set up a town market that would bring together infidels of the surrounding areas and Muslims of the Ottoman and Germiyan begliks.[16]

Insofar as the gaza ethos is concerned, we have seen in the last chapter that it was intimately tied to a code of honor. Old camaraderies, favors, promises, and bonds carried a certain weight. Surely they could be broken, but the breaking of bonds needed to be given meaning within that code. The supporters of Osman preferred to tell the story of Osman's attack on the tekvur of Bilecik, his former ally, as something that occurred only after Osman had heard that the tekvur was about to play a trick on him. On the other hand, there is no reason to expect that some of those friendships did not continue. Alexios Philanthropenos was so respected by the Turks that they were willing to drop the 1323 siege of Philadelphia "remembering the kindness and valor he had displayed in 1295."[17] The most-acclaimed warriors of such frontier conditions have always been those who could, while upholding their own cause with courage and determination, display statesmanly compassion and magnanimity toward the enemy. Salāḥ al-Dīn al-Ayyūbī (Saladin) is probably the best-known example of a medieval warrior who elegantly combined these two, seemingly contradictory, qualities.[18]

As neighborly or chivalric as Osman's relations with other Bithynians may have been, some of those relations eventually turned sour as he set out to expand his domain. Maybe some tension was always inherent in such relationships, not just between Muslim and Christian but also between coreligionists. Different pieces of the Bithynian puzzle may well have been living with an awareness of the temporary nature of the post-Lascarid arrangement. The conversation that leads to Osman's argument against his brother's suggestion of burning and destroying starts with Osman's question as to the best methods of gathering soldiers and conquering lands. At least one of those neighbors was to become a permanent addition to Osman's political community, however. Miḫal, the headman of the village of Harmankaya, apparently joined Osman's exploits quite early in the latter's career.[19] It is not clear when he converted to Islam, but some sources write of the resentment felt by some gazis of this "infidel" among them who had been participating in and apparently enjoying the benefits of their raids. While this may seem odd to some modern scholars, we have seen in the last chapter that even the canonical sources on "war for the faith" did not dismiss such cooperation offhand. In any case, Miḫal did convert after a point, and his descendants, known as the Sons of Miḫal or the House of Miḫal (Miḫaloğulları or Āl-i Miḫal), enjoyed the foremost rank among the gazis in Ottoman service, though their relationship to the House of Osman was not always free of tension. It has been pointed out that Osman's relation to Miḫal, from a relatively equal partnership to vassalage to full incorporation in a new hierarchical structure, can be seen as the beginning of a particularly noteworthy pattern in "Ottoman methods of conquest."[20]

The picture of Osman's rivals would be incomplete without considering another "ethnic group" in post-Mongol Anatolia. Although some of them eventually became assimilated (or some left for central Asia with Timur after 1402), certain people called Tatar are distinguished from the Türkmen of the ucāt and appear as foes of the Ottomans. These seem to be the non-Oğuz Turks and Mongols who were, or had been, associated with the Chingisid polity. Many of them had moved to the western

Anatolian frontiers and made up pieces of the intricate ethnopolitical puzzle there. Some, perhaps most, of them were pagan. In any case, the little band of Ertoğrıl and Osman apparently engaged in confrontations with the Çavdar Tatars in the land of the Germiyan in addition to competing with the House of Germiyan itself. Though the Ottoman chronicles do not refer to him, Cakü Beg of Göynük, mentioned in al-ʿUmarī, must have been one of these Mongol/Tatar foes.[21] In fact, surmising from some Ottoman traditions, this rivalry with the Tatars and the Germiyan was higher in the early Ottoman agenda than the one with local Christians. The Christians may have been easier to cooperate with or subjugate and assimilate compared to the Tatars, who must have had more formidable military skills and possibly also strong political claims among Turco-Mongol tribes. In the early fifteenth century when Timur came into the area, the Tatars — still a distinct group and still not at ease with Ottoman supremacy — switched over to the side of the world conqueror, who sent them messages like the following to steal away their, evidently fickle, allegiance to Bāyezīd: "we have the same ancestors . . . you are therefore truly a shoot from my stock . . . your last king was Artana who died in the Faith and the greatest king in the realms of Rum was your least servant . . . why should you be slaves of a man who is a son of slaves set free by Al-i Saljuk?"[22] The defeated and imprisoned Bāyezīd is reported to have beseeched Timur to "not leave the Tatars in this country, for they are material for wickedness and crime. . . . and they are more harmful to the Muslims and their countries than the Christians themselves."[23]

It is impossible to determine the extent to which Osman acted with a long-term strategy. He may well have been following his predatory instincts and acting on the spur of the moment. But he cannot have missed the potential implications for the future of the family ties he knotted for himself and his son. One of his marriages was to the daughter of a sheikh who is said to have been at the head of a prosperous community of dervishes and pastoralists in the frontier. Since Sheikh Ede Bali and the wedding of his daughter to Osman appear at the end of the undoubtedly apocryphal dream story, and the two stories are narratologically closely linked to one another, the veracity of the marriage has been doubted as well.[24]

That a certain Sheikh Ede Bali indeed lived in western Asia Minor in the first half of the fourteenth century can no longer be doubted because he is mentioned in Elvān Çelebi's hagiographical work, written in 1358/59.[25] The affiliation of the sheikh with the Vefā'ī-Baba'ī mystical order in this source tallies perfectly with our information from other sources concerning the presence of representatives of that order around the early Ottomans. Geographically, Bithynia makes good sense for Baba'īs to have chosen to settle in, since they were pushed in that direction by Seljuk forces during the slaughter that followed the Baba'ī Revolt of 1239–41. Finally, the Ottoman ties to the Baba'ī, especially if strengthened by a wedding alliance with the family of a leading sheikh of that order, would seem to be part of the explanation for their hostile relations with the House of Germiyan. The latter had, after all, been rewarded by the Seljuks for their services in the repression of the Baba'ī uprising.

Apz, who relates the liaison between the families of Osman and Ede Bali on the authority of one of the sheikh's descendants, also reports that Ede Bali had kinship ties through marriage to two other notable families: that of Çandarlı Ḫalīl and that of Tāceddīn-i Kürdī, well-known scholars who are among the early arrivals from areas with more-established educational institutions to enter Ottoman service. Even if a fifteenth-century chronicler, for some odd reason, were to make up such an intricate web of marital associations connecting three prominent families with many living descendants, it is hard to imagine how it could be accepted when such claims implied entitlements to so many resources. Later archival sources once again lend some credence to the assertions of Ede Bali's family: not only do land surveys identify various plots in Söğüt as Osman's endowments to the sheikh, but also a document refers to him specifically as Osman's father-in-law.[26]

It can only be conjectured that marrying his son Orḫān to the daughter of the tekvur of Yarhisar was likewise tied, at least partly, to political strategy. The legendary account of the way Osman crashed the wedding ceremony between the same bride and the tekvur of Bilecik, a friend up to that point, and carried her off suggests that part of the plan may have been to prevent an alliance between the two tekvurs.

Marriage strategies were built into the political gamesmanship in which Osman exerted himself with increasing success, which no doubt was partly due to some military undertakings. Of these we know nothing with certainty until the Battle of Bapheus, Osman's triumphant confrontation with a Byzantine force in 1301 (or 1302), which is the first datable incident in his life. Pachymeres, the chronicler who relates this event, adds that Osman enticed "many Turks" from the Meander region and from Paphlagonia to join his forces.[27] There is no reason to assume that all those warriors became permanent additions to Ottoman forces. Some of the begs were from neighboring polities that had their own identities, claims, and possibly rivalries with the Ottomans, at least for a while. Among the troops that defeated the Byzantine army in Bapheus, Pachymeres mentions a certain 'Alī Amourios, who has been identified as a member of the Çobanoğlu family, which held the most prominent position in the Paphlagonian uc in the thirteenth century. Three years later that coalition between Osman and 'Alī had broken up since the latter "appeared willing to pass into Byzantine service, asking for the area near the Sangarios from Andronikos II."[28]

Of the nameless volunteers in Bapheus, some well-rewarded ones might have stayed on and become "Osmanlı," but others, either at periods of Ottoman inactivity or because their expectations were not met, might have joined another chief if he was getting ready for what promised to be a lucrative raid, which often entailed sending out the news with the hope of luring volunteers. There must have been a good deal of warrior sharing or, to put it more competitively, body snatching among chieftaincies with ill-defined boundaries and only rudimentary structures of authority other than tribal ones, whatever tribalism implied in the early fourteenth century. As late as the 1330s, beglik forces consisted to a large extent of "swing warriors," who were ready to respond to calls of gaza by different chiefs.[29]

Despite such fluctuations, both Osman's following and his ability to attract volunteers at moments of raiding activity must have grown. Still, the budding beglik was so small in the 1310s that the Mevlevī order, when it sent out emissaries to make "spiritual vassals" of gazi begs of the frontiers, did not bother with the Ottomans. For quite some time, they were not the foremost representatives of frontier energy. This arguably helped the Ottoman emirate to construct its political traditions and institutions more gradually and solidly than some of the others—and much less conspicuously, for it was not touched by the wrath of the Ilkhanids, who, in the 1310s and 1320s, sent their governor to the western Anatolian frontiers in order to subdue the begs assuming too much autonomy. Rashīd al-Dīn, the Persian chronicler of the Ilkhanids, and even Aḳsarāyī, who personally participated in central state operations to subdue the frontier begs, do not refer to Osman among the various warlords they name.[30] For quite some time, he and his son fought only local battles while the House of Aydın, for instance, faced off against various international forces in the Aegean area.

This relative inconspicuousness must have been yet another advantage of the location of Osman's base of power. There was also the fact that Söğüt happened to be both an easily defended hill site and a town right by the major road that skirted the hill and extended from Constantinople to Konya.[31] This might not have mattered at other times, but the political fragmentation in the region had rendered small units much more significant than before. Above all, however, the first and foremost advantage, as noted by various scholars, turned out to be the proto-Ottomans' position at the very edge of the frontier. Their initial confrontations may have been with the Germiyanid and Tatar tribes, but when they turned their attention to the towns of Byzantine Bithynia, no other polity could rival their military-strategic and sociopolitical position as neighbor-insiders. And in the competitive world of the marches, nothing succeeded like success. The little enterprise headed by Osman and sons achieved a series of lucrative raids and conquests of small Bithynian towns, and their success lured not only other warriors but also dervishes and scholar-scribes into their midst.

According to Yaḫşi Faḳīh, news of another Ottoman achievement spread and lured another kind of population into Osman's domains: "the justice and generosity" of the early Ottomans, relates Apz, probably on the authority of the son of Orḫān's imam, lured fleeing peasants of the conquered territories back to their villages. "Their means turned out to be better than at the time of infidel rule so that even people of other lands started to arrive."[32] Modern scholars who write about Turkish conquests as a kind of "liberation movement" that spread justice, equity, and tax breaks to Muslims and non-Muslims are generally and to a large extent accurately perceived as engaging in chauvinistic apologetics. But how are we to interpret this assertion by a late medieval historian? He too may be propagandizing of course but even propaganda reflects a certain concern with the principles embedded in it. The theme of the conquerors' interest in the lot of the subjugated people in fact runs through many frontier narratives. In some of the anonymous chronicles, the Ottoman administration of the fifteenth century is bluntly criticized for not taxing its non-Muslim subjects as fairly and mildly as it used to. This concern for fiscal moderation is corroborated by the Ottoman law codes to the extent that these later sources shed light on the earlier practices. The preamble to the 1530 law code of Bayburt, for instance, sets the whole code in a comparative perspective by pointing out that the people of the area were unable to bear the burden of the previous laws of (Akkoyunlu Uzun) Ḥasan. Thus, "some exactions have been cancelled and some reduced" under the new regime of the Ottomans, who realize that the well-being of their subjects is "the reason of the longevity of the state and of order in the realm."[33] The early Ottomans apparently faced a competitive situation in terms of fiscal moderation, too; at least one of their rivals, Umur Beg of Aydın, proudly announced in an inscription in Denizli that he had abolished a local tax.[34]

This should not be surprising, however; nor can it be equated with modern apologetics. There were pragmatic considerations here as the wording of the law code itself makes clear: relative leniency and equity could ease the tensions between rulers and subjects, especially when such rule was quite young and possibly precarious. Moreover, decades of political instability and nomad and raider activity had devastated a good part of the countryside in Anatolia and also led to depopulation; any enterprise that looked forward to a serious political future would want to have producing, tax-paying subjects in its domains. The dislocation of the agrarian population was caused to a large extent by Turkish tribal movement, raiding, and colonization, but if any of those tribes or raiders were to settle down to rule, their priorities would naturally need to be redefined.

In this context, it is worth reconsidering the dream narrative, which, from Apz through Hammer, Gibbons, his critics, and Lindner, has somehow figured in all accounts of early Ottoman history. At least since Hammer, these historians have also been aware that similar dream legends adorn the foundation narratives of many other states. To a hyper-rationalist sensibility, this implies that the story ought to be dismissed altogether or understood merely as a device for satisfying the "psychological needs of the population" in the sense of massaging their superstitious piety (and fooling them?) into submission.[35] If one is not satisfied with the underlying assumption of pure and simple gullibility, however, one might profit from Roy Mottahedeh's brilliant suggestion, on the basis of examples from medieval Islamic history, that such dream narratives can also be seen to embody a compact of sovereignty.[36] Osman, like many other warriors in the region, must indeed have dreamt of rulership, in the nonspecific sense of dreaming. At some point after his emergence, he or his descendants advanced the story of the dream to give his political bid the sanction of a divine compact, but the consensus on the veracity of the dream, as in all compacts, implied not only that the House of Osman's power should be accepted because it had divine sanction but also that the House of Osman had some obligations in return. Did the dream not include a promise (and a vow?) of security and prosperity for the subjects? In a way, then, the dream narrative served as one method of working toward a political consensus.

If the dream legend can be read as a compact, the interpreter (Ede

Bali or 'Abdül'azīz or Ḥācī Bektaş) can be seen as the notary of its contractual character. He is the one who verifies it and provides it with legitimacy in the public sphere. This is not different from the role that is said to have been given to a sheikh at each accession when he girded the new ruler with a sword and thereby, I would add, notarized the transfer of power and reconfirmed the compact.[37] Unfortunately, the early history of that ritual, eventually a sphere of contestation between different Sufi orders just like the identity of the interpreter of Osman's dream, is shrouded in mystery. It is not even clear that such a ritual did in fact take place in the fourteenth century. As for the dream legend itself, it must have been elaborated, at least as we have it, after the emergence of a sedentary preference among the Ottomans since it clearly offers a particularly sedentary vision of the future under their rule, as Lindner has insightfully pointed out in analyzing its manifest content.

Whatever the role of fiscal moderation in rendering Ottoman rule acceptable or tolerable, this must have been buttressed by the security that would come to an area under some stable rule, be it Ottoman or otherwise, after protracted turmoil, caused by Ottomans or others. In the case of northwestern Anatolia, the peasants of the area were so frustrated that they were ready to follow the rebellion of a pseudo-Lachanes in 1294.

All this was certainly facilitated by the decline in the direct interest of Byzantine central government in that area.[38] As the empire's political attention in the post-Lascarid period turned toward the west, Bithynia lost some of its significance and its defenses were neglected. The disappointment of imperial subjects of the area was probably compounded, as Lindner points out, by the fact that they had enjoyed a high level of security and stability under Lascarid rule from Nicaea. From the point of view of the Ottomans, however, this "backwater" status of Bithynia at the time turned out to be advantageous not just because of the weak defensive system they encountered but also because they could expand and build without attracting too much attention from the larger powers. In this neglected area whose Christian inhabitants seem to have been disenchanted with their imperial government, there would also be a better chance of gaining former Byzantine subjects to the Ottoman side or at least of having them become resigned to, if not welcome, the establishment of Ottoman power.

The point about Byzantine neglect of Bithynian defenses should not be exaggerated, however. In fact, the nature of the interest shown by Constantinople once again underscores the advantageous position of

Osman's chiefdom. Michael Palaeologus devoted some attention to the region in 1280–81: in addition to leading an expedition there, he repaired some fortresses, built new ones, and took measures to render the banks of the Sangarius inaccessible to the Turkish forces that had to cross the river to raid Bithynian settlements. Andronicus II spent nearly three years there between 1290 and 1293. These efforts were not in vain in terms of blocking Turkish attacks in the area that had been the most vulnerable, namely, directly to the west of the Sangarius. The area around Tarsius (Tersiye/Terzi Yeri), which lay along the favorite invasion route over the bridge of Justinian, had witnessed the most intense raider action in the immediate post-Lascarid era. Had this situation continued, a chieftaincy based in Paphlagonia could have gained the upper hand. The Byzantine fortifications were eventually captured, of course, but not from across the river. To that extent, imperial policies had been successful. The Ottomans, based as they were in a more southerly, and originally less prominent, location compared to the forces of Paphlagonia, moved "along the river from the south, rendering the fortresses obsolete."[39]

The initial Ottoman move up along the river and westward into Bithynia occurred in the few years following the Battle of Bapheus when they started to make a name for themselves outside the area and to attract aspiring warriors. Only with hindsight does that expansion seem so crucial. In the first two decades of the fourteenth century, looking at western Anatolian frontiers overall, the scene of action in the Aegean area must have been much more glamorous, especially since Ottoman encroachments into Byzantine territory apparently suffered a lull between 1307 and 1317.[40] No matter what the Ottomans had achieved in the first decades of the fourteenth century, they could not yet measure up to the emirates of Aydın and Menteşe. And no matter how many warriors, dervishes, and scholars Osman attracted to his growing community, some of the other begliks did better. According to figures provided by al-ʿUmarī, which must be based on the realities of the 1320s, there were begliks that could muster larger forces than could the House of Osman. Already by 1312, the House of Aydın had built an architectural complex centered on an Ulu Cami, a cathedral mosque, indicating lofty claims and abundant funds on a scale that the Ottomans were unable to match until the 1330s.[41]

To the extent that the presence of the begliks was a constant challenge to the Byzantine Empire, it would take no more than a few decades for the Ottoman one to emerge as the main thrust of that challenge. In his depiction of the principalities in the frontiers of western Anatolia, the Arab geographer al-ʿUmarī would single out the Ottomans as constantly engaged in warfare with Byzantium and often the effective side. When Ibn Baṭṭūṭa toured the emirates of the region in the 1330s, he described Orḫān as "the superior of all the Türkmen emirs in terms of land, army, and wealth."[42] It ought to be remembered, however, that the Arab traveler was in the area before Umur Beg of Aydın (r. 1334–48) undertook his most daring and lucrative raids, which seem to have made him the most illustrious gazi leader for a while and propelled him to play a role in the factional struggles of Byzantine imperial government. Orḫān came into this scene somewhat later, but once he did, he made full use of the advantages offered by the position and the internal political strength of his emirate mentioned by the two Arab authors who described it.

However, all the strategic advantages and circumstantial opportunities would not have meant anything had the Ottomans not acted upon them with some vision, though this vision was probably redefined and sharpened along the way. It is not possible to say much with certainty here for the period when Osman was beg, but obviously his hold over the tribe continued while the tribe itself kept changing. Marriage alliances were struck with at least two important neighbors, an influential dervish and a Christian tekvur. Another tekvur from a neighboring village joined the warriors under Osman's command and eventually converted to Islam. Aspiring youths were invited from different parts of Anatolia to join in military undertakings and some were undoubtedly incorporated. Raids also produced slaves, some of whom became trusted members of the chieftainship, as in the case of Balabancık, who is said to have been assigned important duties in the siege of Bursa. It is also reported, though there is no way of verifying this for the earliest periods, that gentle treatment of subjects lured peasants from other areas (or those who had fled?) to settle in the lands under Osman's control. Later archival documents contain records of donations of land or revenue made by Osman to dervishes and, in larger numbers, to faḳīhs, who seem to have served as imam-judges but were overshadowed by the better-educated kadis later in the fourteenth century.[43]

There were hostilities with some of the neighbors such as the menacing House of Germiyan and Tatar tribes in the vicinity. And some of the other relations could not be maintained on neighborly terms, as symbiotic as they once may have been, when political aspirations led to raids and more serious military undertakings like sieges and conquests of fortified towns. In all these ventures, Osman and his warriors acted with good tactical and strategic sense that eventually led them to take control over Bithynia. Halil İnalcık has recently demonstrated that Osman's conquests show a clear military logic.[44]

By the mid-1320s the Ottomans had a complex enough military-administrative structure to have struck coins in their own name, to assign offices to slaves and eunuchs, to establish waqfs, to issue written documents (in Persian), and to gain possession of as important a city as Bursa. But the most important breakthrough for the chieftaincy in those years may well be that it survived Osman's death without a loss to the integrity of the polity. There may have been some angry voices and some objections, but for all we know, Orḫān replaced his father with the realm intact. Since Orḫān was not the only son, why were Osman's domains not divided among the heirs? If the Ottomans had followed Turco-Mongol practice, as the other begliks around them did, Orḫān could still have been the commander-in-chief over the other brothers and their combined forces, but the brothers would have their own designated functions and domains. This, of course, is the practice followed by the Chingisids and the Anatolian Seljuks, the two greater political traditions the begliks knew something about.[45]

According to the Ottoman chronicler tradition, Orḫān offered the chieftainship to his brother 'Alā'eddīn, but the latter preferred the life of a dervish while occasionally playing the role of an advisor. Even if this story is taken at face value, it fails to account for a number of other brothers of Orḫān who are named in the 1324 waqf deed but never mentioned in the chronicles.[46] In any case, Orḫān's inheritance does not seem to have been contested, and Osman's patrimony was not divided. It would not be meaningful to look for an "Ottoman policy of succession" on the basis of one case, especially one that is so full of obscurities. Furthermore, a systematic study of the succession patterns in the other begliks remains to be conducted before a detailed comparison can be made, but none of them was as successful as the Ottomans in preventing the fissiparous dynamics of inter-generational transition over the long run. Unigeniture in one generation is not unheard of in those emirates, yet eventually they all gave birth to splinter polities whereas the Ottomans came up with unigeniture again and again, even though it was systematized only with Meḥmed II's codification of fratricide.

Ottoman practices in this respect seem to have struck contemporaneous observers, too, as unusual. As we discussed in the last chapter, most of the fifteenth-century chroniclers claim that, at least starting with Bāyezīd I, fratricide had become the norm, which they clearly see as a deviation from some better, older practice. The YF-Apz narrative also finds something remarkable about Orẖān's accession: it is related here that Osman, while he was still alive, deliberately gave the reins to Orẖān so that the young man would be accepted during his father's lifetime, which implies that Osman intended to leave no room for challenges to his son's inheritance of the Osmanlı tribe and lands.[47] Apz may be fictionalizing Osman's designs, but clearly the fifteenth-century historian found something peculiar in the Ottoman practice of unigeniture and set out to explain it. It is in fact more likely that this passage comes directly from Yaẖşi Faḳīh, the son of Orẖān's imam, whom we can expect to have been well informed on this matter. In any case, it is certain that the Ottoman practice had already started to look odd in the beginning of the fifteenth century; Shāhrūẖ, son of Timur and heir to a polity that claimed to be the supreme representative of the Chingisid political tradition, scolded Meḥmed I, whom the Timurids treated as their vassal. The latter, in an uninhibited avowal of Ottoman uniqueness, responded that "the Ottoman sultans from the beginning have made experience their guide and refused to accept partnership in government."[48]

Coincidences may have played a role here, such as 'Alā'eddīn's alleged disinterest in worldly power, but it is difficult to account for so many successive cases of unigeniture as merely a series of flukes. Besides, Meḥmed Çelebi seems to have done his historical homework in arguing that the Ottomans did not seem to have ever taken warmly to the idea of sharing; Orẖān's brotherly suggestion to Alā'eddīn is reported to have been not that they share the realm but that the latter be the "shepherd." In each generation, this reluctance to divide the realm manifested itself: with Murād I (r. 1362–89) and Bāyezīd I (r. 1389–1402) both decisively eliminating the challenges raised by their brothers and/or sons; with none of the princes during the Interregnum (1402–13) pursuing any other goal than seizing control over an undivided realm; with Murād II (r. 1421–51) again having to deal with contenders from the family in an all-out struggle; and with Meḥmed II (r. 1451–81) finally legislating fratricide as the culmination of a centralist logic whose goal was to eliminate all tendencies toward fragmentation. The struggle between Meḥmed II's sons led to Prince Cem's unusual suggestion of sharing the realm, but by then he had lost the struggle and his brother would have none of it. Looking at Ottoman succession practices over the long run, it is clear that they continued, until the seventeenth century, the Inner Asian tradition of giving each heir a sphere of influence within the family dominions and a chance for future rulership, but adapted that tradition to their own vision of a strong central government. An appanage was no more than a princely fief; once one of the princes reached the throne to replace their father, the others would be dispossessed and, after Orḫān at least, eliminated. No "neo-eponymous" dynasty emerged out of Osman's clan. Over the long run, the Ottomans proved to be better students of history than their competitors, not just in the policy of succession but also in the way they dealt with other real and potential challenges to centralization of power, as we shall see next.

Into the Limelight and the Rise of Tensions

If the Ottomans had grown relatively removed from the limelight of "international politics," they found the opportunity to catch up when Byzantine factionalism pulled them into a wider orbit and took them across the Sea of Marmara into Thrace. Among the Turco-Muslim principalities of western Anatolia, it was the House of Aydın whose support was first sought by Kantakouzenos, one of the main contenders to the imperial title. Eventually, two other principalities, flanking the southern side of the Sea of Marmara, became deeply involved in the factional strife of the empire. These were the chiefdom of Orḫān to the southeast and that of the Karasi to the southwest of Marmara facing Thrace.

Very little is known about the history of the Karasi emirate.[49] The Ottoman chronicles are particularly muddled in those sections that cover the relations between these two neighboring rivals. One thing is certain, however, and of major significance for early Ottoman history: the Karasi had a group of particularly accomplished and renowned warriors who could teach the Ottomans a thing or two about crossing over into Thrace, which presented premium raiding territory. Once Orḫān eliminated the House of Karasi and annexed its realm, those warriors passed into his service and provided valuable military leadership in transplanting gazi activity across the Dardanelles, which was initially made possible by the invitation of Kantakouzenos, who needed the Turkish warriors against his foes.

Having incorporated those mighty warriors, however, the Ottomans also took on a serious potential challenge to their control over gaza activity. It is impossible to date several important "internal" political developments in the Ottoman principality with precision in the fourteenth century, but that potential challenge seems to have turned into a real one in the 1360s and 1370s, possibly related to the loss of Gelibolu to Amadeo of Savoy. For a decade when one of the major links between the two peninsulas (Anatolia and Thrace) was severed, some of the gazis of Thrace apparently entertained notions of independence from Ottoman control even if they were originally commissioned by the Ottomans. This was part of the rules of the game after all; the House of Aydın, too, had established itself as an autonomous principality in a region where they had originally been sent in the name of the House of Germiyan.

The most prominent among these independent-minded warriors was a certain Ḥācī İlbegi, one of the former Karasi warriors. Perhaps he was the conqueror who was later identified as Seyyid ʿAlī Sulṭān, the protagonist of the hagiography analyzed in the last chapter.[50] It seems highly likely that the central figure of that (later) Bektāşī cult was built around, or conflated with, a warrior who had strong claims to taking the credit for moving gazi activity into Thrace. Even if that is not the case, it is obvious on the basis of Ottoman sources that Ḥācī İlbegi was credited by some with the crucial victory over Serbian forces in 1371. And it is also stated in those chronicles, though some prefer to omit the relevant passage, that Ḥācī İlbegi was killed by a commander loyal to Murād I, Orḫān's son. Maybe none of this is true; still, these reports indicate that there were some who questioned Ottoman claims to being in charge of the frontiers. Namely, the centrifugal tendencies had risen to the fore in the 1370s, and the Ottomans were facing the kind of crisis that had led in many other states in the region to the emergence of splinter polities headed by successful warlords.

The Ottomans withstood that challenge, however, partly by coopting other warlords and by taking swift and violent measures, none of which could be effectively carried out had they not been developing a sophisticated ruling apparatus. And it is certainly not coincidental that the Ottomans invented the cornerstone of their centralizing political technology in that conjuncture, during or right after the crisis of the 1370s. Observing the loosening of the bonds that had held the warriors together when the head of the House of Osman was one of them, now that the Ottoman beg was turning into a sultan, the budding state created a new army, *yeñi çeri,* that consisted of youths from slave backgrounds so that their sole loyalty would be to the sultan.

We have already seen that the institutional complexity of Osman's principality emerged quite early. Or, to state it more cautiously, those elements that eventually provided it with institutional complexity were present earlier than depicted in the frontier narratives, which describe an egalitarian, institutionally naive enterprise until the arrival of the Çandarlı family. They conveniently omit, for instance, the existence of vezirs (perhaps three) before Çandarlı Ḳara Ḫalīl.[51] Starting with Ḫalīl, three generations of this family monopolized top offices in the administration and played a major role in the building of sophisticated structures of governing that buttressed the centralizing tendency of the Ottoman polity, much to the resentment of the gazis and their supporters. The sources that voice that resentment, given their ideological position and narrative strategies, tend to associate the "beginning" of all evils and tensions with the Çandarlı and with Bāyezīd I, as we saw in the last chapter.

Despite their hypercritical reception, or outright rejection, of these sources, many modern scholars seem to have fallen for the image of a pristine community before the arrival of those nasty sophisticates. Particularly those who argue against the gaza thesis fail to appreciate how early in its formation the Ottoman polity had contact with its relatively sophisticated neighbors and came under the influence of sedentary administrative traditions in both the Perso-Islamic and the Byzantine modes.

Sedentarization, which entailed eventual alienation from nomadic ways and from nomads themselves, was only one aspect of this transformation, and the nomads were only one of the elements to be adversely affected by it. That is a relatively better known part of early Ottoman history and will not concern us here. A more comprehensive view of the emergence and trajectory of Ottoman power is gained by looking at it as a coalition of various forces, some of which were eventually driven to drop out of the enterprise or subdued or marginalized. In other words, it was a history of shifting alliances and conflicts among various social forces which themselves were undergoing rapid transformation while constantly negotiating their position within the polity.

Indeed, if anything characterized medieval Anatolian frontiers, and possibly all frontiers, it was mobility and fluidity. The Ottoman success was due to the fact that they harnessed that mobility to their own ends while shaping and taming it to conform to their stability-seeking, centralizing vision. Of course there were limits on both set by natural and social parameters, but still one could move from place to place, allegiance to allegiance, and identity to identity with an ease and acceptability hard to even imagine in more-settled societies. People not only crossed from one side of the frontier to the other but also moved from one faith to another and from one ethnic identity (which usually also meant from one name) to another with frequency. All this commotion had a solemn cosmic significance in the minds of the actors because it was, or one could occasionally and selectively remember it to be, played out in the name of a much larger struggle between two competing transcendental visions: Islam and Christianity. The *Dāniṣmendnāme,* as we saw in the last chapter, captured the urgency of this in two of its major characters for whom the crossing occurred in such haste, after a sudden flash of enlightenment, that neither one of them had time to change his or her name, overtaken by the joy of having found the right side and too eager to join the fight for its supremacy.

The sociopolitical order created by these frontier conditions developed a general reluctance to recognize an aristocracy, a freezing of inheritable distinction in specific lineages, even after settling down. A system like the *devshirme,* whereby children of non-Muslim peasant families were recruited, "Ottomanized," and then brought to the highest positions of government, could be conceivable only in a state born of those frontier conditions.

The potentialities of mobility and fluidity found their ultimate representation and congealed into "awe-inspiring centrality" (i.e., charisma) in the persons of the babas, religious mystical leaders of the tribal and (newly settled?) peasant populations, who could change into birds or, slipping into things more ferocious, lions or whatever they wished to be and fly or roar over vast spaces unleashing their arsenal of alchemical weaponry. The most illustrious example is of course the Ḥācī Bektaş of later legend, who was sent from Khorasan to Anatolia in the form of a dove and turned out to be the baba of babas. The Ottomans also relied on the services of many of these babas and cultivated and patronized them in the earlier stages of their state building. Eventually, however, the more established and urbane Sufi orders were preferred by the Ottoman state while some of the earlier allies became opponents. The Safavids were able to gain followers among not only the tribes but also some of the closely related groups of dervishes who were ready to adopt Shi'ism. The aẖī bands, on the other hand, the guild-like quasi-Sufi associations of men in urban areas, including the small towns around and later within the Ottoman principality, lost their once considerable autonomy as they were turned into guilds much more strictly controlled by the government.

Another social group that suffered from the centralization of power in the growing Ottoman polity and the eventual adoption of an imperial mode of administrative and intellectual life was that of the frontier warriors, led by the begs of the uc. Given the paucity of sources, it is impossible to pinpoint precisely the early tensions that manifested themselves between the House of Osman and its allies and warriors. Such tensions are naturally built into any political structure, and the example of ʿAlī Amourios from the first few years of the fourteenth century again comes to mind as an early falling out between Osman and one of his fellow warriors. Some of Osman's early allies were his Bithynian Christian neighbors, many of whom found themselves incorporated if not eliminated. As the power of Osman and Orḫān grew and as their principality began to acquire the characteristics of a sedentary administration, there must have been gazis and others within that principality who felt left out. That there was opposition among the neighboring warriors is clear from the rivalries the Ottomans faced. A much deeper, structural tension emerged among the gazis, who were accustomed to seeing themselves as partners of the begs of the House of Osman. Their resentment goes at least as far back as the third quarter of the fourteenth century when the Ottoman ruler not only appropriated their independently conquered areas in Thrace but also imposed a tax on their most important booty: slaves. The reign of Murād I (1362–89) represents a major turning point in the process of outgrowing the petty chiefdom of the frontier that the Ottoman principality had been until the middle of the century. The creation of two offices in particular signal that major developments toward statehood were under way.

Murād was the one who appointed a ḳāḍīʿasker for the first time.[52] This signifies that by then social stratification had crystallized to such a degree that it necessitated the recognition of a distinction between the *ʿaskerī* (military-administrative) class and the rest of the society. While the creation of this new position could also be attributed to the belated arrival of the influence of traditions from previously established administrative centers (or, more specifically, of Seljuk institutions), the two explanations are not mutually exclusive.[53] The arrival and acceptance of a particular institution could only be possible when it made sense, when the development of the accepting society required or at least could comfortably accommodate that change. Through the appointment of a special judge for the ʿaskerī class, Murād took an important step in the delineation of boundaries around the ruling class vis-à-vis the people (as well as himself?).

It is again under Murād I that some warriors are appointed to be *uc begleri* (lords of the frontier) for the first time in the Ottoman principality.[54] This is significant first in terms of the sociopolitical differentiation it implies between a self-conscious central power and frontier warriors whose role is defined *vis-à-vis and by* the center. It is an announcement of the fact that the military-political elite was no longer a band of more or less equal warriors and of its corollary that the beg from the Ottoman family was claiming to be more than *primus inter pares.* That Murād I is reported to have been harsh enough to personally execute those pashas and begs who committed acts of disobedience against him but mellow toward those who showed due obedience and that he was the first to be given the lofty title of *ḫünkār,* or sultan, appear as more than idiosyncratic character traits in this context.[55] In fact, this character portrait drawn of Murād reads like an encapsulation of the most basic elements of his reign's political history, which might be summarized as the elaboration of a sultanic attitude to governing. The appointment of begs of the frontiers also indicates the emergence of a schizoid mental topography in Ottoman political imagination in the same old pattern that divides the land between a core area (*iç il*?) and an uc.

Although the crisis of the 1370s was overcome, its legacy seems to have survived, and not only in the form of a cult built around its main protagonist. Thanks to Orhan Şaik Gökyay's masterful demonstration, we now know that Sheikh Bedreddīn, the "heretical" leader of perhaps the most significant, albeit failed, revolutionary movement in Ottoman history (1416), was the son of not the kadi but the gazi of Simavna.[56] This fits in nicely with the reports that Bedreddīn's father was a companion of Ḥācī İlbegi. At any rate, Sheikh Bedreddīn, the son of a gazi and the daughter of the Byzantine commander whose fortress he had captured, did not advocate forced conversion or brutal repression of the Christians but a utopian synthesis of different faiths, among other things, and he and his lieutenants managed to gather thousands of Muslims and Christians willing to fight against the Ottoman army. Bedreddīn's message lacked single-minded, adversarial proselytizing zeal not despite but because he came from a gazi milieu.

This cooperative and syncretistic spirit is reminiscent of the earliest days of Ottoman power in Bithynia. It was inspired and led by a sheikh who was the son of a gazi; furthermore, one of his father's comrades was an even more illustrious gazi who may have become, or whose legacy was fused with that of, a venerated saint of a "heterodox" syncretistic sect. Opposition to Ottoman central power now converged with attitudes that the government was learning to define as heterodoxy and became a guiding force among certain segments of the frontier warriors and dervishes as well as the nomads.

Not all gazis turned rebels or heretics, of course. Just as not all dervishes embraced heterodoxy and not all tribes ran to the Safavid cause when it presented itself as a political, religious, and cultural option from the second half of the fifteenth century onward. We cannot expect such complex social groups to act en masse. At least the tripartite division of modern political taxonomy—radical, moderate, and conservative—could be applied to the social categories under consideration in terms of their political attitudes, and all three modes are undoubtedly present at any given time in some measure. Not all heirs of the Baba'ī-Vefā'ī tradition went through the radicalization that eventually prevailed among the followers of the cult of Ḥācī Bektaş; some, like Apz, came closer to an emerging Ottoman orthodoxy along Sunni lines. The cult of Ede Bali, too, seems to have remained outside the Bektāşī sphere of influence that subsumed various other cults built around holy figures of the thirteenth and fourteenth centuries. At certain conjunctures when the relative position and power of a social group are undergoing a major qualitative change, radical action is likely to appear preferable to larger segments of that group, or at least those who prefer radical action are likely to become more visible and confrontational, as seems to have been the case in Thrace around 1370.

Unlike Ḥācī İlbegi or Bedreddīn's father and their followers, many "moderate" or "accommodationist" gazis continued their activities in the Balkans, but there was no doubt that they were doing so in the service of the Ottoman state, unlike the early days of relative autonomy. Still, whenever the opportunity presented itself or the circumstances demanded, some gazis opposed the Ottoman state. The important thing is that the gazis are discernible as a specific social group with its own lifestyle, alliances, and conflicts.

Were the gazis who supported the Ottoman family stupid? A relatively centralized state could provide security. It could also render future campaigns more profitable. Thus, to accept tolerable levels of subordination could naturally be a reasonable choice for some of the warriors. What constituted "tolerable" levels must have changed over time and was most certainly measured differently by different warriors according to circumstances and personal inclinations.

Starting from a conception that brought together various elements of the social and cultural reality of the ucāt—booty seekers, metadox dervishes, leaders of nomadic tribes (defined as inclusive entities), recently converted ex-Christians, all of them perceiving and legitimizing their struggle with reference to a higher cause whenever appropriate—the gaza spirit gradually was subjected to a more orthodox interpretation after the taste of the emerging settled Sunni administrators. This is by no means to be seen as an absolute change. Even after the transformation, it never incorporated notions of forced conversion or noncooperation with Christian neighbors or abstinence from armed conflict with other Muslim begs. İnalcık has demonstrated that what happened between Osman and Köse Miḫal appears as a recurrent structural feature of Ottoman methods of conquest at least through the fifteenth century.[57] By the end of that century, heirs to early gazi traditions had clearly fallen out of the Ottoman mainstream. While Apz and the writers of the anonymous chronicles adopted a voice that claimed to champion the more or less authentic continuation of the initial gaza traditions, representatives of the new religious or courtly bureaucracies invoked the gaza in their own "alien" conception, unable to capture the souls of those who saw themselves heirs to earlier traditions. It is worth remembering in this context that the Safavids gained the allegiance of tribes and dervishes not only by religious propaganda but also by championing the "real gaza."

With respect to the Ottoman expansion in the Balkans, the significance of colonization and settlement that accompanied military victories has been pointed out. This may well be the most important factor to point out, but again it is one of many factors, including chance (as in the earthquake that destroyed the Gelibolu fortress). The fragmentary nature of political power in the Balkans and the related problem of the two churches certainly mattered. Since Iorga, many historians have emphasized that the Ottomans reduced the fiscal burden of the Balkan peasantry, who had long suffered rapacious petty lords. More important than the amount of the tax burden may be the systematic and consistent nature of Ottoman administration after uncertainty and chaos. The Ottomans themselves no doubt contributed to that uncertainty and chaos for a while, but when they established their power, one could expect consistency and order. With so many "decisive" battles that sealed Ottoman presence in the Balkans (Sırpsındığı, 1371; Kosovo, 1389; Varna, 1444; Second Kosovo, 1448), one also would like to know much more about Ottoman military strategies and use of technology since these undoubtedly played an important role in our story. Detailed studies are needed, from techniques of cannon casting to allocation of firearms.

There is no doubt, however, that after the suppression of the Bedreddīn Revolt, Turco-Muslim presence in the Balkans finally became equivalent to an Ottoman presence. There were still some cases of serious insurgency but only as claims to local autonomy or as bids by various, not all of them real, Ottoman princes, of whom the Byzantines and the

Venetians seem to have had a nearly endless arsenal. While these challengers were released one after the other like Hollywood sequels, their audience share kept diminishing after Muṣṭafā "the Impostor," Murād II's uncle, was eliminated in 1422.

A distinct group of uc begleri is delineated by İnalcık in his study of the Ottoman political factions in the 1430s and 1440s.[58] At that time, they appear as the leading members of the "war party" that stood once again in opposition to the Çandarlı family, who led the party that stood for accommodation with the imperial government of Byzantium. This was probably the last time the frontier warlords played a meaningful role in strategic decisions affecting the general direction of Ottoman policy; and they appeared to have won the upper hand with the abdication of Murād II and the first enthronement of Meḥmed II in 1444—a precarious victory that was reversed within two years by a Çandarlı-instigated revolt of the ḳul army. The centralizing logic of the Ottoman state had reached such a maturity by that time that even though Meḥmed II's second enthronement in 1451 brought along a more aggressive policy toward Byzantium and the conquest of Istanbul, the fulfillment of these gazi dreams did not lead to a permanent strengthening of the frontier lords in the Ottoman political system. Just as Çandarlı Ḫalīl was murdered by the Conqueror soon after the conquest, some of the leaders of the "war party" from among the uc begleri were put to death soon thereafter.

Perhaps more significant is the Conqueror's highly symbolic act of abolishing an ancient frontier custom. It is reported in Apz and some of the later chronicles that since the time of Osman (and it does not matter whether the custom was really established at that time) the Ottoman rulers would respectfully stand up at the sound of martial music as a sign of readiness for gaza. As the conqueror of Constantinople, however—namely, having achieved the ultimate goal of Anatolian frontier culture—the young sultan apparently perceived himself to have surpassed that culture and its primitive etiquette; he is reported to have abandoned the practice of standing up.[59]

How could Meḥmed II have continued to obey the terms of vassalage implied by the ceremony of standing up in respect when martial music was played? Just as the Abbasid caliph or the Seljuk sultan would send *ṭabl ve ʿalem* (drums and banner) to their vassals, Meḥmed himself was now in a position to dispatch those insignia to lesser powers ready to recognize the Ottoman dynasty as their superior. In less than two centuries the Ottomans had transformed themselves, at least in their historical consciousness, from recipients to granters of insignia of vassalage. Whereas legend related that Osman had received "drums and banner" from Alā'eddīn, the Seljuk sultan, and accepted the latter's overlordship, Meḥmed II dispatched the same items to Mengli Giray, the Crimean khan, bringing someone who was no less than a descendant of the House of Chingis under the overlordship of the House of Osman.[60]

Even though the century following the conquest of Constantinople may appear to have continued to be a glorious time for the Balkan gazis as one reads the gests (*ġazavātnāmes*) recording their deeds, it was a passing glory and was enjoyed only at the cost of increasing subservience to the central state. In 1457, for instance, when Meḥmed II ordered a final assault on and capture of the Belgrade fortress, the frontier warriors of the Balkans protested. "If Belgrade is conquered," they said, according to Apz, "we will have to plow the land."[61] These gazis were obviously aware of where the central state's policy was leading. Even though they undertook numerous exploits and obtained substantial booty in the next few decades, they were increasingly reduced to provincial fief-holders, that is, agriculturalists, losing the last traces of their ancestors' status as mobile and independent frontier warriors. Just as with the nomads, the frontier warriors' activities were controlled and regularized, and they were tied to designated pieces of land in accordance with the administrative logic of the classical Ottoman order.

Unfortunately, the rich cultural traditions and considerable literary as well as architectural patronage of the gazi milieu have not been sufficiently studied, crippling our understanding of some very significant developments involving the gazi circles in the fifteenth century.[62] Why did Prince Cem (1459–95) commission the collection of gazi lore built around the vita of Ṣarı Ṣalṭuḳ? His interest in things Turkish at a moment of an increasing turn to cosmopolitanism in Ottoman cultural life does not seem coincidental if we remember also that he named one of his sons Oġuz. By that time, it was rare for members of the Ottoman family to receive Turkic names, and a symbolically charged name like Oġuz stands out in particular.[63]

In the *Ṣalṭuḳnāme* compiled for Prince Cem, various passages suggest that the book is intended to serve as a rapprochement between the Ottoman family, or that particular prince, and the gazi circles. It is reported here, for instance, that for four years the gazis of Rūm struck coins and had the ḫuṭbe (Friday sermon) read in Ṣalṭuḳ's name—ultimate symbols of sovereignty, reflecting an audacious resistance to accepting Ottoman hegemony. Ṣalṭuḳ himself, however, is said to have disapproved of such action, accepted the superior right of the House of Osman in these matters, and invited all the gazis to gather around Osman's family. *Ṣalṭuḳnāme* suggests that at the time of its composition, ca. 1474, the gazis felt they were not getting a fair return for their services.

Once again, the conquest of Constantinople and the making of that city into the capital, the seat of power, constitute the crucial moment in this regard because they represent the crystallization of a political vision that marginalizes the gazis. Much before the conquest, according to the narrative, which is written after Edirne lost its role as the capital, Ṣalṭuḳ visits that region and warns the Muslim rulers of the future:

> Whoever wishes to conquer [all of] the land of Rūm, must be stationed in Endriyye. And whoever wishes to destroy the infidels and the enemy, should remain in Edirne since it is the hearth of the gazis. There is no better place for gaza than that. This world is like a ring; Rumelia is the seal of the ring and the middle of that seal is Endriyye. Whoever has this [land of] Rūm like a seal on his finger, the center [could also be read as "the capital"] of his ring should be this site. It is the inner sanctum of [the land of] Rūm.

The holy man also prophesies that a sultan named Meḥmed will appear and conquer Constantinople; that city will eventually be destroyed due to "corruption, adultery, sodomy, and tyranny," but not Edirne "unless Muslims give up gaza."[64] Later, during the siege of the Byzantine capital, Ṣarı Ṣalṭuḳ appears to Meḥmed II in a dream and gives him the keys to the city but urges the young sultan to keep these keys in Edirne and never to neglect the latter city since it is the "ancient and holy abode of the gazis."[65]

Do we not find here an expression of the gazis' dismay at the ascendancy of a *ḳapıḳulu*-dominated central administration in Istanbul? The compiler of the *Ṣalṭuḳnāme* also reports that Cem promised to reside in Edirne, the "abode of gazis," if he became sultan. For the gazis, this was a promise of a change of policy that would restore their honor and power. For Cem, it defined his clientele in his future bid for the sultanate.[66] The opposition to Cem in his later struggle (1481–82) for the throne indeed came from some key grandees and the ḳapıḳulu army, who favored and managed to enthrone Bāyezīd. Thereafter, the ascendancy of a ḳul-based administration was sealed, and the gazis never again played as significant a role in guiding the Ottoman polity. The resentment of the pro-Edirne party may have lived on for a while; it is probably not coincidental that in the succession struggles (1511–12) of the next generation one particular historian, Rūḥī of Edirne, criticized Selīm, the candidate of the ḳul soldiery and the eventual winner.[67]

The moving of the capital away from Istanbul, however, retained its symbolic charge in Ottoman political history until the final days of the empire. When ʿOs̱mān II (r. 1618–22) wanted to curb the power of the ḳul army, he threatened to move the capital to another city, rumored to be Bursa, Edirne, or Damascus. Then in 1703, the Janissaries (together with the guilds and the ulema of Istanbul) walked in revolt to Edirne, where Sultan Muṣṭafā II (r. 1695–1703) had been residing for years intending to reestablish it as the Ottoman capital according to rumors; after Muṣṭafā II was forced to abdicate, the newly chosen Sultan Aḥmed III (r. 1703–30) was taken back to Istanbul only after he promised that he would not leave it. In the 1810s, it is reported, Maḥmūd II (r. 1808–38) would threaten the Janissaries that if they did not restrain their excesses, he would take his family and move out of Istanbul. And finally, the choice of Ankara as the capital of the Turkish republic needs no further comment as the symbol of an ultimate rupture from the Ottoman political order.

These incidents do not have anything to do with the gazi circles; it would be an anachronism to talk of the frontier warriors as a political force after the sixteenth century. Yet the thread binding these incidents, from Cem's promise to reside in Edirne to the choice of Ankara as the capital of the Turkish republic, whose establishment spelled the end of the Ottoman dynastic regime, is clear: in the "long durée" of Ottoman political history, the political tension of "Istanbul versus another city" represented a symbolically potent axis that defined different sociopolitical interests, preferences, and visions. In the *Ṣalṭuḳnāme,* we find the first occurrence of this axis (in the form of Istanbul versus Edirne), along whose lines a meaningful opposition to the central state can be identified.

In the fifteenth century, this opposition came from the gazi circles of Rumelia because the definitive consolidation of Ottoman imperial policies after the conquest of Istanbul represented the final blow to their autonomy, which had been eroding since at least the 1370s. Some of the authors of that era who had been steeped in the gazi milieu and were able to understand their plight managed to convey their sense of resentment in an interconnected corpus of narratives, the *Tevārīḫ-i Āl-i ʿOs̱mān,* which enables us to follow the history of the Ottoman dynasty as the increasing alienation of the ruler from the mores, customs, and lifestyle of an idealized frontier society of a bygone era.

It would not be realistic to attempt an exhaustive account of the precise nature of the gazis' role in early Ottoman history and of their relations with other social groups such as the dervishes, the nomads, or the ḳapıḳulus. The main aim here has been to demonstrate the possibility of speaking of a gazi milieu in medieval Anatolia. The gazis are discernible as a specific social group during the first two centuries of Ottoman history. Whatever the significance of the role they played in the emergence of the Ottoman state, they were not imaginary creations of the Ottoman ulema as relentless fighters against the infidels. They represented a specific segment of the medieval Anatolian frontier society with their own customs and lore, interests and alliances, within a coalition that had so much success that it eventually devoured some of its members.

Like so many other elements of that coalition, such as the pastoralist tribes and the eventually heterodox dervishes, the gazis, too, represented a concrete social group which was eventually left out of the ruling stratum as an imperial, centralized polity emerged under the leadership of the House of Osman, who had once been one of their kind, one of the gazi begs. An illustrative example of this change is the case of Miḫaloğlu ʿAlī Beg, sixteenth-century heir to a long and illustrious line of frontier lords, descendants of one of Osman's renowned fellow warriors, who was told to curtail his gaza activity according to the decisions of the Sublime Porte. Whereas a raid used to be a matter of local or regional proportions and of basically personal gain for a gazi in terms of its immediate consequences, it had by then become a matter in the realm of international Realpolitik. So, when Süleymān the Magnificent struck a peace treaty with the Habsburgs and intended to keep it, Miḫaloğlu was ordered to refrain from conducting raids into their territory. What that meant for the gazi is captured in a witty simile by Nihālī, a kadi and a poet who was known as the Caʿfer of Galata because of his indulgence in wine, which often took him to the pubs in that part of Istanbul: "To give ʿAlī Beg [a commander's position in] an uc and to forbid him to operate it is like giving me the judgeship of Galata and telling me not to drink."[68]

Epilogue

The Creation of an Imperial Political Technology and Ideology

They say that Murad had a dream one night, which he then related and all the Turks believed it to be prophetic: he saw a man dressed in white garments, like a prophet, who took the ring that his son was wearing on his middle finger and transferred it to the second finger; then he took it off and put it on the third; after he had passed the ring to all five fingers, he threw it away and he vanished. Murad summoned his hodzas and diviners and asked them to interpret this dream for him. They said: "Undoubtedly, the meaning is that only five kings from your line will reign; then another dynasty will take over the kingdom." Because of this dream it was decided that no members of the old, noble families, i.e., the Turahanoglu, the Mihaloglu, or the Evrenos, would be appointed beglerbegs or viziers and that they should be restricted to the office of the standard-bearer of the akıncı, i.e., the horsemen who owe military service and receive no salary when they form the vanguard during campaigns. There is another family of this kind, called Malkoçoglu. These standard bearers are under the command of the beglerbeg. All these families had hoped to reign but, because of Murad's dream, they were deprived of their former considerable authority.[1]

Tension between state building and frontier activity that could generate alternative or spin-off enterprises had proven to be a structural weakness of many medieval Turco-Muslim political formations throughout southwestern Asia. Rival members of a ruling family or successful warriors who may have been a part of the original conquest activity, or even governors of outlying provinces, could and did establish their own, often short-lived, dynasties that would either replace an existing dynasty or, more often, snatch an autonomous realm from its grip. Frontier regions that allowed ambitious rivals to build alternative foci of power, legitimacy, and political alliances were laboratories for such experiments and catalyzed the dynamics of fragmentation. Warriors may have been united under the dream of conquest (in the name of the faith) but their dreams diverged when it came to the distribution of power after the conquest. It was the peculiar success of the House of Osman to pursue its own dream of absolute power to the exclusion or subjugation of other dreamers.

With the conquest of the Byzantine capital in 1453, the inveterate dream and the most cherished goal of numerous medieval Muslim polities in the shifting frontier regions of southwestern Asia, dominated first by Arabs and later by Turks, was realized. Ironically, this achievement also spelled the definitive end of the frontier areas (the ucāt) as assembly plants of new political enterprises and of the Ottoman polity as a frontier principality. The most succinct expression of that transformation may be Meḥmed the Conqueror's decision not to stand up at the sound of martial music, as he well knew his ancestors used to. He was thus abandoning one of the hallowed traditions of earlier Ottomans as frontier warriors, who would show their respect for the call to gaza through this practice. This was not an abandonment of the devotion to the principle of gaza, since martial music as a reminder of the Ottoman duty to struggle for the faith would still be regularly played at the gates of the palace; it was rather the expression of a fundamental change in the relationship of the House of Osman and of the Ottoman state to that principle and its representatives. Being a gazi was not the primary component of the Ottoman ruler's multiple identity anymore; he was first and foremost a sultan, a khan, and a caesar, "the ruler of the two seas and the two continents," as Meḥmed the Conqueror called himself on the inscription at the gate of his new palace in his new capital.

The making of Constantinople into a Muslim city was an ideal shared by Muslim warriors and their followers for centuries, but making it into the capital of the state or making it into the kind of capital envisioned by Meḥmed II was by no means the intention of all the conquerors. Meḥmed's throne city was part of a political project that was vehemently opposed in some circles. The project involved building a highly centralized imperial administrative apparatus that was to serve under the House of Osman, which took pride in its gazi past but which now defined itself in a new fashion. The process of centralization can be traced back to earlier Ottoman history of course, but now it was given its most systematic and radical formulation. Hierarchies of power in Ottoman political society were sharply delineated, and frontier warriors definitively subjugated, along with several other groups whose forerunners had been partners in the early Ottoman enterprise, to the domination of the central administration.

The process of centralization was not linear, because the nature of the political configuration that was emerging through conquest was always contested. It was *one* of the dynamics of earlier Ottoman history and turned out to be the dominant one in determining the shape of the state that was built at the end of that competitive process.

The century following the conquest of Constantinople witnessed not only further conquests to expand the empire as territory but also institutional developments that consolidated the empire as state. Codification, the creation of impersonal bureaucratic procedures, the increased reliance on slave-servants as administrators, and the institution of a state-controlled scholarly hierarchy were the most important elements in the process of consolidation that brought centralized absolutism to its apex (within limits set by various constraints, of course). These were paralleled by the creation of an Ottoman imperial idiom in architecture, poetry, and historiography. Both the institutional and the cultural parameters that were set and finetuned around the mid sixteenth century were considered the classical expressions of the Ottoman political technology and ideology by later generations, as the empire entered a phase of decentralization towards the end of that century.

It was also in the sixteenth century that people began to realize, or began to deal with an earlier realization, that some of the ways of the earlier Ottomans did not exactly conform to the norms of orthodox Islam as understood by its learned representatives serving the Sunni state. Two glaring transgressions among institutionalized practices were the establishment of pious endowments with cash (cash waqf) and the recruitment of the children of non-Muslim subjects for service as ḳuls of the Sublime Porte (devshirme). The former implied regular returns for money, or in other words interest, while the latter implied forced conversion of populations that should have been free of such interference according to the covenant known as the *dhimma* that the Ottomans otherwise upheld. The devshirme, as a crucial ingredient of the Ottoman administrative apparatus in the classical age, does not seem to have invited more than minimal debate. Cash waqf, on the other hand, turned out to be the subject of intense controversy and divisiveness among the religious and legal scholars, as the Ottoman state was trying to find the right dose of flexibility without stepping outside orthodoxy. Even those who allowed cash endowment to continue were aware that it was not practiced elsewhere in the Muslim world but was born under the peculiar circumstances of a frontier environment.

Then, too, some voices were raised against certain holy figures of an earlier era whom frontier folk and march principalities had idealized without much concern for their orthodoxy. Ṣarı Ṣalṭuḳ, for instance, was characterized as a Christian ascetic by Ebūssuʿūd Efendi (d. 1574), Süleymān's Grand Mufti, and legends about Aḫī Evren were ridiculed by Münīr Efendi of Belgrade (fl. early 17th century), who wanted artisans to follow an ideologically correct line. The shrine of Seyyid Gazi, and the order of Ḥācī Bektaş, were now seen to have fallen into the hands of heretics. In the end, neither the cash waqf nor the cults of these figures were suppressed, which is due, to some extent, to the relative lack of rigidity in Ottoman orthodoxy and also to the insufficiency of the technologies of control available to a pre-modern state. Still, the waqf and the cults were rendered questionable, circumscribed, and, especially in the case of cults, marginalized vis-à-vis the political classes.

Just as fellow warriors and allied social forces of the frontier era had to be subjugated or eliminated in order to establish the supremacy of Ottoman power, so their legacy had to be tamed or suppressed or marginalized in order to consolidate that power. The Ottoman state, like any of its counterparts, was constructed not only in reality but also, thanks in part to historians, in the imagination of people.

Abbreviations

AB	İ. H. Uzunçarşılı. *Anadolu Beylikleri ve Akkoyunlu, Karakoyunlu Devletleri*. Ankara, 1937.
Apz	ʿĀşıḳpaşazāde (fifteenth-century Ottoman historian)
BMGS	*Byzantine and Modern Greek Studies*
BSOAS	*Bulletin of the School of Oriental and African Studies*
DOP	*Dumbarton Oaks Papers*
EI	*The Encyclopedia of Islam*
İA	*İslâm Ansiklopedisi*
IJMES	*International Journal of Middle East Studies*
JOS	*Journal of Ottoman Studies*
JTS	*Journal of Turkish Studies*
MOG	*Mitteilungen zur osmanischen Geschichte*
OA	Oxford Anonymous
OE	E. Zachariadou, ed. *The Ottoman Emirate (1300–1389): A Symposium Held in Rethymnon, 11–13 January 1991*. Rethymnon, 1993.
SI	*Studia Islamica*
TSF	Philip S. Khoury and Joseph Kostiner, eds. *Tribes and State Formation in the Middle East*. Berkeley, 1990.
TSK	Topkapı Sarayı Kütüphanesi (Topkapi Palace Library)
WZKM	*Wiener Zeitschrift für die Kunde des Morgenlandes*
YF	Yaḫşi Faḳīh (author of lost chronicle, Apz's main source)
ZDMG	*Zeitschrift der Deutschen morgenlandischen Gesellschaft*

Notes

Preface

1. H. A. Gibbons, *The Foundation of the Ottoman Empire* (Oxford, 1916); M. F. Köprülü, *Les origines de l'empire ottoman* (Paris, 1935); P. Wittek, *The Rise of the Ottoman Empire* (London, 1938).

2. For a new exercise, see Halil İnalcık, "Comments on 'Sultanism': Max Weber's Typification of the Ottoman Polity," *Princeton Papers in Near Eastern Studies* 1(1992):49–72.

3. It seems rather appropriate that the villain's name brings to mind Jorge Luis Borges (although Eco may have been initially unaware that this character would turn out to be the murderer, as he claimed in his *Postscript to the Name of the Rose,* trans. W. Weaver [San Diego, 1984], 28), the most antihistorical and antinarrative of postmodern authors.

4. See Peter Burke, *The Historical Anthropology of Early Modern Italy: Essays on Perception and Communication* (Cambridge, 1987); and N. Z. Davis, *Fiction in the Archives: Pardon Tales and Their Tellers in Sixteenth-Century France* (Stanford, 1987).

5. Sir Moses Finley, *Ancient Slavery and Modern Ideology* (New York, 1980).

6. Halil Berktay, *Cumhuriyet İdeolojisi ve Fuat Köprülü* (Istanbul, 1983); idem, "The 'Other' Feudalism: A Critique of Twentieth Century Turkish Historiography and Its Particularisation of Ottoman Society" (Ph.D. diss., University of Birmingham, 1990); Martin Strohmeier, *Seldschukische Geschichte und türkische Geschichtswissenschaft: Die Seldschuken im Urteil moderner türkischer Historiker* (Berlin, 1984); Michael Ursinus, "Byzantine History in Late Ottoman Turkish Historiography," *BMGS* 10(1986):211–22; idem, "'Der schlechteste Staat': Ahmed Midhat Efendi (1844–1913) on Byzantine Institutions," *BMGS* 11(1987):237–43; idem, "From Süleyman Pasha to Mehmet Fuat Köprülü: Roman and Byzantine History in Late Ottoman Historiography," *BMGS* 12(1988): 305–14. The translations by Gary Leiser in part serve a similar end of stocktaking, especially since they are enlarged with annotations, additional footnotes,

and introductions, even though the introductions are not critical: *A History of the Seljuks: İbrahim Kafesoğlu's Interpretation and the Resulting Controversy* (Carbondale and Edwardsville, 1988); M. F. Köprülü, *The Origins of the Ottoman Empire* (Albany, 1992); idem, *Some Observations on the Influence of Byzantine Institutions on Ottoman Institutions* (Ankara, 1993); and idem, *Islam in Anatolia after the Turkish Invasion* (Salt Lake City, 1993). For works on the gaza thesis, see n. 56 in chapter 1 below. Hereafter, the simplified spelling of "gaza" will be used.

Introduction

1. Albert Hourani, "How Should We Write the History of the Middle East?" *IJMES* 23(1991):130. The name of the eponym of the dynasty will hereafter be spelled in its simplified form of "Osman," primarily for the sake of practicality. It is, moreover, uncertain that his given name was ʿOṣmān, from the Arabic ʿUthmān, as will be argued in chapter 3.

2. This usage does not appear in European languages but was common in Arabic, Persian, and Turkish.

3. Both the politico-military and the religio-cultural history of those four centuries is given magisterial treatment in Speros Vryonis, *The Decline of Medieval Hellenism in Asia Minor and the Process of Islamization from the Eleventh through the Fifteenth Century* (Berkeley, 1971).

4. Claude Cahen, "Kilidj Arslan II," *EI*, new ed., s.v.

5. Ibid. For a general survey of Seljuk history (as well as the histories of other Turco-Muslim polities and populations) in Anatolia, see idem, *La Turquie pré-ottomane* (Istanbul, 1988); also see Osman Turan, *Selçuklular Zamanında Türkiye* (Istanbul, 1971). The Seljuks of Rūm are seen within the larger context of Seljuk history in the Middle East in idem, *Selçuklular Tarihi ve Türk-İslâm Medeniyeti*, 4th enl. ed. (Istanbul, 1993), and in Gary Leiser, trans. and ed., *A History of the Seljuks: Ibrahim Kafesoğlu's Interpretation and the Resulting Controversy.*

6. For the background, causes, and unfolding of the rebellion, see Ahmet Yaşar Ocak, *Babaîler İsyanı* (Istanbul, 1980).

7. On Seljuk caravanserais, see Kurt Erdmann, *Das anatolische Karavanserail des 13. Jahrhunderts* (Tübingen, 1961); and M. Kemal Özergin, "Anadolu'da Selçuklu Kervansarayları," *Tarih Dergisi* 15(1965):141–70. The most recent treatment of the world economy in the relevant era is Janet Abu Lughod, *Before European Economy: The World System,* A.D. *1250–1350* (New York, 1989). A detailed look at the changes in medieval Anatolian economy after the Turkish invasions is included in Michael Hendy, *Studies in the Byzantine Monetary Economy, c. 300–1450* (Cambridge, 1985).

8. Elizabeth A. Zachariadou, *Trade and Crusade: Venetian Crete and the Emirates of Menteshe and Aydın (1300–1415)* (Venice, 1983). On the international fair, see Faruk Sümer, *Yabanlu Pazarı: Selçuklular Devrinde Milletlerarası Büyük Bir Fuar* (Istanbul, 1985), which includes a detailed summary translation into English and the Arabic originals of the sources. For a general assessment of Mongol rule in Anatolia, see idem, "Anadolu'da Moğollar," *Selçuklu Araştırmaları Dergisi* 1(1969):1–147. A proliferation of local minting at the end of the thirteenth

century is mentioned in Rudi P. Lindner, "A Silver Age in Seljuk Anatolia," in *Türk Nümismatik Derneğinin 20. Kuruluş, Yılında İbrahim Artuk'a Armağan* (Istanbul, 1988).

9. Marshall Sahlins, *The Islands of History* (Chicago, 1985), 79.

10. 'Āşıkpaşazāde, ed. Giese, 9–10. The translation is a modified version of the one given by Lindner, *Nomads and Ottomans in Medieval Anatolia* (Bloomington, 1983), 37.

11. On that theory, see Terence Spencer, "Turks and Trojans in the Renaissance," *Modern Language Review* 47(1952):330–33; Agostino Pertusi, "I primi studi in Occidente sull'origine e la potenza dei Turchi," *Studi Veneziani* 12(1970):465–552; S. Runciman, "Teucri and Turci," *Medieval and Middle Eastern Studies in Honour of Aziz Suryal Atiya*, ed. S. Hanna (Leiden, 1972), 344–48; and F. L. Borchardt, *German Antiquity in Renaissance Myth* (Baltimore, 1971), 85, 292.

12. The passage appears in the only historical work that can be called an official chronicle under Meḥmed, and it was written in Greek: Michael Kritovoulos, *History of Mehmed the Conqueror,* trans. C. T. Riggs (Princeton, 1954), 181–82.

13. Lawrence Stone, "The Revolution over the Revolution," *New York Review of Books,* 11 June 1992, 47–52.

14. Norman Cantor, *Inventing the Middle Ages: The Lives, Works, and Ideas of the Great Medievalists of the Twentieth Century* (New York, 1991).

15. Two detailed narrative accounts have appeared to which the reader can now refer: Colin Imber, *The Ottoman Empire, 1300–1481* (Istanbul, 1990); and Halil Inalcık, "The Ottoman Turks and the Crusades, 1329–1451," in K. M. Setton, general ed., *A History of the Crusades,* vol. 6, *The Impact of the Crusades on Europe,* ed. H. W. Hazard and N. P. Zacour (Madison, 1989), 222–75.

16. The term is used in the historiography of Muslim cultures to denote cases like that of "the petty kings who ruled the tribes of western Asia after the death of Alexander the Great" (definition given by J. W. Redhouse, *A Turkish and English Lexicon* [Istanbul, 1890], s.v.).

17. For a sympathetic assessment of his work, see J. R. Barcia, ed., *Américo Castro and the Meaning of the Spanish Civilization* (Berkeley, 1976).

18. The case of India, invaded and then ruled in large part by Muslim conquerors in its "medieval" history, obviously presents many parallels to both Anatolia and Iberia. See, for instance, the inflammatory title of a scholarly article by A. L. Srivastava: "A Survey of India's Resistance to Medieval Invaders from the North-West: Causes of Eventual Hindu Defeat," *Journal of Indian History* 43(1965):349–68.

19. See p. 190 in the lead essay by C. E. Bosworth to "Othmanli," *EI,* new ed., s.v. The fascicule that contains this entry appeared in 1993.

20. National historiographic projects, European or otherwise, eliminated more than ethnic diversity of course. Cultural and social diversity of all kinds could be marginalized or "otherized" and deemed to lie beyond "us." See, for instance, Herman Leibovics, *True France: The Wars over Cultural Identity, 1900–1945* (Cambridge, Mass., 1993). In fact, it is not always possible to distinguish ethnic and cultural diversity; the term "ethnic" is only awkwardly applied to

prenational societies. On national history as linear narrative, see Homi K. Bhabha, ed., *Nation and Narration* (London and New York, 1990).

21. Though this is not the place to discuss this issue in detail, I should note that some of my comments here are based on the observation that the history of most of the world seems to be written in two spheres, the national and the international, that do not always communicate well with each other. Individual historians may in fact produce different kinds of histories for these different spheres. At any rate, for the history of many nations there are two different consensuses, if not more. Only some non-Western nations have had their national version internationally recognized, even then with many differences. Besides, for every nationalist proposition that achieves international recognition, objections are bound to be raised by "hostile" nationalist traditions. Hence, there is never full international recognition, but if scholars and institutions of the Western world accept a proposition, that proposition becomes the dominant, thus "international," position at large.

22. The process of Islamization, which implied Turkification over the long run in Anatolia and, to a lesser extent, in the Balkans, must naturally be studied against the background of migrations and conversions. On both of those issues, we lack statistical information, which is a serious obstacle to dealing (if this is at all desirable) with the numerical dimensions of the ethnoreligious concoction. Some have tried nonetheless. Osman Turan estimates that since Turkish immigration was constant and conversion to Islam was not mandatory, ethnic Turks outnumbered Islamized Christians in a ratio of 70:30. See his "L'islamisation dans la Turquie du moyen âge," *SI* 10(1959):137–52, where these numbers are not even tentatively substantiated. Mükrimin Halil Yınanç provides another daring estimate that there were more than 1,080,000 Türkmen tribesfolk in Asia Minor at the end of the thirteenth century on the basis of highly dubious, general figures given in medieval narrative sources. See his *Türkiye Tarihi Selçuklular Devri,* vol. 1, *Anadolu'nun Fethi* (Istanbul, 1944), 174–76. For a serious study at the micro level, see H. Lowry, Trabzon Şehrinin İslâmlaşma ve Turkleşmesi, 1461–1583 (Istanbul, [1981?]). Recent developments in genetic research have facilitated the return of racially oriented investigation and may, alas, address the issue at hand.

23. For a discussion of the main differences of opinion, see N. Todorov, *The Balkan City, 1400–1900* (Seattle, 1983), 13 ff., who portrays the generally accepted (non-Turkish) view as follows:

> [T]he destructive force of invasion turned numerous areas of the Balkans into a desert for a prolonged period, and . . . the local population, routed by the invader, exterminated and taken into slavery, declined to the extent that all the more fertile plains became populated by the Turks.

On the Turkish side, see, for instance, M. Akdağ, *Türkiye'nin İktisadî ve İçtimaî Tarihi,* 2 vols. (Istanbul, 1974):

> It is clear from both Byzantine and Turkish sources that Turks and the people of Byzantium intermingled with no animosity of either religious or national nature, and procured their mutual needs from one another. (1:463)

> Anatolian Christians, who suffered much poverty under Byzantine rule and on the eve of the Mantzikert victory, benefited from the economic vitality and prosperity that came

about when these lands passed to the Turks. Villages, towns, and cities became more populous and prosperous. Even if it were true that Christians left their places and homes out of fear during Turkish conquests and fled here and there, this can be considered only for limited strata of the rich and for some of the ecclesiastical class. (1:473)

Another version of this argument has been to emphasize that Turkish conquests were for a cause; thus Ö. L. Barkan mentions the "compelling power of the Turkish sword that represented a new cause" (trans. H. Berktay, in his "The 'Other' Feudalism," 15).

24. For late Ottoman views on Byzantine history, see the articles by M. Ursinus, cited above in Preface, n. 6.

25. See Eleanor Searle, *Predatory Kinship and the Creation of Norman Power, 840–1066* (Berkeley, 1988).

26. Mahmut R. Gazimihal, "İstanbul Muhasaralarında Mihaloğulları ve Fatih Devrine Ait Bir Vakıf Defterine Göre Harmankaya Mâlikânesi," *Vakıflar Dergisi* 4(1958):125–37.

27. İ. Kaygusuz, *Onar Dede Mezarlığı ve Adı Bilinmeyen Bir Türk Kolonizatörü: Şeyh Hasan Oner* (Istanbul, 1983), 10.

28. Passage from the *Künhü'l-aḫbār* of Muṣṭafā ʿĀlī discovered, translated, and cited by Cornell H. Fleischer, *Bureaucrat and Intellectual in the Ottoman Empire: The Historian Mustafa Âli (1541–1600)* (Princeton, 1986), 254.

1. The Moderns

1. See, for instance, Georges Dumézil, *The Destiny of a King,* trans. A. Hiltebeitel (Chicago, 1973): "a literary work does not have to set forth a theory: it is the hearer's or the reader's task to perceive the providential design which has arranged the events in the order in which the work presents them and with the results it describes. Yet it is the design that justifies these events and results, and gives them a meaning" (p. 115).

2. Though the compositional history of this extremely important text is still unclear, the episode about Osman is common, with some differences that do not matter for this discussion, to both the versified and the prose version, which were put into writing in the fifteenth century. For the version in verse, see *Manẓûm Hacı Bektaş Velî Velâyetnâmesi (İlk Velâyetnâme),* ed. Bedri Noyan (Aydın, 1986), 261–80 of text. For the one in prose, see *Vilâyet-nâme: Manâkıb-ı Hünkâr Hacı Bektâş-ı Velî,* ed. and trans. into modern Turkish by Abdülbaki Gölpınarlı (Istanbul, 1958), 71–75.

3. Richard Knolles, *The General Historie of the Turkes* (London, [1610?]); see "The Author's Induction to the Christian Reader." Samuel Johnson is cited by E. F. Gibbon, whose own opinion of Knolles is not so positive: "Yet I much doubt whether a partial and verbose compilation from Latin writers, thirteen hundred folio pages of speeches and battles, can either instruct or amuse an enlightened age, which requires from the historian some tincture of philosophy and criticism." *The History of the Decline and Fall of the Roman Empire,* 7 vols., ed. J. B. Bury (London, 1914), 7:25–26 n. 66.

4. Knolles entitled his English translation *The Six Bookes of a Commonweale.* The French original came out in 1576, the English translation in 1603.

5. Joseph von Hammer-Purgstall, *Die Geschichte des osmanischen Reiches,* 10 vols. (Pest, 1827–35).

6. Nicolae Iorga, *Geschichte des osmanischen Reiches nach den Quellen dargestellt,* 5 vols. (Gotha, 1908–13). An uncritical but accurate overview is given by M. M. Alexandrescu-Dersca [Bulgaru] in two versions: "N. Iorga, historien de l'empire ottoman," *Balcania* 6(1943):101–22; and *Nicolae Iorga—A Romanian Historian of the Ottoman Empire* (Bucharest, 1972).

7. To begin his analytical chapter (*Geschichte,* 1:456) Iorga wrote, for instance:

> Um die Entwicklung des osmanischen Reiches zu verstehen, um sich von den Ursachen des schwachen christlichen Verteidigung, der grossen Anzahl der Renegaten, der Bereitwilligkeit so vieler christlicher Völkerschaften, das türkische "Joch" auf sich zu nehmen, von der ausserordentlichen Seltenheit der Aufstände—gab doch eine einmal eroberte Stadt niemals Zeichen der Unzufriedenheit mit ihrem Lose, und während all der grossen Kriegszüge der Franken und Ungarn schloss sich unter dem Zeichen des Kreuzes kommenden Gästen nirgend ein irgendwie beträchtlicheres Kontingent einheimischer Bauern an, um am heiligen Werke der "Befreiung" teilzunehmen—, um sich von all dem Rechenschaft zu geben, ist es erforderlich, sich die wahren Eigenschaften der Osmanen und ihr wirkliches Leben klarzumachen.

8. H. A. Gibbons, *The Foundation of the Ottoman Empire* (Oxford, 1916).

9. *The Turkish Letters of Ogier Ghislein de Busbecq,* trans. E. S. Forster (Oxford, 1927), 55; Gibbons, *Foundation,* 50.

10. Gibbons, *Foundation,* 51.

11. Todorov rightly points out the genealogy of this view, from Hammer through Iorga to Grousset, though it had never been expressed so strongly. See *Balkan City,* 46.

12. Gibbons, *Foundation,* 75. Gibbons was not any milder on "degenerate" Byzantines approaching the end of their empire. He continued on the same page: "But when we compare the early Osmanlis with the Byzantines . . . it is the Osmanlis who must be pronounced the fittest. They were fresh, enthusiastic, uncontaminated, energetic. They had ideals; they had a goal."

13. C. Diehl, *Byzantium: Greatness and Decline,* trans. N. Walford (New Brunswick, N.J., 1957), 290. The original French version was published in 1926.

14. N. Iorga, *Byzance après Byzance: Continuation de l'"Histoire de la vie byzantine"* (Bucharest, 1935). Also see his *Histoire de la vie byzantine* (Bucharest, 1934), 3:159–60. All this is tied, naturally, to the claim that the Ottomans did not have the requisite "forms of life" (*Lebensformen* or *formes de vie* in the languages used by Iorga, key concepts in his understanding of history) for the establishment of an empire. See idem, *Geschichte des osmanischen Reiches* (Gotha, 1908), 1:264.

15. Friedrich Giese, "Das Problem der Entstehung des osmanischen Reiches," *Zeitschrift für Semitistik und verwandte Gebiete* 2(1924):246–71.

16. J. H. Kramers, "Wer war Osman?" *Acta Orientalia* 6(1928):242–54.

17. William L. Langer and Robert P. Blake, "The Rise of the Ottoman Turks and Its Historical Background," *American Historical Review* 37(1932):468–505; the citations are from pp. 497 and 504.

18. Köprülü, *Les origines de l'empire ottoman.* A Turkish edition, with some minor changes and a new introduction by the author, was published in 1959: *Osmanlı İmparatorluğunun Kuruluşu* (Ankara). An annotated English translation of that edition has appeared as *The Origins of the Ottoman Empire,* trans. and ed. Gary Leiser (Albany, 1992).

19. Paul Wittek, *Das Fürstentum Mentesche* (Istanbul, 1934). A Turkish translation was made by a student of Köprülü: *Menteşe Beyliği,* trans. O. Ş. Gökyay (Ankara, 1944).

20. Paul Wittek, *The Rise of the Ottoman Empire* (London, 1938).

21. Wittek, *Mentesche,* 35.

22. Mehmet Fuat Köprülü, "Bizans Müesseselerinin Osmanlı Müesseselerine Te'siri Hakkında Bâzı Mülâhazalar," *Türk Hukuk ve İktisat Tarihi Mecmuası* 1(1931):165–313. "Les institutions byzantines ont-elles joué un rôle dans la formation des institutions ottomanes?" *VIIe Congrès International des Sciences Historiques: Résumés*... (Warsaw, 1933), 1:297–302, is a French summary of this work, which is now published as a book in three languages: *Alcune osservazioni intorno all'influenza delle istituzioni bizantine sulle istituzioni ottomane* (Rome, 1953); by the original title in Turkish, with additional notes by Orhan Köprülü (Istanbul, 1981); *Some Observations on the Influence of Byzantine Institutions on Ottoman Institutions,* trans. G. Leiser (Ankara, 1993).

23. The introduction of Durkheimian sociology is attributed to Ziya Gökalp, the sociologist who was the mentor of a whole generation of nationalists in the early twentieth century. As a student of "Gökalp's disciple, Mehmed Fuad Köprülü," Halil İnalcık is conscious of this legacy; see his "Impact of the *Annales* School on Ottoman Studies and New Findings," *Review* 1(1978):69–70. İnalcık has also written a more detailed assessment of Gökalp's sociology: "Sosyal Değişme, Gökalp ve Toynbee," *Türk Kültürü* 3/31(May 1965):421–33.

24. Köprülü, *Origins,* 24.

25. Lucien Fevbre, "Review of Köprülü, Les origines de l'empire ottoman," *Annales: ESC* 9(1937):100–101. Lengthy passages of this review were cited with relish by Köprülü in his introduction to the Turkish edition; see pp. xxi–xxiii in the English translation.

26. Köprülü, *Origins,* xxiii. Here I had to change the translator's "had" to "have" because it is a more accurate rendering of the tense in the original Turkish sentence ("*mışlardır*" and not "*mışlardı*") and thus of the likelihood that there is an implicit critique of Wittek here, always appreciated as a good philologist even by his critics. Köprülü had already raised the same criticism against Wittek's "monocausal" explanation more directly in "Osmanlı İmparatorluğunun Etnik Menşei Meseleleri," *Belleten* 7(1943):285–86.

27. Köprülü, *Origins,* 11–21.

28. Ibid., 86–87.

29. Ibid., 87–88.

30. The sun-language theory claimed, on the basis of a heliocentric view of the origin and nature of human languages, that Turkish was the Ur-language from which all civilized languages derived. See Büşra Ersanlı Behar, *İktidar ve Tarih: Türkiye'de "Resmi Tarih" Tezinin Oluşumu (1929–1937)* (Istanbul, 1992), 175–81.

31. While it may be accurate to state that "the greatest single influence on modern perceptions of early Ottoman history has been the work of the scholar Paul Wittek," it is misleading to add that Wittek's gaza thesis "appealed to everyone: Turkish nationalists can see Wittek's gazis, or Holy Warriors, as the embodiment of Turkish-Islamic heroism" (Imber, *The Ottoman Empire,* 12–13). There was a good deal of shared ground between Wittek and Köprülü; in addition to what has been mentioned, we should note that Köprülü, along with many other Turkish scholars before and after Wittek, accepted that there were gazis in medieval Anatolia and that Osman and some of his followers and descendants belonged in that category. But this is surely not the same thing as subscribing to the gaza thesis. While some of his articles were translated, Wittek's book was not published in Turkish until 1971 (translated by Güzin Yalter and first published as *Beiheft* to İ. H. Danişmend's *İzahlı Osmanlı Tarihi Kronolojisi,* and then as fascicule no. 1 in *Batı Dillerinde Osmanlı Tarihleri* [Istanbul, 1971], 3–52). An earlier translation by Fahriye Arık is cited in Uzunçarşılı, *Osmanlı Tarihi,* vol. 1 (Ankara, 1947), 97–98, but it remained unpublished. Arık herself was not convinced by Wittek and wrote an article to prove (but it ultimately turned out to be wrong) that a symbol on Orḫān's coins was the tribal sign of the Kayı. As for Uzunçarşılı, arguably the most widely read historian of republican Turkey, and always more comfortable as a chronicler, he did not overtly subscribe to any thesis. To the extent one can discern an explanatory model in his works, he is closer to Köprülü not only because he accepts the Kayı tribal origins but also because he emphasizes the role of the aḫīs, the dervishes, and early institutionalization based on Turco-Muslim models. Most importantly, the notion of descent-based tribalism reigned supreme in Turkey, and this alone should caution the historiographer against universalizing Wittek's appeal. Also see n. 67 below. As in the case of Togan (see n. 38 below), many Turkish scholars were uncomfortable with implications of religious fanaticism. A Russian translation of Köprülü's book appeared in 1939 (Moscow). A Serbo-Croatian translation, with a laudatory introduction by Nedim Filipović, was published before the Turkish edition: *Porjeklo Osmanske Carevine* (Sarajevo, 1955).

32. Aydın Taneri would argue, for instance, that Mevlānā Celālüddīn Rūmī is not only Turkish but a Turkish nationalist; see his *Mevlânâ Âilesinde Türk Milleti ve Devleti Fikri* (Ankara, 1987).

33. George Georgiades Arnakis, *Hoi protoi othomanoi* (Athens, 1947).

34. Robert Lee Wolff's review was published in *Speculum* 26(1951):483–488.

35. Arnakis, *Hoi protoi othomanoi,* 246.

36. A. Zeki Velidî Togan, *Umumî Türk Tarihi'ne Giriş,* 3d ed. (Istanbul, 1981), esp. see 332–33.

37. Ibid., 333–35. In the same work (341), he also delineated what he interpreted to be Kipchak (as opposed to Oğuz) influences in early Ottoman usages. Togan also engaged in an exchange with Köprülü which may be called the second Kayı controversy: Köprülü still insisted that Osman's ancestry was from the Kayı branch of the Oğuz Turks while Togan raised the possibility that it may have been from the eastern Turkish Kay.

38. Ibid., 317–51. On the religiosity of the early Ottomans, Togan writes: "Since their level of civilization was incomparably lower than, say, the begs of

Kastamonu or Germiyan, they were detached from Islamic fanaticism, though they were Muslim" (336–37).

39. Mustafa Akdağ, "Osmanlı İmparatorluğunun Kuruluş ve İnkişafı Devrinde Türkiye'nin İktisadi Vaziyeti," in two parts, *Belleten* 13(1949):497–571, 14(1950):319–418. Critiqued by Halil İnalcık, "Osmanlı İmparatorluğunun Kuruluş ve İnkişafı Devrinde Türkiye'nin İktisadî Vaziyeti Üzerinde Bir Tetkik Münasebetiyle," *Belleten* 15(1951):629–84.

40. Akdağ, *Türkiye'nin İktisadî ve İçtimaî Tarihi*, 2d ed., 2 vols. (Istanbul, 1974). The original publication date is 1959.

41. See, for instance, the citations from Akdağ in the Introduction, n. 21, above.

42. Vryonis, *The Decline of Medieval Hellenism*. Also see his response to the reviews of this book, "The Decline of Medieval Hellenism . . . ," *Greek Orthodox Theological Review* 27(1982):225–85.

43. Vryonis, "The Decline," 278.

44. Ibid., 262–63.

45. Ernst Werner, *Die Geburt einer Grossmacht—Die Osmanen (1300–1481): Ein Beitrag zur Genesis des türkischen Feudalismus*, 2d ed. (Berlin, 1972). A Turkish translation, by Y. Öner, was published in 198?–88: *Büyük Bir Devletin Doğuşu—Osmanlılar*, 2 vols. (Istanbul).

46. Also see Werner's "Panturkismus und einige Tendenzen moderner türkischer Historiographie," *Zeitschrift für Geschichtswissenschaft* 13(1965):1342–54. In solidarity with Marxist historians of Balkan socialist republics, Werner's main objection was to the position that the Ottoman expansion brought all sorts of benefits to the Balkan peoples.

47. For a more recent defense of his position and of G.D.R. historiography against "bourgeois" medievalists, see Werner's "Einleitung" (with Matschke) and "Ökonomische und soziale Strukturen im 10. und 11. Jahrhundert," in *Ideologie und Gesellschaft im hohen und späten Mittelalter*, ed. E. Werner and K.-P. Matschke (Berlin, 1988).

48. Werner, *Geburt*, 18. After the Second World War, Köprülü abandoned his scholarly career and entered political life as one of the founders of the Democratic Party. In the early 1950s, when the cold war raged strong, he served as minister of foreign affairs in Turkey's staunchly pro-American government.

49. Köprülü, *Origins*, 24. I changed Leiser's "antipathy" to "conflict." The Turkish version has *zıddiyet*. Emphases are mine.

50. İnalcık, "The Question of the Emergence of the Ottoman State," *International Journal of Turkish Studies* 2(1980):71–79.

51. Wittek, *The Rise*, 34.

52. Ibid., 42.

53. Paul Wittek, "De la défaite d'Ankara à la prise de Constantinople," *Revue des Études Islamiques* 12(1938):1–34.

54. See, for instance, Michael W. Doyle, *Empires* (Ithaca and London, 1986): "These Anatolian Turkish tribesmen were stamped with a strikingly militant culture (ghazi fanaticism), an Islamic equivalent of the Crusaders" (106), or Perry Anderson, *Lineages of the Absolutist State* (London, 1979): "ghazi out-

look — a militant, crusading Muslim faith that rejected any accommodation with the Infidel" (362).

55. I certainly do not wish to imply that no original contributions were made to the study of the period. In addition to various relevant works on late Byzantine history, which we cannot attempt to summarize here, some solid new research was produced on individual principalities, such as the monographs by İ. H. Uzunçarşılı, H. Akın, Y. Yücel, N. Varlık, and Ç. Uluçay and B. Flemming's study of Hamidili and Teke. Of great value in illuminating not only the activities of the other begliks but also the early Ottomans is the impressive body of studies produced by E. Zachariadou, who combined Muslim, Byzantine, and Latin sources for important discoveries. (See the Selected Bibliography under these names.) This research was not generated directly by the debate concerning the rise of the Ottoman state, however.

For research and debate on the Kayı, see Köprülü's introduction to the Turkish edition of his work (pp. xxv–xxvi in the English translation).

56. Rudi Paul Lindner, *Nomads and Ottomans;* G. Káldy-Nagy, "The Holy War (*jihād*) in the First Centuries of the Ottoman Empire," *Harvard Ukrainian Studies* 3/4(1979–80):467–73; R. C. Jennings, "Some Thoughts on the Gazi-Thesis," *WZKM* 76(1986):151–61; Colin Heywood, "Wittek and the Austrian Tradition," *Journal of the Royal Asiatic Society* (1988):7–25; idem, "Boundless Dreams of the Levant: Paul Wittek, the *George-Kreis,* and the Writing of Ottoman History," ibid. (1989):30–50; Colin Imber, "Paul Wittek's 'De la défaite d'Ankara à la prise de Constantinople,'" *JOS* 5(1986):65–81; idem, "The Ottoman Dynastic Myth," *Turcica* 19(1987):7–27; idem, "The Legend of Osman Gazi," *OE,* 67–76. Also see idem, *The Ottoman Empire,* introduction. A similar attitude to the gaza thesis is displayed in the philological analyses of Şinasi Tekin in his "Türk Dünyasında Gaza ve Cihad Kavramları Üzerinde Düşünceler," in two parts in *Tarih ve Toplum* 19(1993):9–18 and 73–80. It has been a happy coincidence to see that Dr. Feridun Emecen of Istanbul University has recently produced a critique of Tekin's position, as well as some of the works mentioned in this note, that makes an argument close to mine and uses some of the same evidence; I am grateful to him for showing me his "Gazâya Dair: XIV. Yüzyıl Kaynakları Arasında Bir Gezinti," *Hakkı Dursun Yıldız'a Armağan* (Istanbul, forthcoming).

57. Lindner, *Nomads and Ottomans,* 2. For further elaboration of this point, see also his "What Was a Nomadic Tribe?" *Comparative Studies in Society and History,* 1982, 689–711. For a critique of Lindner's understanding of tribalism, see Richard Tapper, "Anthropologists, Historians, and Tribespeople on Tribe and State Formation in the Middle East," *TSF,* 48–73.

58. Lindner, *Nomads and Ottomans,* 2.

59. The predilection to pass inquisitorial judgment on Muslims who display certain tendencies that are considered uncanonical can also be observed, as Muhsin Mahdi points out, among the historians of thought who are ready to place medieval Muslim philosophers like Ibn Sīnā (Avicenna) outside the community of believers. See his "Orientalism and the Study of Islamic Philosophy," *Journal of Islamic Studies* 1(1990):73–98.

60. Jennings, "Some Thoughts," 155, 153.

61. Káldy-Nagy, "Holy War," 470. See also p. 469 for the same point made with respect to earlier Turkish warlords such as Artuḳ (d. 1091).

62. It seems more appropriate to read the change in naming practices as a question of identity rather than one of sincerity, reflecting a deemphasis on the Turkic traditions in the self-definition of the early Ottomans as formulated by M. Kunt, "Siyasal Tarih, 1300–1600," in *Türkiye Tarihi,* ed. S. Akşin (Istanbul, 1987–88), 2:36–37.

63. R. P. Lindner, "Stimulus and Justification in Early Ottoman History," *Greek Orthodox Theological Review* 27(1982):216.

64. Michel Mazzaoui, *The Origins of the Safavids: Šiʿism, Sufism, and the Ġulat* (Wiesbaden, 1972).

65. *Al-Şaḳāʾiḳ al-nuʿmāniyya,* trans. Mecdī Efendi, as *Ḥadāʾiḳuʾş-şaḳāʾiḳ,* ed. A. Özcan (Istanbul, 1989), 31–33.

66. On human sacrifice, see Vryonis, "Evidence of Human Sacrifice among Early Ottoman Turks," *Journal of Asian History* 5(1971):140–46. For an assessment of the applicability of shamanism to our case, see İ. Kafesoğlu, *Eski Türk Dini* (Ankara, 1980) and the unpublished M.A. thesis of A. Karamustafa (McGill University, 1981). For a survey of the anthropological critique of the reading of unorthodox practices as survivals, see C. Stewart, *Demons and the Devil* (Princeton, 1991), 5–12.

67. In arguing for the Köprülü-inspired tribal origins of the Ottoman state as opposed to Wittek's gazi thesis, some Turkish scholars, too, felt gazis would have to have been devout Muslims. Faruk Demirtaş, "Osmanlı Devrinde Anadolu'da Kayılar," *Belleten* 12(1948): "Had the early Ottomans been a society composed of gazis, as a European scholar claims, they would have taken devout Muslim names as opposed to the national names most of them bore" (602).

68. W. Barthold, *Turkestan down to the Mongol Invasion,* 4th ed. (London, 1977). The original in Russian appeared in 1900 and an English edition in 1928.

69. Ibid., 215.

70. Ibid., 312.

71. In the first half of this century, Orientalists were much more certain that corporate organizations existed in medieval Islam and that gazis were part of that phenomenon. Barthold, for instance, speaks of "the guild of warriors for the Faith" (ibid., 214–15).

72. Lindner, "Stimulus," 219. Naturally, the same question could have been raised with regard to tribalism. If it was the motive force, as Lindner suggests, were the Ottomans the only group in Anatolia to "go tribal"? If so, that requires some historical explanation of Osman's unique method. If not, why were the others unable to succeed? Due to greater success enjoyed by Osman as a chieftain? But then the same point could be made within the framework of the gaza thesis. If, on the other hand, there are reasons for tribalism to work more successfully in Bithynia than elsewhere, the same can be said for gaza.

73. İnalcık, "The Question of the Emergence," 74–75.

74. Ibid., 76.

2. The Sources

1. There are, however, four documents attributed to Osman's chieftainship. The first three, from later sources, are clearly apocryphal. For references and

discussion, see Irène Beldiceanu-Steinherr, *Recherches sur les actes des règnes des sultans Osman, Orkhan et Murad I* (Munich, 1967), 59–77. The fourth one, despite some traces of having been later touched up, as Taeschner and Wittek pointed out, seems to contain an authentic kernel of an endowment deed issued in 1323 by Aspurça Ḫātūn, one of Orḫān's wives (ibid., 78–82).

2. Apz, ed. Giese, 10–11. The attribution of illiteracy, though not at all unbelievable in the case of Osman, could also be read as a topos used to underline the role of divine inspiration in the deeds of a holy warrior. On the inconsistent and vague role of the sword in later accession rituals, see F. W. Hasluck, *Christianity and Islam under the Sultans,* ed. Margaret M. Hasluck (Oxford, 1929), 2:604–22.

3. An undated coin was discovered by İbrahim Artuk; see his "Osmanlı Beyliğinin Kurucusu Osman Gâzî'ye Ait Sikke," in *Social and Economic History of Turkey (1071–1920),* ed. O. Okyar and H. İnalcık (Ankara, 1980), 27–33. Lindner has more recently referred to one issued in 1299 in Söğüt; see his "A Silver Age in Seljuk Anatolia," in *İbrahim Artuk'a Armağan* (Istanbul, 1988), 272.

4. Reproduced in facsimile and discussed in İ. Hakkı Uzunçarşılı, "Gazi Orhan Bey Vakfiyesi," *Belleten* 5(1941):277–88 and pls. LXXXVI, LXXXVII. For further discussion of this document, see Beldiceanu-Steinherr, *Recherches,* 85–89.

5. There were at least four other begs with the title of Şücā'eddīn in Anatolia in that generation: another Orḫān, this one from the House of Menteşe, who has an inscription in Milas dated 1330 (Uzunçarşılı, *AB,* 73); Yaḫşi Ḫān bin Karasi, emir of Bergama (ibid., 99); İnanç Beg of Ladik, whose name and title appear on an inscription of 1335 (ibid., 56); and a certain Uğurlu(?) in central Anatolia, mentioned in *Al-'Umarī's Bericht über Anatolien in seinem Werke "Masālik al-abṣār fī mamālik al-amṣār,"* ed. F. Taeschner (Leipzig, 1929), 31.

6. Cited in Elizabeth A. Zachariadou, "Pachymeres on the 'Amourioi' of Kastamonu," *BMGS* 3(1977):57–70. İnalcık argues ("Osmān Ghāzī's Siege of Nicaea and the Battle of Bapheus," *OE*) that "it is not plausible that Turcomans from such a distant region as the Meander came to join 'Osmān" (80) and that those volunteers must have come from the nearer area of Afyonkarahisar. This does not change my argument in terms of communication among Türkmens from different principalities.

7. Several histories of Turkish literature concentrate only on works produced in Turkish, but for a more comprehensive look at works produced in thirteenth- and fourteenth-century Anatolia in Arabic, Persian, and Turkish, see the lists in Uzunçarşılı, *AB,* 259–62 and 209–23, including discussion of the authors and the patrons. Monographs on individual begliks also have useful sections on intellectual life. The most informative and substantive discussion of the literary scene, accompanied by analyses of individual works, is by Alessio Bombaci: *La Turchia dall'epoca preottomana al XV secolo,* part 1 of A. Bombaci and S. Shaw, *L'impero ottomano* (Turin, 1981). Also see relevant chapters in C. Cahen, *La Turquie pré-ottomane* (Istanbul, 1988).

8. See Rudi Paret, *Die legendäre Maghāzī-Literatur: Arabische Dichtungen über die muslimischen Kriegszüge zu Mohammeds Zeit* (Tübingen, 1930); Aldo Gallotta, "Il Şalṣāl-nāme," *Turcica* 21–23(1991):175–90; Peter Heath, "A Critical Review of Modern Scholarship on *Sīrat 'Antar Ibn Shaddād* and the popular *sīra,*" *Journal of Arabic Literature* 15(1984):19–44.

9. Irène Mélikoff, *La geste de Melik Dāniṣmend: Étude critique du Dāniṣmendnāme,* 2 vols. (Paris, 1960); and idem, *Abū Muslim: Le 'porte-hache' du Khorassan dans la tradition épique turco-iranienne* (Paris, 1962). Also see P. N. Boratav, "Baṭṭāl," *İA,* s.v. On Arabic legends that constitute the basis of the Turkish literature on Seyyid Baṭṭāl Gazi, see the collected articles of Marius Canard in *Byzance et les musulmans du Proche Orient* (London, 1973). A fifteenth-century text of the Baṭṭāl legend in Turkish is now being edited by George Dedes in his ongoing dissertation (Harvard University).

10. A critical edition of Ebū'l-ḫayr-i Rūmī's *Ṣalṭuḳnāme* is published by Ş. H. Akalın in 3 vols: vol. 1 (Ankara, 1988); vol. 2 (Istanbul, 1988); vol. 3 (Ankara, 1990). The Topkapı Palace MS (H. 1612) is published in facsimile, with an introduction by F. İz, 6 vols. (Cambridge, Mass., 1986).

11. *Ṣalṭuḳnāme,* ed. Akalın, 1:5. For the *Ḥamzanāme* cycle in Turkish, see Lütfi Sezen, *Halk Edebiyatında Hamzanâmeler* (Ankara, 1991); on 'Aşkar, see 64–65. Note that the horse is of even more remote origins; before Ḥamza, it served Isḥāḳ, son of Ibrāhīm (Abraham).

12. This unique manuscript is in the collection of Şinasi Tekin, who has published two articles on it: one introducing the work and the other providing the text as well as an analysis of the section on gaza. See, respectively, his "XIVüncü Yüzyıla Ait Bir İlm-i Hâl: Risāletü'l-İslām," *WZKM* 76(1986): 279–92; and "XIV. Yüzyılda Yazılmış Gazilik Tarikası 'Gaziligin Yolları' Adlı Bir Eski Anadolu Türkçesi Metni ve Gazâ/Cihâd Kavramları Hakkında," *JTS* 13(1989):109–204.

13. For the history of different textual renderings of the epic, see Mélikoff, introduction to *La geste de Melik Dāniṣmend.*

14. The same point about 'İzzeddīn's patronage of the epic is made by Cahen, *La Turquie pré-ottomane,* 335. The site of Seyyid Baṭṭāl's burial appeared in a dream to Ümmüḫān Ḫātūn, 'Alā'eddīn's mother, according to later legend. Al-Harawī, the Arab traveler who visited the area in 1173, mentions the shrine of Baṭṭāl in that "strange frontier town"; *Guide des lieux des pèlerinages,* ed. and trans. J. Sourdel-Thomine (Damascus, 1952–57).

15. See Mélikoff, *La geste de Melik Dāniṣmend,* 2:128–29.

16. Ibid., 197. The emphasis is mine.

17. Next to the tomb attributed to Seyyid Baṭṭāl Gazi is one where his beloved, known as *kral kızı* (the king's daughter), is said to be buried.

18. Ibid., 42.

19. See *Dedem Korkudun Kitabı,* ed. Orhan Ş. Gökyay (Istanbul, 1973), 83–97. The following translations are from the *Book of Dede Korkut,* trans. G. Lewis (Middlesex, England, 1974), 117–32.

20. This was, of course, not the only marriage between Turkish and Christian ruling houses in medieval Anatolia, but the first (of eleven) between the Comneni and the Türkmen of that region, as mentioned in A. Bryer, "Greek Historians on the Turks: The Case of the First Byzantine-Ottoman Marriage," in *The Writing of History in the Middle Ages: Essays Presented to Richard William Southern,* ed. R. H. C. Davis and J. M. Wallace-Hadrill (Oxford, 1981), 471–93, which is about the Ottoman prince Orḫān's marriage to the daughter of Kantakouzenos in 1346. Citing an unpublished M.A. thesis by G. E. Rakintzakis (University of Birmingham, 1975), Bryer writes that "between 1297 and 1461, thirty-four or

more Byzantine, Trapezuntine, and Serbian princesses married (in order) Mongol khans and ilhans, Turkish emirs, and Türkmen begs" (481).

21. The section on the exploits of Umur Beg is translated in *Le Destān d'Umūr Pacha*, ed. and trans. Irène Melikoff-Sayar (Paris, 1954).

22. When the Ottoman armada sailed into the Aegean in 1470, a Venetian observer reported that "the sea looked like a forest" (cited in Imber, *The Ottoman Empire*, 201). As late as in the seventeenth century, Ottoman sailors of the Aegean Sea are said to have sworn "for the sake of Umur Gazi." See Tuncer Baykara, *Aydınoğlu Gazi Umur Bey* (Ankara, 1990), 47.

23. Ibid., 46–48. Had Osman been defeated by the Germiyan or Orḫān by the Karasi, this is how their Bithynian exploits might have appeared in a Germiyan or Karasi chronicle.

24. According to a variant of this story, recorded in Anatolia in the 1930s, it was Sofia, another Byzantine lady, who gave the keys of the Birgi fortress to Umur Beg; see Himmet Akın, *Aydınoğulları Tarihi Hakkında Bir Araştırma*, 2d rev. ed. (Ankara, 1968), 26.

25. Two related versions of this tale are studied in Wittek, "The Taking of the Aydos Castle: A Ghazi Legend and Its Transformation," in *Arabic and Islamic Studies in Honor of Hamilton A. R. Gibb*, ed. G. Makdisi (Cambridge, Mass., 1965), 662–72.

26. *Düstūrnāme*, 84–85: "görişüp esenleşüp qardaş olur."

27. Ibid., 106.

28. Ibid., 107. According to Gregoras, the Byzantine chronicler (cited in Bryer, "Greek Historians," 477), Kantakouzenos had strong brotherly feelings for Umur Beg so that the two were like Orestes and Pylades.

29. For a comparison of the Ottoman chronicles and the *Düstūrnāme* with regard to this episode, see E. Zachariadou, "Yahshi Fakih and His Menakib," forthcoming in the proceedings of the Turkish Historical Association Congress held in 1989.

30. According to Islamic prophetology, revelations to four prophets—David, Moses, Jesus, and Muḥammad—were given written form; the "four books" thus subsume the scriptures of all of the Abrahamic religions. "Seventy-two" is a standard number for "all" the peoples or languages. In the later and more "historical" vita of the sailor-gazi Ḫayreddīn (Barbarossa, d. 1546), too, one of the protagonists is distinguished by knowing foreign tongues, among which Greek is particularly emphasized: *Il "Ġazavāt-i Ḫayreddīn Paša" di Seyyid Murād*, ed. Aldo Gallotta (Naples, 1983), 12r–v. Because he knew other languages and because he was such a good conversationalist, "wherever Oruç Re'is [the elder brother of Ḫayreddīn Barbarossa] went, old and young infidels gathered around him and conversed with him." The modern Turkish publication, not a scholarly edition but based on some manuscripts not used by Gallotta, mentions that Oruç knew "all languages." See *Barbaros Hayreddin Paşanın Hatıraları*, ed. E. Düzdağ (Istanbul, 1973), 1:65.

31. The citations are from Stephen J. Greenblatt's "Improvisation and Power," in *Literature and Society*, ed. E. Said (Baltimore, 1980), 57–99. Even though the author of this brilliant article is cautious enough to note that this kind of empathy is not exclusively a Western mode, he still states (61) that it is characteristically Western and "greatly strengthened from the Renaissance on-

ward." A student of Islamic history like myself would want to further relativize and qualify these remarks. Throughout the medieval era, it was precisely through rendering the Christian and Jewish (and all kinds of other) truths into "ideological constructs . . . that bear a certain structural resemblance to one's own set of beliefs" (62) that Muslims were so successful in spreading the rule and the message of Islam.

32. On the inappropriateness of the modern concept of toleration in the medieval context, see J. M. Powell, ed., *Muslims under Latin Rule, 1100–1300* (Princeton, 1990).

33. A. Y. Ocak, "Bazı Menâkıbnâmelere Göre XIII. ve XV. Yüzyıllardaki İhtidâlarda Heterodoks Şeyh ve Dervişlerin Rolü," *JOS* 2(1981):31–42.

34. Elvān Çelebi, *Menāḳibü'l-Ḳudsiyye fī Menāṣibi'l-Ünsiyye,* ed. İ. Erünsal and A. Y. Ocak (Istanbul, 1984).

35. Ibid., line 1546.

36. This is how Ocak reads this passage; see his "İhtidâlarda Heterodoks Şeyh ve Dervişlerin Rolü," 38.

37. On Ḥācī Bektaş as Saint Charalambos, see Vryonis, *Decline of Medieval Hellenism,* 372; on Elvān Çelebi as a friend of Saint George, see Hans Dernschwam, *Tagebuch,* ed. F. Babinger (Leipzig, 1923), 203.

38. Vasilis Demetriades, "The Tomb of Ghazi Evrenos Bey at Yenitsa and Its Inscription," *BSOAS* 39(1976):328–32.

39. So at least claims Mu'allim Nācī in his report of A.H. 1315 to the sultan; Istanbul University Library, TY 4127, quoted in Konyalı, *Söğüt'de Ertuğrul Gâzi Türbesi ve İhtifali* (Istanbul, 1959), 48.

40. Osman Turan, for instance, writes of "Shi'i Türkmen sheikhs like Ḥācī Bektaş and Buzagı Baba," two thirteenth-century holy figures; see his article in *Köprülü Armağanı,* 542. It is quite typical still for a student of religious history to write that Sheikh Bedreddīn "prit contact avec des Turkmènes chi'ites et il commença à enseigner des idées batinites" (M. S. Yazıcıoğlu, *Le Kalâm et son role dans la société turco-ottomane aux XVe et XVIe siècles* [Ankara, 1990], 259). Yazıcıoğlu is following Uzunçarşılı, whose encyclopedic works on Ottoman history are among the many authoritative texts that have rendered such characterizations routine. The most influential authorities, however, have been Köprülü and Gölpınarlı. The Baba'īs have also made it as Shi'is into Moojan Momen's *An Introduction to Shi'i Islam* (New Haven, 1985); see pp. 97, 103. For a thoughtful consideration of this issue, see C. Cahen, "Le problème du Shi'isme dans l'Asie Mineure turque préottomane," in *Le Shi'isme imâmite* (Paris, 1970).

41. Köprülü, *Origins,* 103. Also see this depiction of the thirteenth century in Köprülü's "Anadolu Selçukluları Tarihinin Yerli Kaynakları," *Belleten* 7(1943): 379–458: "this was a time when anti-Sunni Sufi brotherhoods and doctrines were rapidly spreading in Anatolia, especially among the nomadic tribes and peasants" (Gary Leiser, trans., *The Seljuks of Anatolia: Their History and Culture according to Local Muslim Sources* [Salt Lake City, 1992], 53).

42. A. Y. Ocak, *Babaîler İsyanı* (Istanbul, 1980) (based on Ocak's dissertation, which was published in its original French in 1989). The publication of this work was followed by an interesting discussion that helped me begin to question some assumptions of medieval Anatolian religious history. See M. Bayram, "Babaîler İsyanı Üzerine," *Fikir ve Sanatta Hareket,* 7th ser., 23(March 1981):16–

28; and Ocak, "Babaîler İsyanı'nın Tenkidine Dair," *Fikir ve Sanatta Hareket,* 7th ser., 24(September 1981):36–44. Now also see Ocak, *Osmanlı İmparatorluğunda Marjinal Sûfîlik: Kalenderîler (XIV–XVII. Yüzyıllar)* (Ankara, 1992).

43. See the works of Mikail Bayram, for instance, who argues that Baba Ilyās, Ḥācī Bektaş, Aḫi Evren, and other "Sunni" leaders of the "Sunni" Türkmen population were portrayed as heretical and Shi'i by their enemies, the pro-Mongol collaborators and Mevlevīs. Esad Coşan argues that Ḥācī Bektaş was Sunni and not a Baba'ī; see the introduction to *Maḳālāt,* ed. Coşan (Ankara, [1983?]), esp. pp. xxxvi–xxxviii). Needless to say, these revisions must be seen within the context of current ideological tensions in Turkey; Coşan himself is a sheikh of the Naḳşibendī. On the other side, it has been customary to see Ḥācī Bektaş as a Shi'i since at least Köprülü's influential article "Anadolu'da Islāmiyet," *Darülfünūn Edebiyāt Fakültesi Mecmū'ası* 2(1922). The politicization of these issues should be obvious from the fact that the manuscript on the basis of which Köprülü claimed that Ḥācī Bektaş was a Twelver Shi'i (Coşan misleadingly presents this as Köprülü's sole evidence) was in the General Directorate of the Police! Coşan's publication was immediately countered by a facsimile edition by the Bektaşī-'Alevī circles: *Makaalât ve Müslümanlık,* ed. Mehmet Yaman (Istanbul, 1985). Both the publisher's preface and the editor's long introduction are implicit polemics against Coşan's views.

44. It should be noted in this context that Sheikh Abū'l-Wafā' (Tāc al-'Ārifīn, d. 1101 or 1107), from whom Baba Ilyās's spiritual descent is traced, was Sunni according to his hagiography but not so rigid as not to be well disposed toward 'Alevīs or tolerate Kurds who neglected their religious obligations. See Alya Krupp, *Studien zum Menāġybnāme des Abu l-Wafā' Tāǧ al-'Ārifīn,* part 1: *Das historische Leben des Abu l-Wafā' Tāǧ al-'Ārifīn* (Munich, 1976), 54–55.

45. For a more detailed discussion, see Akın, *Aydınoğulları,* 53–54.

46. For these names, see I. Uzunçarşılı, *Kütahya Şehri* (Istanbul, 1932), 27–28. The second one appears in an eyewitness report of the 1277 battle, cited in Ḳalḳaşandī's *Ṣubḥ al-A'ṣā,* trans. F. Sümer, Yabanlu Pazarı, 64–95; see p. 91.

47. Yaşar Yücel, *Anadolu Beylikleri Hakkında Araştırmalar I: Çoban-oğulları Beyliği, Candar-oğulları Beyliği, Mesalikü'l-ebsara Göre Anadolu Beylikleri,* 2d ed. rev. (Ankara, 1991), 43. The same beg is called, among other things, *ḳāhirü'l-kefere* (the Subduer of the Infidels) in an inscription stone that stands on a medrese erected by his command but finished after his death in 1328–29 (ibid., 152). As Yücel suggests (42), he may indeed be the model for a certain beg called Muẓaffereddīn in the *Ṣalṭuḳnāme* to whom various struggles against the infidels from his base in Kastamonu are attributed.

48. See Zachariadou, "Pachymeres on the 'Amourioi' of Kastamonu."

49. Uzunçarşılı, *Kütahya Şehri,* 72.

50. Akın, *Aydınoğulları,* 105.

51. Uzunçarşılı, *AB,* 122.

52. Eflākī, *Manāḳıb al-'Ārifīn,* 2 vols., trans. T. Yazıcı (Ankara, 1959–61), 2:225–26.

53. Ibn Baṭṭūṭa, *Tuḥfatu'n-nuẓẓār fī ġarā'ibi'l-amṣār wa ajā'ibi'l-asfār,* 4 vols., ed. and trans. C. Defrémery and B. R. Sanguinetti (Paris, 1853–58), 2:305–6.

54. A. Bryer, "Han Turali Rides Again," *BMGS* 11(1987):202.

55. The differences go much farther than those indicated by Şerif Mardin in

the introduction to his *Religion and Social Change in Modern Turkey: The Case of Bediüzzaman Said Nursi* (Albany, 1989). See the comparisons made by Ş. Tekin on the basis of several canonical works in his introduction to "XIV. Yüzyılda Yazılmış Gazilik Tarikası."

56. See the books by R. Peters and the ones edited by J. T. Johnson and J. Kelsay in the bibliography.

57. For instances of such ambivalence from pre-Islamic Arabia and from Byzantium, see F. Donner, "The Sources of Islamic Conceptions of War," in Johnson and Kelsay, eds., *Just War and Jihad,* 35 and 38–39.

58. See "Ghazā," *EI,* new ed., s.v.

59. See Tekin, ed., "XIV. Yüzyılda Yazılmış Gazilik Tarikası." This source also reminds us that it would be wrong to present the political culture of the frontiers in contrast or in no relation to that of areas under more central control. While they may have evolved under peculiar circumstances and developed their own peculiar cultural modes, the frontiers were not absolutely divorced from other traditions.

60. War is, after all, a form of contact and a potential means of exchange. For some interesting cases of technological cross-fertilization through military confrontations, see A. D. H. Bivar, "Cavalry Equipment and Tactics in the Euphrates Frontier," *DOP* 26(1972):281–312; Eric McGeer, "Tradition and Reality in the *Taktika* of Nikephoros Ouranos," *DOP* 45(1991):129–40.

61. Katia Galatariotou, "Structural Oppositions in the Grottaferrata *Digenis Akritas*" *BMGS* 11(1987):29–68.

62. Another parallel between the two narratives, noted by G. Lewis (*The Book of Dede Korkut,* n. 81 on p. 204), is that the young warriors, after winning the hands of their companions, create some tension with the in-laws since they refuse to be wed without seeing their own parents.

63. The point has been made and successfully applied to the Akritic cycle by Michael Herzfeld, "Social Borderers: Themes of Conflict and Ambiguity in Greek Folk Song," *BMGS* 6(1980):61–80.

64. Wittek, *Mentesche,* 46.

65. *Il "Ġazavāt-i Ḫayreddīn Paša" di Seyyid Murād,* 76r., ed. Aldo Gallotta (Naples, 1983).

66. F. İz, ed., "Maḳāle-i Zindancı Maḥmūd Ḳapudān," *Türkiyat Mecmuası* 14(1964):111–50. A German translation was published earlier by A. Tietze: "Die Geschichte vom Kerkermeister-Kapitän: Ein türkischer Seeräuberroman aus dem 17. Jahrhundert," *Acta Orientalia* 19(1942):152–210. On this work and its interpretation as a frontier narrative, see my forthcoming article in *Hesperis-Tamuda* (based on a paper presented at the conference on "Maghrib et les ottomans" held at Université Mohammed V, Rabat, April 1992).

67. See M. Colakis, "Images of the Turk in Greek Fiction of the Asia Minor Disaster," *Journal of Modern Greek Studies* 4(1986):99–106.

68. Galatariotou, "Structural Oppositions," 51.

69. For references to Greek and Armenian nationalist readings of the Digenis legend that naturally run counter to the thrust of my argument here, see ibid., 54, n.77. One could easily find similarly nationalist readings of the Turco-Muslim legends.

70. Keith Hopwood, "Türkmen, Bandits and Nomads: Problems and Per-

ceptions," in *Proceedings of CIEPO Sixth Symposium: Cambridge . . . 1984,* ed. J.-L. Bacqué-Grammont and E. van Donzel (Istanbul, 1987), 30. The second part of the sentence is accurate but it does not justify the implication in the first part, namely, that "the conflict between pastoralist and sedentary farmer" has no basis in reality (which is the way the word "construct" seems to be used). Why cannot both be valid, but in varying degrees in different times and places? In any case, Hopwood is certainly right in underlining the bias of historiography toward focusing only or primarily on conflict and in indicating that "[m]ore work like that of Prof. Bryer on Byzantino-Turkic relations in the Empire of Trebizond [citing Anthony Bryer's "The Pontic Exception," *DOP* 29(1975)] needs to be done to elucidate the integrative features of the Türkmen conquest" (30). Hopwood himself cautions against overlooking conflict and exaggerating complementarity in a more recent article: "Nomads or Bandits? The Pastoralist / Sedentarist Interface in Anatolia," *Byzantinische Forschungen* 16(1991):179–94.

71. Galatariotou, "Structural Oppositions." For a balanced discussion of raiding economy, the claim of operating for the sake of one's faith, and an honor code all working together in another environment, see C. W. Bracewell, *The Uskoks of Senj: Piracy, Banditry, and Holy War in the Sixteenth-Century Adriatic* (Ithaca, 1992).

72. "The enemy thus in Digenes is not the Arab for the Byzantine, nor the Byzantine for the Arab. The people whom Digenes consistently puts down are coloured neither by race nor by creed, but by their contempt for the unwritten rules of the code of honour. Such is Digenes' conflict with the apelatai. The apelatai are the main villains of the story" (Galatariotou, "Structural Oppositions," 48). On who the apelatai may have been, see ibid.

73. Aḥmad Ibn ʿArabshāh, *Tamerlane, or Tımur the Great Amir,* trans. J. H. Sanders (London, 1936), 201.

74. Galatariotou, "Structural Oppositions," 44–45.

75. Cited in Tekin, "XIVüncü Yüzyıla Ait Bir İlm-i Hâl," 286.

76. See section edited by Tekin in "XIV. Yüzyılda Yazılmış Gazilik Tarikası," 162. This situation was not necessarily hypothetical. Pachymeres, the Byzantine chronicler, for instance, writes that some of the Byzantine soldiers in the district of Nicaea served the Turks as guides when their tax exemptions were abolished by the emperor after the seat of government moved back to Constantinople (cited in İnalcık, "Siege of Nicaea," *OE,* 79). Notwithstanding its negative moral connotation, the fact that *müdārā* (feigned peace) was a legally sanctioned category of behavior vis-à-vis infidels must have provided Muslim frontier warriors with some flexibility even when they needed or wanted to be canonically correct. On this notion, see H. J. Kissling, *Rechtsproblematiken in den christlich-muslimischen Beziehungen, vorab im Zeitalter der Türkenkriege* (Graz, 1974). Moreover, this was not the only relevant category; on *istimālet* (conciliatory policy), see İnalcık, "Methods of Conquest."

77. For the efficacy of this argument, see Vryonis, *Decline of Medieval Hellenism,* 435. Based on a critical survey of some late Byzantine hagiographies, Zachariadou concludes (in a paper delivered at Princeton University in 1987) that churchmen were wary of this sentiment because it was gaining currency and leading many Christians to convert to Islam.

78. Ṭaşköprīzāde, *Al-Şaḳā'iḳ,* 28–29.

79. Apz, ed. Giese, 9.

80. Ibid.

81. Related among the events of A.H. 139 in Balādhurī's *Kitāb Futūḥ al-Buldān,* trans. P. K. Hitti in *The Origins of the Islamic State,* 2 vols. (1916; New York, 1968), 292.

82. Topkapı Palace Archives, E. 5584.

83. Cited in J. F. Richards, "Outflows of Precious Metals from Early Islamic India," in *Precious Metals in the Later Medieval and Early Modern Worlds,* ed. J. F. Richards (Durham, N.C., 1983), 195.

84. The same point has already been made by Ménage in "The Beginnings of Ottoman Historiography," in *The Historians of the Middle East,* ed. B. Lewis and P. M. Holt (London, 1962): "The fact that many campaigns are directed against Muslim states is irrelevant, for these fellow-Muslims are regarded as hindering the ghazā" (177–78).

85. Ibn 'Arabshāh, *Tamerlane,* 170–71.

86. See S. Walt, *Origin of Alliances* (Ithaca, 1990), 206–12.

87. See G. Moravcsik, *Byzantinoturcica,* 2 vols., 2d ed. rev. (Berlin, 1958), 2:108–9. This is Lindner's reference for his argument that "when chroniclers of the stature of . . . Pachymeres, John Cantacuzenus, and Nicetas Gregoras know nothing of such a zeal animating their enemies, it is reasonable to doubt its existence." See his *Nomads and Ottomans,* 6. The same argument is made by Jennings, "Some Thoughts," 158–59.

88. Lindner, *Nomads and Ottomans,* 14.

89. Eva de Vries-Van der Welden argues that this is a misreading of Palamas's account, which, she feels, reflects mutual animosity and hatred rather than moderation; see the chapter on Palamas in her *L'élite byzantine devant l'avance turque à l'époque de la guerre civile de 1341 à 1354* (Amsterdam, 1989). Indeed, it is worth mentioning that she disagrees with the whole scholarly tradition treated in this book since she feels that there was not much (any?) room for moderation, tolerance, and conciliation in the attitudes of the Turks in medieval Anatolia.

90. For Palamas's captivity, see Anna Philippidis-Braat, "La captivité de Palamas chez les Turcs: Dossier et commentaire," *Travaux et Mémoires* 7(1979):109–221. It is still not clear who the *xiónai* are in Palamas's account. Earlier propositions for reading *hoca* or *ahi* seem far-fetched, as Michel Balivet rightly argues in his "Byzantins judaïsants et Juifs islamisés: Des 'kühhân' (kâhin) aux 'xiónai' (xiónios)," *Byzantion* 52(1982):24–59, but his suggestion of *kāhin* is not fully satisfactory either since it relies on a misinterpretation of Turkish phonology (the second vowel of *kāhin* is not dropped in the accusative: namely, the accusative of *burun* is *burn-u,* as Balivet points out, but that of *kāhin* is *kāhin-i* since the first vowel is a long one). For the *xiónai* problem, also see Philippidis-Braat, 214–18.

91. For an account of Plethon's life and thought, see C. M. Woodhouse, *George Gemisthos Plethon: The Last of the Hellenes* (Oxford, 1986); for his Jewish tutor in the "court of the barbarians," see pp. 24–29. An Orientalist's assessment of Plethon's experience in the Ottoman court can be found in Franz Taeschner, "Georgios Gemisthos Plethon, ein Beitrag zur Frage der Übertragung von islamischen Geistesgut nach dem Abendlande," *Der Islam* 18(1929):236–43; and

idem, "Georgios Gemisthos Plethon, ein Vermittler zwischen Morgenland und Abendland zu Beginn der Renaissance," *Byzantinisch-Neu-griechische Jahrbücher* 8(1929–30):100–113. Taeschner's arguments for Islamic "influences" on Plethon are refuted in Milton V. Anastos, "Plethon's Calendar and Liturgy," *DOP* 4(1948):185–305, esp. 270 ff.

92. The world of the gazis does not seem to have been totally devoid of formalization either. Objects often reported to have been sent by higher authorities in the caliphate or sultanate apparently symbolized some formal ties of vassalage; also, various caps are mentioned as markers of distinction between different kinds of affiliation, including spiritual ones (as in the case of the House of Aydın and the Mevleviyye). Nevertheless, there is no indication that inclusion in gazi bands or the adoption of such a title was predicated upon any particular ritual. Wittek, along with many other scholars of his generation, would have the gazis organize their lives, relations, and ceremonies much more formally and uniformly than I see it. See his *The Rise,* 37–40. This is in part related to assumptions about a far-reaching, often underground, network of various "heterodox" associations in the medieval Middle East: guilds, futuwwa, bāṭinī esotericists. The most elaborate depiction of that alleged network and tight organization can be found in the works of Louis Massignon, and it is clear in his case that the historian's imagination was partly shaped by the reality and phobia of international communism. See, for instance, his "La futuwwa ou la pacte d'honneur artisanale chez les travailleurs musulmanes," *La Nouvelle Clio,* 1952. The works of Taeschner, whose identification of futuwwa as "Islamisches Ordensrittertum" was highly influential on Wittek and many others; see C. Cahen, "Futuwwa," *EI,* new ed., s.v.

93. See, for instance, the documents published by A. Refik [Altınay], "Osmanlı Devrinde Rafızîlik ve Bektaşîlik," *Darülfünun Edebiyat Fakültesi Mecmuası* 8/2(April 1932):21–59. Further relevant literature is cited in A. Y. Ocak, *Osmanlı İmparatorluğunda Marjinal Sûfîlik: Kalenderîler (XIV–XVII. Yüzyıllar)* (Ankara, 1992), 189–92; also see S. Faroqhi, "Seyyid Gazi Revisited: The Foundation as Seen through the Sixteenth- and Seventeenth-Century Documents," *Turcica* 13(1981):90–122.

94. "Al yeşil giyinmiş gerçek gazili / Ali nesli güzel imam geliyor." (Accompanied by the *real* gazis dressed in red and green / the beautiful imam from the line of ʿAlī is coming). C. Öztelli, ed., *Bektaşi Gülleri* (Istanbul, 1985), 202. This and various other poems in this collection (and in others) that sing the praises of gazis like Seyyid Baṭṭāl Gazi (p. 263) or of ʿAlī's "gaza" should also remind us that gaza is not a specifically Ottoman or a necessarily Sunni ideology. The Safavids, too, fought as gazis, especially in the earlier stages of their enterprise. The poems of Shah Ismāʿīl (alias Ḫaṭāʾī) frequently invoke the three social forces that also appear in the sources of late-Seljuk and post-Seljuk Anatolia: the aḫī, the abdāl, the gazi. See *Il Canzoniere di Šāh Ismāʿīl Ḫaṭāʾī,* ed. Tourkhan Gandjei (Naples, 1959), passim. In the case of Anatolia, Apz added a fourth and even more enigmatic category: the *bacıs* (sisters).

95. *Ein Mesnevi Gülschehris auf Achi Evran,* ed. F. Taeschner (Hamburg, 1930). The 1360 recasting of the *Dānişmendnāme* by ʿĀrif ʿAlī must also be mentioned here as a fourteenth-century frontier narrative, even though it deals

with a relatively remote period. As for the hagiographies of several thirteenth- and fourteenth-century figures, such as those of Ḥācī Bektaş, Ṣarı Ṣalṭuḳ, and Seyyid Ḥārūn, it must be noted that those were recorded much later.

96. One was completed just before the end of the century, in 1398. It was written for Ḳāḍī Burhāneddīn, a medrese-educated scholar-statesman who ruled in Sivas as a representative of the Ilkhanid-Seljuk tradition and not as a frontier warrior. This Persian chronicle is quite polished and informative on political events in fourteenth-century Anatolia but is clearly not a frontier narrative of conquest and proselytization. See *Bazm u razm,* ed. F. M. Köprülü (Istanbul, 1928). Its author, 'Abdül'azīz, had been brought from the court of Baghdad. Another Persian chronicle, a (600-couplet) *Shāhnāma* of the House of Karaman as a sequel to Dehhānī's *Shāhnāma* of the Seljuks (of Rūm?), was allegedly written by Yarcānī for Karamanoğlu 'Alā'eddīn Beg, who held power in the latter part of the same century. Neither of these two *Shāhnāmas* is extant; instead we have a Turkish chronicle written by Şikārī in the beginning of the sixteenth century which cites the other two and claims to be in part a Turkish prose translation of Yarcānī's work. See *Şikârî'nin Karaman-oğulları Tarihi,* ed. M. Koman (Konya, 1940), 8–9. On this source, also see Lindner, *Nomads and Ottomans,* 145–47. There is very little that can be added to Köprülü's survey of early Anatolian sources in his "Anadolu Selçuklu Tarihinin Yerli Kaynakları"; now also see the English translation of this work with updated references: *The Seljuks of Anatolia,* trans. Gary Leiser. For a more recent survey of relevant hagiographic works (in Arabic, Persian, and Turkish) from the thirteenth to the sixteenth century, see A. Y. Ocak, *Kültür Tarihi Kaynağı Olarak Menâkıbnâmeler* (Ankara, 1992), 46–59.

97. Obviously, the issue of literacy must also be considered in this discussion, but given our present state of knowledge on the matter, not much can be said. The number of medreses was slowly growing in the fourteenth century, and there was increased demand for scribal services. But the sites where one could acquire literacy skills and obtain some education were not limited to formally designated schools. Dervish lodges and homes must also have offered such possibilities; Apz, for instance, in all likelihood obtained his education in the lodge. Naturally, the history of early Ottoman literacy involves much more than the possibilities for education within the early Ottoman world since we are also dealing with many migrants and converts who offered skills acquired elsewhere. For early Ottoman medreses starting with the first one (established ca. 1331), see M. Bilge, *İlk Osmanlı Medreseleri* (Istanbul, 1984).

98. Ménage, "Beginnings," 170.

99. On Ḥamzavī, see Franz Babinger, *Die Geschichtsschreiber der Osmanen und ihre Werke* (Leipzig, 1927). To the same author is attributed an early chronicle of which no copies have ever been identified and to which no date can presently be assigned.

100. *Selçuḳnāme,* TSK, R.1390. Professor Şinasi Tekin of Harvard University is currently preparing a critical edition of this text through a comparison of the cited manuscript with other extant copies. I am grateful to him for enabling me to make use of his early draft.

101. It is not known when exactly the tales of Dede Korkut were written

down, but it was not earlier than the fifteenth century. Based on the fact that the author is buttering up both Akkoyunlu and Ottoman rulers, it has been suggested that the composition belongs to someone living in the undefined borderlands between the two states during the reign of Uzun Ḥasan (1466–78). See Boratav, *100 Soruda Türk Halkedebiyatı* (Istanbul, 1969), 46–47. G. Lewis, on the other hand, dates the composition "fairly early in the 15th century at least" (*The Book of Dede Korkut,* 16–19). In addition to questions concerning the time the stories can be traced back to, or when they were composed in the shape we have them (which is what G. Lewis is asking and which could have been accomplished orally), we must ask when a decision was made to render the composition in written form. In this respect, the reference to the Ottomans is more significant than Lewis considers. On the other hand, the seemingly interpolated paragraph about Korkut Ata and his prophecy concerning Ottoman glory in the Book of Dede Korkut appears also in Yazıcızâde's history of the Seljuks, written ca. 1436; see G. Lewis, n. 140. Also see Bryer, "Han Turali Rides Again."

102. Abū Bakr Ṭihrānī-Isfahānī, *Kitāb-i Diyārbakriyya* (in Persian), 2 vols., ed. N. Lugal and F. Sümer (Ankara, 1962–64). This work must also be seen in a continuum with the fourteenth-century Persian chronicles of the Karamanids and of Kadi Burhāneddīn, who were, in many ways, more faithful to Seljuk traditions than the Ottomans ever were.

103. This anonymous work is reproduced, apparently verbatim, in the Oxford Anonymous manuscript and (from the latter) in the *Cihānnümā* of Neşrī. See İnalcık, "Rise of Ottoman Historiography," and Ménage, "Beginnings."

104. First noted by A. Karahan, "XV. Yüzyıl Osmanlı Dinî Edebiyatında Mesneviler ve Abdülvasî Çelebi'nin Halilnâme'si," *Estratto dagli Atti del III Congresso di Studi Arabi e Islamici . . . 1966* (Naples, 1967). The full text is given in Ayhan Güldaş, "Fetret Devri'ndeki Şehzadeler Mücadelesini Anlatan İlk Manzum Vesika," *Türk Dünyası Araştırmaları* 72(June 1991):99–110.

105. E. H. Ayverdi, *Osmanlı Mi'mârîsinde Çelebi ve II. Sultan Murad Devri, 806–855 (1403–1451)* (Istanbul, 1972), 195–96. It is possible that he was simply enlarging or restoring (was it perhaps destroyed by Timur's forces?) a mosque built earlier by Orḫān, but Ertoġrıl was after all Orḫān's grandfather and the principality was small enough for Söğüt to be meaningful at that time. Meḥmed I's interest in Söğüt was the only occasion when Osman's descendants turned their attention to that little hometown of theirs in Anatolia until the eighteenth century.

106. On these "calendars," see Osman Turan, ed., *Istanbul'un Fethinden Önce Yazılmış Takvimler* (Ankara, 1954); Nihal Atsız, ed., *Osmanlı Tarihine Ait Takvimler* (Istanbul, 1961); V. L. Ménage, "The 'Annals of Murād II,'" *BSOAS* 39(1976):570–84.

107. On the "imperial project" and its critique as embodied in popular legends about the history of Constantinople and of the Hagia Sophia, see S. Yerasimos, *La fondation de Constantinople et de Sainte-Sophie dans les traditions turques* (Paris, 1990). Though my own understanding of the interrelationships of the fifteenth-century chronicles is somewhat different from that of Yerasimos, I agree with his general argument.

108. The articles by İnalcık and Ménage in *Historians of the Middle East,* ed.

B. Lewis and P. M. Holt (London, 1962), are indispensable beginnings for any work on early Ottoman historiography. While they deal primarily with the interrelationships of the early texts, these articles also contain many pointers about the politico-ideological context in which the chronicles must be understood. Also see İnalcık, *Fatih Devri Üzerinde Tetkikler ve Vesikalar* (Ankara, 1954); and idem, "Meḥmed I," and "Murād II," *İA,* s.v. On the incorporation of various antinomian movements into the Bektāşiyya, see Irène Melikoff, *Sur les traces du Soufisme turc* (Istanbul, 1992); and Ahmet Karamustafa, *God's Unruly Friends* (Salt Lake City, 1994).

109. Naturally, not all scholars fit into this neat bipolar schema, which nonetheless remains a useful and valid one for our discussion. Exceptions will be mentioned in what follows.

110. Lindner, *Nomads and Ottomans,* 19.

111. This view of fifteenth-century Ottoman historiography, with the exception of the notion of tribalism, is shared by Gibbons, Arnakis, Káldy-Nagy, Jennings, Imber, and, to a large extent, Lindner.

112. V. L. Ménage, "The Menāqib of Yakhshī Faqīh," *BSOAS* 26(1963):50–54.

113. Lindner, *Nomads and Ottomans,* 22.

114. İnalcık, *Fatih Devri;* and idem, "The Policy of Mehmed II towards the Greek Population of Istanbul and the Byzantine Buildings of the City," *DOP* 23(1970):231–49.

115. The unmitigated joy of the frontier warriors in the early Ottoman era, not very different from a similar ethos reflected in the Viking sagas, is brilliantly captured by Yahya Kemal Beyatlı, the classicizing Turkish poet from the turn of this century: "Bin atlı akınlarda çocuklar gibi şendik / Bin atlı o gün dev gibi bir orduyu yendik" (We were happy like children in those raids with one thousand horsemen / We defeated a giant army that day with one thousand horsemen). This should not be taken to imply that there was an indiscriminate appreciation of warfare and that there were no anti-war sentiments. But the raiders apparently felt that as long as fighting was bound to occur, one might as well have one's heart in it. On anti-war poetry in Anatolian Turkish, see İlhan Başgöz, *Folklor Yazıları* (Istanbul, 1986), 81.

116. Hereafter, the Yaḫşi Faḳīh menāḳib will be abbreviated YF.

117. Wittek, "The Taking of the Aydos Castle."

118. Ibid. It may of course be questioned whether Apz indeed reflected the mentality of "the earliest Ottoman times" here, but at least it is clear that he was quite close to the spirit of other frontier lore, such as that analyzed in the earlier part of this chapter.

119. In this unique episode in Apz's chronicle, which in all likelihood comes from YF, it is suggested to Osman that he obtain permission from the Seljuk sultan, but Osman finds the Osmanlis' mission of gaza a sufficient cause to sanction the reading of the ḫuṭbe in his own name. Here we clearly have the use of the gaza as a legitimizing principle in opposition to claims (of the Timurids and their protégés in Asia Minor?) that the Ottomans were upstarts who needed the suzerainty of a legitimate central power.

120. Ménage, "On the Recensions of Uruj's 'History of the Ottomans,'"

BSOAS 30(1967): 314–22; Elizabeth Zachariadou, "The Menaqib of Yahshi Fakih," unpublished; Jacques Lefort, "Tableau de la Bithynie au XIIIe siècles," *OE*, 101–17; Clive Foss, "The Homeland of the Ottomans," unpublished.

121. Yerasimos, *La fondation de Constantinople et de Sainte-Sophie.*

122. Neşrī, ed. Taeschner, 25; ed. Unat and Köymen, 78–79.

123. Neşrī, ed. Taeschner, 29; ed. Unat and Köymen, 92–95.

124. In one of Neşrī's known sources, the Oxford Anonymous (hereafter abbreviated OA), there is a passage on Osman's election, "evidently taken from Yaziji-oghlu" (V. L. Ménage, *Neshrī's History of the Ottomans* [London, 1964], 13). While relating some interesting and seemingly authentic tribal traditions concerning the electoral process, Yazıcızāde does not mention Dündar or any other rivals. The whole section on Osman after his election, where his rivalries with family members may have been recorded, is missing in the extant manuscript. If there is a family fight in the missing part of this source, it is unlikely to have been with Dündar since the OA does not mention any brothers of Ertoğrıl. This source is now published, but its editors (who have not used Ménage's work) have maintained the older mistaken identification with Rūḥī-i Edrenevī: "Rûhî Târîhi," ed. H. E. Cengiz and Y. Yücel, *Belgeler* 14–18(1989–92):359–472. Thus the editors have also "completed" the text by filling in the missing section on Osman from a copy of the chronicle of Rūḥī.

125. İbn Kemāl, *Tevārīḫ-i Āl-i ʿOsmān,* vol. 1, ed. Ş. Turan (Ankara, 1970), 65–66, 129–30.

126. Anonymous, ed. Giese, 14. The episode is set in the context of Osman's death. Orḫān offers the chieftainship to his brother ʿAlā'eddīn, who has no such claims but a few useful administrative reforms to suggest.

127. It is even conceivable, as argued once by Wittek and seconded by İnalcık, that there may have been a fuller version of Apz than the redactions, editions, and copies we now have; see İnalcık, "The Rise of Ottoman Historiography," 154.

128. Ed. Babinger, 6; ed. Atsız, 22.

129. Ed. Atsız, 394, in Osmanlı Tarihleri, ed. Atsiz (Istanbul, 1947).

130. See *Manzûm Hacı Bektâş Veli Vilâyetnâmesi,* ed. Bedri Noyan (Aydın, 1986). In light of the information provided by Noyan (pp. 6–9), it seems that the objections of both Gölpınarlı and, for different reasons, Coşan with respect to the authorship of Mūsā b. ʿAlī of the version in prose are not warranted. Gölpınarlı's identification of Firdevsī as the author of the versified version is probably still accurate, however.

131. Such conflicts between the dictates of interstate relations (Byzantine, Mongol, Seljuk) and local conditions of the frontiers were apparently common. For an interesting case having to do with a neighbor of Osman, see E. Zachariadou, "Pachymeres on the 'Amourioi' of Kastamonu."

132. İbn Kemāl, *Tevārīḫ-i Āl-i ʿOsmān,* 1:129: "baʿżı rāvī eydür ʿOṣmān Beg ʿamusi Dündar'ı, ki başında serdārlıḳ sevdāsı var idi, bu seferde helāk itdi . . . żarar-i ʿāmmdan ise żarar-i ḫāṣṣ yegdür . . . diyü urdı öldürdi."

133. Başbakanlık Arşivi, Tahrir Defteri 453, f. 258b. See Ö. L. Barkan and E. Meriçli, eds., *Hüdavendigâr Livası Tahrir Defterleri* (Ankara, 1988), 255. Previously cited in İ. Uzunçarşılı, *Osmanlı Tarihi* (Ankara, 1947), 1:104 n. 2, who takes it as certain that this Dündar Beg is Osman's uncle.

134. The "realism" of this investigation, the primary purpose of which has

been to see whether these stories about Ertoġrıl's and Osman's generations may have been partially based on real events even if they come from later sources, is not meant to preclude a symbolic reading of those historical traditions. I have already cited Sahlins's observation that the real and the symbolic are not mutually exclusive. Just like the Romans once again, the Ottomans seem to have historicized certain mythical structures to such an extent that these Romans of the Muslim world appear almost free of myths: Ottoman histories are, upon a straightforward reading, not legend-filled Shāhnāmes but much more realistic accounts of historical incidents. Still, readers of Dumézil will possibly wonder whether it is not the ancient motif of the tripartite ideology that both Ertoġrıl and Osman, leaders of the two successive generations of state builders, had two brothers in most of the family chronicles. The murder of an uncle, moreover, may be just the kind of sinful act those readers have come to expect of young warriors destined to become kings.

135. Lindner, *Nomads and Ottomans,* 6–7. In terms of the mistaken characterization of gaza as an ideology with particular resonance among "orthodox and sedentary audiences," we should recall the invoking of the same principle by the early Safavids to appeal to the increasingly unorthodox nomadic population of Anatolia and Azerbaijan.

136. See archival sources published in Barkan and Meriçli, eds., *Hüdavendigâr Livası Tahrir Defterleri.* The relevant earlier publication by Barkan, "Osmanlı İmparatorluğunda Bir İskân ve Kolonizasyon Metodu Olarak Vakıflar ve Temlikler," *Vakıflar Dergisi* 2(1942):279–386, selected primarily documents related to dervishes and aḫīs, excluding many that dealt with the faḳīhs. It seems, on the basis of the later publication, that in the generations of Osman and Orḫān, more land was given to faḳīhs than to either dervishes or aḫīs. Though "faḳīh" literally means a jurisconsult, it implied more of an imam (as prayer leader) than a juridical figure in the context of western Anatolia in the late-thirteenth and fourteenth centuries, but looking at the example of Tursun Faḳīh some of these figures, possibly those who had a more impressive education, may also have played a consultative role in legal-administrative matters. On the "faḳīh"s, also see Köprülü, *Islam in Anatolia,* 28.

137. It would be too much of a digression to discuss the second point in detail here. That discussion must await the future publication of the "YF menāḳib" that I have edited experimentally through a comparison of the chronicle of Apz with the anonymous ones, basically following the lead given by Ménage a long time ago. A similar experiment was recently published in Greek translation by E. Zachariadon (Athens, 1992). My basic point is that the critical passages are used by the compilers of the different chronicles not randomly but within the framework of a conscious editorial policy.

138. The use of this word indicates that here the blame is placed squarely on the Ottoman rulers, not on the ruling elite in general.

139. Anonymous, *Tevārīḫ-i Āl-i ʿOsmān* (see *Die altosmanischen anonymen Chroniken,* part 1, ed. F. Giese [Breslau, 1922]). Passages translated in B. Lewis, ed. and trans., *Islam from the Prophet Muhammad to the Capture of Constantinople,* vol. 1, *Politics and War* (New York, 1974), 135–41.

140. The YF-Apz narrative, for instance, describes the meager inheritance left by Osman Beg with great admiration: Apz, ed. Giese, 34.

141. Anonymous, *Tevārīḫ*, in *Islam from the Prophet Muhammad to the Capture of Constantinople,* trans. B. Lewis, 142.

142. See Ernest Gellner's discussion of the relevance of the Ibn Khaldūnian paradigm in dealing with the Ottoman experiment in his "Flux and Reflux in the Faith of Men," in his *Muslim Society* (Cambridge, 1980), 73–77; and idem, "Tribalism and the State in the Middle East," in *TSF,* 109–26. It is true that in terms of its longevity, the Ottoman Empire does not conform to that paradigm, but a closer look reveals that Ottoman history is beset with the general rhythm of tribal-societies-turned-empire-builders as described by Ibn Khaldūn; and later Ottoman intellectuals, once they discovered Ibn Khaldūn, appreciated the relevance of his theory as addressing a phenomenon much more universal than the Arabian and North African states that he took as the basis of his theorizing. See Cornell Fleischer, "Royal Authority, Dynastic Cyclism, and 'Ibn Khaldunism' in Sixteenth-Century Ottoman Letters," *Journal of Asian and African Studies* 18(1983):198–220. The longevity can be explained within that paradigm (as an exception that ultimately confirms the rule) by the bold initiative of the House of Osman in creating an unprecedentedly sophisticated system of an artificial but cohesive household (the *ḳapıḳulları,* often erroneously translated as "the sultan's slaves") just when the tribal/warrior solidarity, or ʿaṣabiyya, was waning. For Ibn Khaldūn's views on the "slave soldier" phenomenon, see David Ayalon, "Mamlūkiyyāt," *Jerusalem Studies in Arabic and Islam* 2(1980):340–49. Ibn Khaldūn's brief narrative on the first century of the Ottomans does not contain any reflection on their institutional peculiarities or any fresh analytical insights. But then, Ottoman peculiarities were not that obvious when the Arab historian wrote and, to the extent they were, systematic information on the subject could hardly have been available to him. The relevant passage from his world history (not the famous *Muqaddimah,* which is a theoretical work) is translated on pp. 161–64 in C. Huart, "Les origines de l'empire ottoman," *Journal des Savants,* n.s., 15(1917):157–66. Another Arab historian, Ibn Hājar (1372–1449), writes that he heard it said a number of times by none other than Ibn Khaldūn that "there was no one to fear with regard to Egypt but the Sons of Osman"; see Şevkiye İnalcık, "Ibn Hacer'de Osmanlılara Dair Haberler," *Ankara Üniversitesi Dil Tarih Coğrafya Fakültesi Dergisi* 6(1948):356 (or p. 351 of her trans.).

143. Ménage, "Some Notes on the Devshirme," *BSOAS* 29(1966):75 n. 48. Note that El Cid of the medieval Iberian frontier also takes one-fifth from his fellow warriors.

144. Cezbī, *Velāyetnāme-i Seyyid ʿAlī Sulṭān,* Ankara Cebeci İl Halk Library, MS 1189; this copy was made in Rebīʿü'l-evvel A.H. 1313/A.D. 1895. Irène Beldiceanu-Steinherr was the first to note the significance of this source for rethinking the Thracian conquests: "La vita de Seyyid ʿAlī Sulṭān et la conquête de la Thrace par les Turcs," in *Proceedings of the 27th International Congress of Orientalists . . . 1967,* ed. D. Sinor (Wiesbaden, 1971), 275–76. On alternative renderings of the Thracian conquests, also see her "La conquête d'Andrinople par les Turcs: La pénétration turque en Thrace et la valeur des chroniques ottomanes," *Travaux et Mémoires* 1(1965):439–61; and idem, "Le règne de Selīm Ier: Tournant dans la vie politique et religieuse de l'empire ottoman," *Turcica* 6(1975):34–48.

145. It is surprising, however, that Bāyezīd I (r. 1389–1402) is mentioned as the ruler of the time, since the Thracian adventures of the Turco-Muslim frontier warriors, including the Ottomans, clearly started under Bāyezīd's grandfather. To the extent one can discern "historical" events in this source, a good many are known to have occurred before even Bāyezīd's father reached rulership. The hagiographer must have "slipped" here because he or she cites a document (*berāt*) to prove that the rights of the assaulted protagonist over his property had been legitimized by the Ottomans themselves; and that document was apparently a deed issued by Bāyezīd. Later archival sources indeed refer to a title deed given by that sultan to Ḳızıl Deli (or the sheikh of the shrine complex named after him?) in 1400/1401; see Tayyib Gökbilgin, *XV–XVI. Asırlarda Edirne ve Paşa Livâsı: Vakıflar - Mülkler - Mukataalar* (Istanbul, 1952), 183. I also had the good fortune to hear Irène Beldiceanu-Steinherr's presentation on Ottoman archival documents concerning that endowment in a symposium on the Via Egnatia, held at the University of Crete, Rethymnon, in January 1994; the proceedings are forthcoming.

146. There are differences between the versions of the anonymous chronicles and of the YF-Apz narrative, but I will disregard them to highlight the comparison with the tales of Ḳızıl Deli.

147. Much more is known about the "historical" Emīr Sulṭān (d. 1429) than about Seyyid ʿAlī and others in his entourage. The former evidently did take part in Ottoman campaigns. A Byzantine account of the 1422 siege of Constantinople relates that he was there along with 500 dervishes. See Ioannes Cananus, *De Constantinopolis Obsidione,* ed. and trans. E. Pinto (Messina, 1977). According to later legends, he was the one who miraculously caused the departure of Timur's troops from Bursa and who girded sultans with swords upon accession or when departing for a campaign. See C. Baysun, "Emīr Sulṭān," *IA,* s.v.

148. Cezbī, *Velāyetnāme,* 18–19. (The manuscript is assigned not folio but page numbers by a modern hand.)

149. See her works cited in n. 144, above.

150. See the vita of Şeyḫ Bedreddīn by his grandson Ḫalīl bin Ismāʿīl. According to this work, Şeyḫ Bedreddīn's grandfather ʿAbdülʿazīz and Ḥācī İlbegi were related. However, while the former was of "Seljuk descent" (*Selçuḳ nesli*) (F. Babinger, ed., *Die Vita [menāqibnāme] des Schejch Bedr ed-dīn Maḥmūd, gen. Ibn Qāḍī Samauna* [Leipzig, 1943], 5), the latter was not, since he was "the seed of a son-in-law" (*gürgen tohumı*) (6).

151. This curious tale is reported in Dimitrie Cantemir's early eighteenth-century history of the Ottoman Empire: *Osmanlı Tarihi,* 3 vols., trans. Özdemir Çobanoğlu (Ankara, 1979), 1:29–30. It is hard to imagine that such a story would be made up in the eighteenth century; Cantemir must have had access to some oral or written tradition. It is also noteworthy that Şeyḫ Bedreddīn's grandson, writing in the early sixteenth century and sanitizing his grandfather's story to forge a rapprochement with the Ottomans, uses a particularly offensive expression, "seed of a son-in-law," to underline that İlbegi was "not of Seljuk descent." The Timurids, too, could be seen as the "seed of a son-in-law," since Timur was no more than a son-in-law (*gürgen*) to the Chingisids, the real bearers of legitimacy.

152. The shrine in Dimetoka, a city conquered by İlbegi according to almost all accounts, was widely known as one of the four or five most-respected cultic sites of the Bektāşī order in the sixteenth century. A poem by Pīr Sulṭān Abdāl refers to various episodes in the vita analyzed above, indicating that the Ḳızıl Deli lore had been elaborated and was in wide circulation by the latter part of the sixteenth century. The motifs of crossing to Gelibolu and being the commander of forty holy warriors are repeated in the poems of this Bektaşī poet and later ones. See Öztelli, ed., *Bektaşi Gülleri,* 121–22, and passim.

3. The Ottomans

1. According to Luṭfī Paşa (grand vezir, 1539–41), who wrote a history of the House of Osman in his retirement, Osman's success partly depended on the fact that he did not make his political bid (*beglenmedi*) so long as the House of Seljuk was "ruler of the time" (*ḥākimü'l-vaḳt*). *Tevārīḫ-i Āl-i ʿOsmān* (Istanbul, 1922–23), 5–6. On the political nature of a tribe, see the apt formulation by Lindner, "What Was a Nomadic Tribe?": "The tribe served, first and foremost, a political purpose: the protection and enhancement of the position of its tribesmen in the face of the wider world" (699).

2. Aptullah Kuran, "Karamanlı Medreseleri," *Vakıflar Dergisi* 8(1969):209–23; see 223 (translation mine).

3. Köprülü argues that Osman's ancestors must have come to Asia Minor with the first Seljuk conquerors (*Origins,* 74–76). His argument, based primarily on the fact that Kayı appears in many different parts of Anatolia as a toponym, is hardly convincing. The whole attribution of Kayı ancestry to the Ottomans is suspect, as will be discussed below. And even if this were true, different clans of Kayı ancestry could have arrived in Anatolia at different times. Köprülü also claims that "older written sources" support his position, but he does not name those sources; a chronicle, for instance, states that "Ertoġrıl left Turkīstān with 340 men of his and came to Rūm along with the Seljuks" (Cengiz and Yücel, eds., "Rûhî Tarihi," 375).

4. This section of the *Selçuḳnāme* is edited in A. S. Levend, *Türk Dilinole Gelişme ve Sadeleşme Safhaları* (Ankara, 1949), 18. A coin issued in the name of Orḫān in 1327 contains a symbol that some scholars were inclined to read as the stamp of the Kayı tribe (see Uzunçarşılı, *Osmanlı Tarihi,* 1:125), but this has been shown to be a misreading. The Kayı symbol appears on Ottoman coins only during the reign of Murād II (1421–51), that is, in Yazıcızāde's lifetime, when the Kayı lineage had been re-remembered. See F. Sümer, *Oğuzlar (Türkmenler): Tarihleri-Boy Teşkilâtı-Destanları,* 3d enl. ed. (Istanbul, 1980), 220.

5. Şükrullāh, *Behçetü't-tevārīḫ,* trans. N. Atsız in idem, *Osmanlı Tarihleri* (Istanbul, 1947), 51. On the political implications of the Oġuz genealogy, see Barbara Flemming, "Political Genealogies in the Sixteenth Century," *JOS* 7–8(1988):123–37; and, Aldo Gallotta, "Il mito oguzo e le origini dello stato ottomano: Una riconsiderazione," *OE,* 41–59. For an original interpretation of the genealogies that include the Biblical-Koranic figures Japheth or Esau as the ancestors of the Ottomans, see S. Yerasimos, *La fondation de Constantinople.* No

matter what Ottoman claims were to a distinguished pedigree, they do not seem to have been taken seriously, at least by their rivals. Timur's derisive letters to Bāyezīd I are well known. A Karamanid chronicle refers to the House of Osman as "*bī-'aṣl*" (lacking a proper lineage, or, upstart); see *Şikârî'nin Karaman Oğulları Tarihi,* ed. M. Koman (Konya, 1946), passim. For a number of different, some rather wild, theories proposed in sixteenth-century sources, mostly outside the Ottoman empire, see Köprülü, "Osmanlı İmparatorluğunun Etnik Menşei Meseleleri."

6. Apz, ed. Giese, 8.

7. Ibid., 16.

8. Togan, *Umumî Türk Tarihi'ne Giriş,* 324–33.

9. For an informative but credulous account of the late-nineteenth-century discovery of the Karakeçili and a revival of the same "tradition" after 1946, see I. H. Konyalı, *Söğüt'de Ertuğrul Gâzi Türbesi ve İhtifali.* Sultan 'Abdülḥamīd II (r. 1876–1909) instigated the discovery of the tomb of "Ertoġrıl's wife" (presumably implying Osman's mother), who remains unnamed in the inscription dated A.H. 1305/A.D. 1887 (ibid., 23). Also see the lame attempt by Mu'allim Nācī, an intellectual writing an Ottoman history for the same sultan, to coin the word "Ertuğrullu" (Istanbul University Library, MS. T. 4127, quoted at length by Konyalı, 46–50). For further information on the Karakeçili in the nineteenth and twentieth centuries, and a collection of some of their early-twentieth-century lore, see Safa Öcal, *Devlet Kuran Kahramanlar* (Istanbul, 1987). Several tribal groups named Karakeçili appear in different parts of Anatolia in the sixteenth century; see F. Sümer, *Oğuzlar.* Those around Kayseri were Christian according to sixteenth-century court records of that city; see M. H. Yınanç, *Türkiye Tarihi Selçuklular Devri* (Istanbul, 1944), 1:167–68. An ethnographer of Anatolian 'Aleviism notes in the 1970s that while the majority of the Karakeçili were Sunni, there were some 'Alevī clans: Mehmet Eröz, *Türkiye'de Alevîlik-Bektâşîlik* (Istanbul, 1977), 28.

10. OA, 376: "Germiyān ili henüz dārü'l-ḥarb idi." Earlier cited in Ménage, *Neshrī's History,* 71. According to Uzunçarşılı and Varlık, the Germiyan were not settled there at least until the 1240s.

11. G. Moravcsik, "Türklüğün Tetkiki Bakımından Bizantinolojinin Ehemmiyeti," *İkinci Türk Tarih Kongresi: Istanbul, 1937* (Istanbul, 1943), 493–98; Richard Hartmann, *Zur Wiedergabe türkischer Namen und Wörter in den byzantinischen Quellen,* Abhandlungen der Deutschen Akademie der Wissenschaften zu Berlin, Klasse für Sprachen, Literatur, und Kunst, no. 6 (Berlin, 1952), 6. For other theories, from the earlier part of this century, concerning Osman's name, see Langer and Blake, "The Rise of the Ottoman Turks," 496 n. 65.

12. F. Taeschner, ed., *Al-Umari's Bericht über Anatolien* 22, line 5: "'Uthmān"; 41, line 18: "Ṭaman." For a list of "misspelled" Anatolian geographical and personal names in this work and their "corrections," see İ. H. Konyalı, *Abideleri ve Kitâbeleri ile Şereflikoçhisar Tarihi* (Istanbul, 1971), 140–42.

13. Cited in M. H. Yınanç, "Ertuğrul Gâzî," *İA,* s.v. Yınanç reads the name as "Utman." Also see the verses cited in Latin-letter transcription (from the same manuscript?) in Gazimihal, "Mihâloğulları," 128, with the name read as "Atman." Osman must have had another (an earlier?) name, whatever the precise

form it took, according to Jean Deny and Adnan Erzi as well: see Deny, "L'Osmanli moderne et le Türk de Turquie," in *Philologicae Turcicae Fundamenta,* vol. 1 (Wiesbaden, 1963), 182–239; Erzi, "Osmanlı Devletinin Kurucusunun İsmi Meselesi," *Türkiyat Mecmuası* 7–8 (1940–42): 323–26. Given that such an impressive array of scholars, independently of each other, reached similar conclusions, it is surprising that Osman's change of name is not taken into account in treatments of his life. It is curious that the title ***hetman*** given to the chieftains of Zaporozhian Cossacks (seventeenth century) derives etymologically from the Turkish word ***ataman;*** see Omeljan Pritsak, "Das erste türkisch-ukrainische Bündnis (1648)," *Oriens* 6 (1953): 268. This particular Turkish word for a leader is not attested in medieval Anatolia; Louis Bazin, however, makes a very good effort to demonstrate that it is plausible for ***ataman*** to have been of ancient usage as a title; see his "Antiquité méconnue du titre d'***ataman***?" *Harvard Ukrainian Studies* 3/4 (1979–80): 61–70.

It should also be noted that Osman's name is misspelled even on his own coin, but in a different fashion. It has the Arabic *thā'* in the middle but the "'alif" is omitted, thus forcing the reader to a shortening of the second syllable, which is a long one in the Arabic original.

14. As we saw in chapter 1 with respect to the arguments made by Demirtaş and Káldy-Nagy, some scholars feel that giving a Turkish name to one's child does imply being less of a Muslim. Among the "reasons for hypothesizing that Ertughrul and his sons were only loosely attached to Islam," Káldy-Nagy writes that "Ertughrul himself, his two brothers, . . . and his two sons . . . had old Turkic, i.e., non-Muslim names." After noting that Osman's original name must have been "Ataman," he adds: "The appropriate question here, then, is: to what extent was Osman — though no longer a pagan — actually imbued with the spirit of Islam when he gave the name Orkhan . . . to several [sic] of his sons . . . ?" ("Holy War," 470).

15. Andronicus III is reported to have designed a plan to help the besieged Bursans but it was not carried out. See A. E. Laiou, *Constantinople and the Latins* (Cambridge, Mass., 1972), 292–93.

16. Apz, 14–15; Osman's discussion with his brother is on p. 16.

17. Laiou, *Constantinople and the Latins,* 292.

18. In the case of Salāḥ al-Dīn, too, there has been concern among scholars to determine the extent to which he was driven by sincere faith or plain ambition. See H. A. R. Gibb, "The Achievement of Saladin," *Bulletin of the John Rylands Library* 35 (1952): 46–60.

19. On Mihāl, see Ayverdi, *Osmanlı Mi'mârîsinin İlk Devri,* 5 n. 3 (the site of Harman Kaya, reported to be his original base), and 150–51 (alleged tomb and ancestors).

20. İnalcık, "Ottoman Methods of Conquest," *SI* 2 (1954): 104–29.

21. Göynük was totally Christian when Ibn Baṭṭūṭa passed through it in 1333.

22. Ibn 'Arabshāh, *Tamerlane,* trans. Sanders, 178. See ibid., 177, on their numbers, strength, wealth, and huge herds. The "king of Artana" (or Eretna) was appointed governor by the Ilkhanids just before the dissolution of their power. Thereafter, he ruled his own principality, styling himself "sultan," in central and eastern Anatolia until his death in 1352.

23. Ibid., 201. This "treachery" may be why Yaḫşi Faḳīh, possibly writing in the post-1402 circumstances, is particularly keen on presenting them as villains.

24. Imber, "Dynastic Myth," n. 1, accuses İnalcık of being so credulous as to take the wedding story seriously.

25. Elvān Çelebi, *Menāḳibü'l-ḳudsiyye,* 169. The editors identify (p. lxxvi) the Sheikh Bali who appears just a few lines earlier as another person. But the name could be a shorter version of Ede Bali, just as Ede Sheikh is used in some later documents. In other words, the consecutive lines about Bali and Ede Bali may refer to the same person. If so, the information given in the lines concerning Sheikh Bali's wealth tallies perfectly with Apz's apologetic report about Ede Bali as a rich herd-owner "whose dervishliness was in his esoteric being." The Turkish translation of the *Burhān-i Ḳāṭi'* (a celebrated Persian dictionary) indicates that "ede" was used for "elder brother" in the Maraş region in the eighteenth century (*Tarama Sözlüğü,* 8 vols. [Ankara, 1963–77], 3:1384). If it had the same meaning and functioned as a title in fourteenth-century western Anatolia, it could easily have been dropped when one wanted to refer to the sheikh by his name (Bali) only.

26. The document (from A.H. 985, in Başbakanlık Arşivi, Mühimme Defterleri 31, p. 237) cannot be conclusive evidence, however, since it is possible that the scribe was too gullible or that this information was accepted dogma by that time. On the other hand, it is worth noting that Apz writes that he received all this information orally from Maḥmūd, Ede Bali's son, and the land surveys give the names of Ede Bali's descendants in this order: his son Maḥmūd, Maḥmūd's son Meḥmed, Meḥmed's sons Maḥmūd and Paşa. Barkan and Meriçli, eds., *Hüdavendigâr,* 282–83. The YF-Apz narrative also refers to a certain Aḫī Ḥasan as Ede Bali's nephew (Apz, ed. Giese, 14). Along with some other evidence of the same nature, this has been taken by Giese as the basis of his argument that Osman and Ede Bali were leading members of the aḫī associations that Ibn Baṭṭūṭa encountered in almost every town he visited in Anatolia; see his "Das Problem der Enstehung des osmanischen Reiches." Even though Giese's theory is farfetched, it is clear on the basis of the documents edited by Barkan and Meriçli that several grants were made to aḫīs by the begs of the fourteenth century, including those of the Ottoman family. The precise contribution of the aḫīs to the Ottoman enterprise remains to be assessed but it cannot be ignored. Many of these documents were already known and used by E. H. Ayverdi, *Osmanlı Mi'mârîsinin İlk Devri,* 8.

27. Zachariadou, "Pachymeres on the 'Amourioi' of Kastamonu."

28. Ibid., 70.

29. See E. Zachariadou, "Notes sur la population de l'Asie Mineure turque au XIVe siècle," *Byzantinische Forschungen* 12(1987):224.

30. See Togan, *Umumî Türk Tarihi'ne Giriş,* 323.

31. The geographical setting of Söğüt is exhaustively analyzed by Clive Foss, unpublished paper. I am grateful to the author for enabling me to make use of this important study. The location alongside a major highway should also be seen in terms of the larger picture of thriving commerce in and around Asia Minor, as mentioned above in the Introduction. In general, the specific material conditions on the ground—not the main concern of this book—in Bithynia as compared to other parts of the peninsula should be studied much more carefully in order to

assess the advantages and potential of different principalities. To what extent did different agricultural activities continue? What kind and level of an interface between pastoralist and agrarian activities can be observed in different parts of Asia Minor? Foss makes an exemplary attempt, in the same unpublished paper, to draw some answers to such questions from a late thirteenth-century endowment deed, for instance. Many other documents of the same sort need to be analyzed, and Byzantine sources brought into the picture. On the ebb and flow as well as the changing nature of productive activity in medieval Anatolia, also see Hendy, *Studies in the Byzantine Monetary Economy*. Akdağ's *Türkiye'nin İktisadî ve İçtimaî Tarihi* is also useful. Begs benefited from such activity in terms of both revenue and booty, of course; their success must have depended, to some extent, on finding the right mixture. For a general look at the sources of wealth for the principalities, see E. Zachariadou, "S'enrichir en Asie Mineure au XIVe siècle," *Hommes et richesses dans l'empire byzantin,* vol. 2: VIIIe–XVe siècle, ed. V. Kravari et al. (Paris, 1991), 215–24. Important information on revenues in Anatolia in the first half of the fourteenth century was discovered in sources concerning Ilkhanid finances by A. Zeki Velidî [Togan], "Mogollar Devrinde Anadolu'nun İktisadî Vaziyeti," *Türk Hukuk ve İktisat Tarihi Mecmuası* 1 (1931): 1–42.

32. Apz, ed. Giese, 19. One of the manuscripts used by Atsız adds that people of other regions came to Osman's domains upon hearing of the "comfort of the infidels here [in Osman's realm]" (102).

33. See *Bayburt Kanunnâmesi,* ed. Leyla Karahan (Ankara, 1990), 16.

34. Tuncer Baykara, "Denizli'de Yeni Bulunan İki Kitâbe," *Belleten* 33 (1969): 159–62. Also see idem, *Aydınoğlu Gazi Umur Bey* (Ankara, 1990), 20–21.

35. See, for instance, the interpretation of a dream attributed to Muḥammad al-Qā'im, the founder of the Sa'dian dynasty of Morocco, who competed with the Ottomans in the midsixteenth century, in Dahiru Yahya, *Morocco in the Sixteenth Century* (Atlantic Highlands, N.J., 1981), 5.

36. On dreams of sovereignty as compacts, see Roy Mottahedeh, *Loyalty and Leadership in an Early Islamic Society* (Princeton, 1980), 69–70.

37. One could see this within a larger context as part of the role that dervishes continued to play for several centuries, certainly throughout Ottoman history, in Islamic political culture, which is said to be devoid of mechanisms of intermediation between the governing elites and the governed. To the extent that legitimacy of power depended on the acceptance and fulfillment of some reciprocal expectations, it involved the intermediacy ("notarization") of figures who were recognized by the public for reasons that were, ordinarily, not state-induced.

38. The decline of interest is only relative of course and even then not valid for the whole period. In her *Constantinople and the Latins,* Laiou shows that Andronicus II (r. 1282–1328) was quite concerned with Asia Minor in the first twenty-two years of his reign. On pseudo-Lachanes, see Lindner, *Nomads and Ottomans,* 7–8.

39. C. Foss, "Byzantine Malagina and the Lower Sangarius," *Anatolian Studies* 40 (1990): 161–83 and plates; see esp. 173–75. For Andronicus II in Bithynia, see Laiou, *Constantinople and the Latins,* 79. Note also the expedition of Catalan troops, dispatched to Asia Minor by the Byzantine empire in 1304, as recorded in Muntaner, *Crónica* (Barcelona, 1951).

40. Laiou, *Constantinople and the Latins,* 247. This impression may be due simply to a gap (mentioned in ibid., 244) in Byzantine narrative sources for a while after 1307, namely, when Pachymeres ended his account.

41. R. M. Riefstahl, *Turkish Architecture in Southwestern Anatolia* (Cambridge, Mass., 1930). The full inscription program of the mosque is given in Akın, *Aydınoğulları,* 104–7.

42. *Al-'Umarī's Bericht über Anatolien,* 22; Ibn Baṭṭūṭa, 2:324.

43. Barkan and Meriçli, eds., *Hüdavendigâr,* passim.

44. İnalcık, "Siege of Nicaea."

45. This does not imply that the appanage system was limited to the Turco-Mongol traditions. The (Persian) Būyids and (Kurdish) Ayyūbids followed similar practices, as did the Merovingians of medieval Gaul. For references to the most important works on the appanage system in the Islamic world, see S. Humphreys, *Islamic History* (Princeton, 1991), 166. For a detailed delineation of its workings in one polity over a considerable stretch of time, also see R. McChesney, *Waqf in Central Asia: Four Hundred Years in the History of a Muslim Shrine, 1480–1889* (Princeton, 1991), passim.

46. Pazarlu Beg is mentioned once by the Byzantine historian Kantakouzenos. Land surveys of the fifteenth and sixteenth centuries refer to some endowments by Pazarlu and 'Alā'eddīn in the Söğüt-Yarhisar area. It has escaped all attention that the YF-Apz narrative (Atsız, 102) refers to a son of Osman's as the one who was in charge of the seasonal migration of the tribe; he remains unnamed but is clearly neither Orḫān nor 'Alā'eddīn.

47. Based on the fact that the endowment deed of March 1324 is issued in the name of Orḫān, Uzunçarşılı has suggested ("Gazi Orhan Bey Vakfiyesi," 282–83) that Osman must have died before that date. But this is not conclusive evidence since there is no reference to Osman as deceased in the document as it now exists, that is, torn, particularly in that part where Osman's name was written, which could have been followed by a formula like "*el-merḥūm.*"

48. Aḥmed Ferīdūn Beg, ed., *Münşe'ātü's-selāṭīn* (Istanbul, 1857), 1:143–44.

49. See the excellent study of E. Zachariadou, "The Emirate of Karasi and That of the Ottomans: Two Rival States," in *OE,* 225–36.

50. Irène Beldiceanu-Steinherr, "La vita de Seyyid 'Alī Sulṭān et la conquête de la Thrace par les Turcs"; idem, "La conquête d'Andrinople par les Turcs"; and idem, Le règne de Selīm Ier."

51. This argument was first made by Uzunçarşılı on the basis of a document he discovered and published in "Osmanlı Tarihine Ait Yeni Bir Vesikanın Ehemmiyeti ve Bu Münasebetle Osmanlılarda İlk Vezirlere Dair Mütalea," *Belleten* 3(1939):99–106. For an exhaustive analysis of this document, which Wittek argued was a forgery, and for references to the considerable body of scholarly literature on it, see Irène Beldiceanu-Steinherr, *Recherches,* 106–10.

52. Uruç bin 'Ādil, *Oruç Beğ Tarihi,* ed. N. Atsız (Istanbul, [1972?]), 39.

53. On the office of the ḳāḍī'asker under the Seljuks, see Turan, *Vesikalar,* 46–47. Note that Ottoman *każā* (juridical system) seems to have evolved in more of a synthesis with the administration of *'urfī* (sultanic/customary) law than Seljuk każā, where *şer'ī* (religious) and *'urfī* spheres remained more clearly differentiated.

54. *Oruç Beğ Tarihi*, ed. Atsız, 41.

55. *Byzantium, Europe, and the Ottoman Sultans, 1373–1513: An Anonymous Greek Chronicle of the Seventeenth Century (Codex Barberinus Graecus 111)*, trans. M. Philippides (New Rochelle, N.Y., 1990), 21. Elizabeth Zachariadou has shown that this source is based primarily on the second edition (Venice, 1573) of Francesco Sansovino's history of the Ottomans; see her *The Chronicle about the Turkish Sultans (of Codex Barberinus Graecus 111) and Its Italian Prototype* (Thessaloniki, 1960) (in Greek). I thank the author for bringing this to my attention and for orally summarizing its contents.

56. Orhan Şaik Gökyay, "Şeyh Bedreddin'in Babası Kadı Mı Idi?" *Tarih ve Toplum* 2(February 1984):96–98. On the popular confusion between kadi and gazi, see Hasluck, *Christianity and Islam under the Sultans*, 710.

57. İnalcık, "Ottoman Methods of Conquest": "The state did not as a rule seek their conversion to Islam as a necessary prerequisite to enrollment in the Ottoman askeri class" (116). Also, being a tribal leader (in the inclusive sense) does not exclude being a gazi; ibid., 119 n. 3. As late as the seventeenth century, there were non-Muslims among the prebendal cavalry, but as isolated cases; see Bistra Cvetkova, *Les institutions ottomanes en Europe* (Wiesbaden, 1978), 5.

58. İnalcık, *Fatih Devri Üzerinde Tetkikler ve Vesikalar*. In the rest of this paragraph, I basically follow this masterpiece of Ottoman political history.

59. Neşrī, ed. Taeschner, 32; ed. Unat and Köymen, 108–9. Apz (ed. Giese, 13–14) relates the practice of standing up and its meaning but not its abolition. In fact, he writes that Ottoman dynasts stood up "until today," implying that this passage (which does not appear in the anonymous chronicles or Uruç) was written before Meḥmed II changed the code; it may again be from the work of Yaḫşi Faḳīh.

60. In A.H. 883/A.D. 1478–79. ʿAbdallāh Ibn Riżvān, *La chronique des steppes Kiptchak, Tevārīḫ-i deşt-i Qipçaq du XVIIe siècle*, ed. A. Zajaczkowski (Warsaw, 1966), 34.

61. Apz, ed. Giese, 138.

62. Machiel Kiel has undertaken some pioneering studies with many relevant examples; see his collected articles in *Studies on the Ottoman Architecture of the Balkans* (Hampshire, Great Britain, 1990). Also note that it was the Sons of Miḫal who built up the complex of the Seyyid Gazi shrine and some other "heterodox" sites in that area. Hayretī, an ʿAlevī poet of the early sixteenth century from Gianitsa, spent most of his life with his patrons among frontier lords, including the Sons of Miḫal and Yaḥyā; see M. Çavuşoğlu and A. Tanyeri, intro. to Hayretî, *Dîvan* (Istanbul, 1981), xi–xv.

63. According to Ebū'l-ḫayr, the compiler, Cem would rather listen to the stories of Ṣarı Ṣalṭuḳ than those of the *Ḥamzanāme* cycle. While this implies at one level a preference of "Turkish" over "Arab" heroes, it should also be read as an affinity felt for a more familiar geography and "history" since the *Ṣalṭuḳnāme* focuses on the spiritual and military conquest of the Balkans, which was of course the legacy and continued concern of the Ottomans in the fifteenth century. To the extent that it is a "Turkish-Arab" dichotomy, one should recognize that this is not necessarily a question of ethnic stock as such identities are understood in our time. Ṣarı Ṣalṭuḳ is identified in the beginning as a descendant of the Prophet

Muḥammad through the line of the earliest Muslim warriors that were engaged in Byzantine Anatolia.

64. *Ṣalṭuḳnāme,* ed. Akalın, 2:241–44.

65. Also see Köprülü, "Anadolu Selçukluları Tarihinin Yerli Kaynakları," 437 (translated in *The Seljuks of Anatolia,* 47–48).

66. That Cem had some political ambitions as early as 1473, when he ordered the compilation of the *Ṣalṭuḳnāme,* also emerges from Angiolello's report of a rather obscure incident. According to the Vicentine page, who was in Ottoman service from 1470 to 1483, there was an attempt to enthrone Cem while his father was on campaign in eastern Anatolia against Akkoyunlu Uzun Ḥasan. The exact nature of the incident can be elucidated only after further research, but there can be little doubt that the Conqueror took the matter seriously; he put Cem's advisors to death upon his return. See I. Ursu, ed., *Historia Turchescha (1300–1514)* (Bucharest, 1909), 48.

67. V. L. Ménage ("Edirne'li Rûhî," 313–14) points out that Rūḥī's chronicle in fact breaks off at the point where Selīm's victory looks inevitable. In his *La fondation,* S. Yerasimos has already underlined the role of Edirne in the resistance to Meḥmed's imperial project, on the basis of a number of works, including the *Ṣalṭuḳnāme* (207–10).

68. *Meşā'irü'ş-şü'erā* of 'Āşıḳ Çelebi, cited in A. S. Levend, *Gazavât-nâmeler ve Mihal-oğlu Ali Bey'in Gazavât-nâmesi* (Ankara, 1956), 196.

Epilogue

1. *An Anonymous Greek Chronicle,* 59–60.

Selected Bibliography

Sources

'Abdü'l-kerīm b. Mūsā. *Maḳālāt-i Seyyid Ḥārūn*. Edited by Cemal Kurnaz. Ankara, 1991. Supersedes earlier edition by Ç. Uluçay in *Belleten* 10(1940):749–78.

'Abdü'l-vaṣī Çelebi. "Der vaṣf-i ceng-i Sulṭān Meḥemmed bā Mūsā vü hezīmet-i Mūsā." From his *Ḫalīlnāme* (wr. 1414). Edited by Ayhan Güldaş, in "Fetret Devri'ndeki Şehzadeler Mücadelesini Anlatan İlk Manzum Vesika," *Türk Dünyası Araştırmaları* 72(June 1991):99–110.

al-Aḳsarāyī, Karīm al-Dīn Mahmūd. *Müsâmarat al-aḫbār wa musāyarat al-aḫyār.* Edited, with notes, by Osman Turan, in *Müsâmeret ül-ahbâr: Moğollar Zamanında Türkiye Selçukluları Tarihi* (Ankara, 1944).

Anagnostis, Johannis. *Selânik (Thessaloniki)'in Son Zaptı Hakkında Bir Tarih: Sultan II. Murad Dönemine Ait Bir Bizans Kaynağı.* Translated by Melek Delilbaşı. Ankara, 1989.

Angiolello, Giovanni Maria. *Historia Turchescha (1300–1514)*. Edited by I. Ursu. Bucharest, 1909. Ursu attributes the text to Donado da Lezze.

Anonymous. *Tevārīḫ-i Āl-i 'Osmān.* TSK, M.R. 700. Modern Turkish transliteration by N. Azamat (Istanbul, 1992).

———. *Die altosmanischen anonymen Chroniken: Tevârîh-i Âl-i 'Osmân.* Edited and translated by F. Giese. Part 1, *Text and Variants.* Breslau, 1922. Part II, *Translation.* Leipzig, 1925.

[Oxford] Anonymous. Bodleian Library, Marsh 313. Published as "Rûhî Târîhi," with facsimile and transcription, by H. E. Cengiz and Y. Yücel in *Belgeler* 14–18 (1989–92): 359–472.

'Āşıḳpaşazāde [Dervīş Aḥmed]. *Menāḳib ü Tevārīḫ-i Āl-i 'Oṣmān.* (1) Critical edition by F. Giese, *Die altosmanische Chronik des 'Āşıḳpaşazāde* (Leipzig, 1929). (2) Edition by N. Atsız in *Osmanlı Tarihleri* (Istanbul, 1947). (3) *Vom Hirtenzelt zur Hohen Pforte: Frühzeit und Aufstieg des Osmanenreiches nach der*

Chronik "Denkwürdigkeiten und Zeitläufe des Hauses 'Osman" vom Derwisch Ahmed, genannt 'Āşık-Paşa-Sohn. Translated (based on the Berlin MS), with notes, by Richard F. Kreutel (Graz, 1959).

'Azīz ibn Ardaşīr Astarābādī. *Bazm u Razm*. Edited by M. F. Köprülü. Istanbul, 1928. Abbreviated translation into German by Heinz Helmut Giesecke, in *Das Werk des 'Azīz ibn Ārdaşīr Āstarābādī: Eine Quelle zur Geschichte des Spätmittelalters in Kleinasien* (Leipzig, 1940).

Beldiceanu-Steinherr, Irène, ed. *Recherches sur les actes des règnes des sultans Osman, Orkhan et Murad I.* Munich, 1967.

Cananus, Ioannes. *De Constantinopolis Obsidione*. Edited and translated by Emilio Pinto. Messina, 1977.

Cezbī. *Vilāyetnāme-i Seyyid 'Alī Sulṭān*. Ankara Cebeci Il Halk Library, MS 1189.

Dānişmendnāme. Edited and translated by I. Mélikoff, in *La geste de Melik Dānişmend*, 2 vols. (Paris, 1960).

Dedem Korkudun Kitabı. Edited by O. Ş. Gökyay. Istanbul, 1973. English translation by G. Lewis, *Book of Dede Korkut* (Middlesex, England, 1974).

Dushan's Code: The Fourteenth Century Code of Serbian Tsar, Stephan Dushan: The Bistritza Transcript. 2d ed., introduction and translation by Durica Krstic. Belgrade, 1989.

Ebū' l-ḫayr-i Rūmī. *Ṣaltuḳnāme*. (1) Facsimile edition of TSK, H. 1612 by F. İz, 6 vols. (Cambridge, Mass., 1986). (2) Critical edition by Ş. H. Akalın in 3 vols.: vol. 1 (Ankara, 1988); vol. 2 (Istanbul, 1988); vol. 3 (Ankara, 1990).

Eflākī. *Manāḳib al-'Ārifīn*. 2 vols. Edited and translated by Tahsin Yazıcı. Ankara, 1959–61.

Elvān Çelebi. *Menāḳibü'l-Ḳudsiyye fī Menāṣibi'l-Ünsiyye*. Edited by İ. Erünsal and A. Y. Ocak. Istanbul, 1984.

Enverī. *Düstūrnāme*. Translated by Irène Mélikoff-Sayar, in *Le destān d'Umur Pacha* (Paris, 1954).

Ferīdūn Beg, Aḥmed, ed. *Münşe'ātü's-selāṭīn*. 2 vols. Istanbul, 1857–59.

Firdevsī-i Rūmī. *Ḳuṭb-nâme*. Edited by İ. Olgun and İ. Parmaksızoğlu. Ankara, 1980.

Gregoras, N. *Rhomäische Geschichte*. Edited and translated by J. L. van Dieten. Stuttgart, 1973.

Gülşehrī. *Ein Mesnevi Gülschehris auf Achi Evran*. Edited by F. Taeschner. Hamburg, 1930.

[Ḥācī Bektaş-ı Velī?]. *Maḳālāt*. (1) Edition in modern Turkish script by Sefer Aytekin (Ankara, 1954). (2) Critical edition by Esad Coşan (Ankara, [1983?]). (3) Facsimile edition of Süleymaniye Library MS Laleli 1500, with introduction by Mehmet Yaman (Istanbul, 1985).

Ḥadīdī. *Tevārīḫ-i Āl-i 'Oṣmān (1299–1523)*. Edited by Necdet Oztürk. Istanbul, 1991.

Ḫalīl b. Ismā'īl b. Şeyḫ Bedrüddīn Maḥmūd. *Menāḳıb-i Şeyh Bedrü'ddīn ibn Isrā'īl*. Istanbul Belediye Kütüphanesi, M. Cevdet MS K.157. A defective copy of this MS was prepared for and reproduced by F. Babinger, in *Die Vita (menāqibnāme) des Schejch Bedr ed-dīn Maḥmūd, gen. Ibn Qāḍī Samauna* (Leipzig, 1943).

Hüdavendigâr Livası Tahrir Defterleri. Edited by Ömer Lütfi Barkan and E. Meriçli. Ankara, 1988.

Hull, D. B., trans. *Digenis Akritas: The Two-Blooded Border Lord (The Grottaferrata Version)*. Athens, Ohio, 1972.

Ibn Arabshāh, Aḥmad. *Tamerlane, or Timur the Great Amir.* Translated by J. H. Sanders. London, 1936.

Ibn Baṭṭūṭa. *Tuḥfatu'n-nuẓẓār fī ġarā'ibi'l-amṣār wa 'ajāibi'l-asfār.* 4 vols. Edited and translated by C. Defrémery and B. R. Sanguinetti. Paris, 1853–58.

Ibn Kemāl [Kemālpaşazāde]. *Tevārīḫ-i Āl-i 'Os̱mān.* Vols. 1, 2, and 7. Edited by Ş. Turan. Ankara, 1970, 1983, 1954.

Ibn Riżvān, 'Abdallāh. *La chronique des steppes Kiptchak, Tevārīḫ-i deşt-i Qipçaq du XVIIe siècle.* Edited by Ananiasz Zajaczkowski. Warsaw, 1966.

Ḳāḍī Aḥmed, Niğdeli. *Al-walad al-shafīq.* Süleymaniye Library MS Fatih 4519.

Knolles, Richard. *The General Historie of the Turkes.* London, 1610.

Kritoboulos, Michael. *History of Mehmed the Conqueror.* Translated by C. T. Riggs, Princeton, 1954.

Lutfī Paşa. *Tevārīḫ-i Āl-i 'Os̱mān.* Istanbul, 1922–23.

Mihailović, Konstantin. *Memoirs of a Janissary.* Translated by Benjamin Stolz. Historical commentary and notes by Svat Soucek. Ann Arbor, 1975.

[Mūsā b. 'Alī?]. *Vilāyetnāme.* Facsimile and modern Turkish edition by A. Gölpınarlı (who attributes the work to Firdevsī-i Rūmī), in *Vilâyet-nâme: Manâkıb-ı Hünkâr Hacı Bektâş-ı Veli* (Istanbul, 1958). The versified version may indeed be by a Firdevsī. The text is edited in modern Turkish transcription in Firdevsi-i Rûmi, *Manzûm Hacı Bektâş Veli Velâyetnâmesi (İlk Velâyetnâme),* edited by Bedri Noyan (Aydın, 1986).

Neşrī [Mevlānā Meḥmed]. *Ǧihânnümâ: Die altosmanische Chronik des Mevlânâ Mehemmed Neschrî.* 2 vols. Edited by F. Taeschner. Leipzig, 1951–55.

———. *Kitâb-i Cihan-nümâ.* 2 vols. Edited by F. R. Unat and M. A. Köymen. Ankara, 1949–57.

Philippides, Marios, trans. *Byzantium, Europe, and the Ottoman Sultans, 1373–1513: An Anonymous Greek Chronicle of the Seventeenth Century (Codex Barberinus Graecus 111).* New Rochelle, N.Y., 1990.

Seyyid Murād. *Il "Ġazavāt-i Ḫayreddīn Paša" di Seyyid Murād.* Facsimile edition of Escorial Library (Madrid) MS 1663, with variants, edited by Aldo Gallotta (Naples, 1983). Modern Turkish translation based on MSS at the University Library of Istanbul, by E. Düzdağ, in *Barbaros Hayreddin Paşanın Hatıraları,* 2 vols. (Istanbul, 1973).

Şikâri'nin Karaman Oğulları Tarihi. Edited by M. Mesud Koman. Konya, 1946.

Şükrullāh. *Behçetü't-tevārīḫ.* Translated by N. Atsız. In *Osmanlı Tarihleri.* Edited by N. Atsız. Istanbul, 1947.

Tekin, Şinasi. "XIV. Yüzyılda Yazılmış. . . ." *JTS* 13(1989):139–204. Edition of section on gaza from *Risāletü'l-Islām,* ms in Tekin's personal library.

Ṭaşköprīzāde, Aḥmed. *Al-Şaḳā'iḳ al-nu'māniyya fī 'ulamā al-dawlat al-'Os̱māniyya.* Translated by Mecdī Efendi, in *Ḥadā'iḳu'ş-şaḳā'iḳ,* edited by A. Özcan (Istanbul, 1989).

Tārīḫ-i Āl-i Selçuḳ. Paris, coll. Schefer, pers. 553. Facsimile edition and Turkish translation by Feridun Nâfiz Uzluk (Ankara, 1952).

Ṭihrānī-Isfahānī, Abū Bakr. *Kitāb-i Diyār-Bakriye.* 2 vols. Edited by N. Lugal and F. Sümer. Ankara, 1962–64.

Tursun Beg. *The History of Mehmed the Conqueror.* Facsimile edition and summary

English translation by Halil Inalcik and Rhoads Murphey. Minneapolis and Chicago, 1978.

Al-'Umarī's Bericht über Anatolien in seinem Werke "Masālik al-abṣār fī mamālik al-amṣār." Edited by F. Taeschner. Leipzig, 1929.

Uruç bin 'Ādil. *Die frühosmanischen Jahrbücher des Urudsch: Nach den Handschriften zu Oxford und Cambridge erstmals herausgegeben und eingeleitet.* Edited by Franz Babinger. Hanover, 1925.

———. [Edirneli Uruç Beg]. *Oruç Beğ Tarihi.* Edited by Nihal Atsız. Istanbul, [1972?]. Contains a poorly reproduced facsimile of Manisa Muradiye Library MS 5506, ff.143–236.

Yazıcızāde 'Alī. *Tevārīḫ-i Āl-i Selçuḳ.* TSK, R. 1391.

Studies

Akdağ, Mustafa. "Sultan Alaeddin Camii kapısında bulunan Hicrî 763 tarihli bir kitabenin tarihî önemi." *Tarih Vesikaları,* n.s., 1/3(1961):366–73.

Akın, Himmet. *Aydınoğulları Tarihi Hakkında Bir Araştırma.* 2d rev. ed. Ankara, 1968.

Alexandrescu-Dersca [Bulgaru], M. M. *Nicolae Iorga—A Romanian Historian of the Ottoman Empire.* Bucharest, 1972.

[Altınay], A. Refik. "Osmanlı Devrinde Rafizîlik ve Bektaşîlik." *Darülfünun Edebiyat Fakültesi Mecmuası* 8/2 (April 1932): 21–59.

Angelov, D. "Certains aspects de la conquète des peuples balcaniques par les Turcs." *Byzantinoslavica* 17(1956):220–75.

Arnakis, G. G. "Gregory Palamas among the Turks and Documents of His Captivity as Historical Sources." *Speculum* 26(1951):104–18.

———. "Gregory Palamas, the Chiones, and the Fall of Gallipoli." *Byzantion* 22(1952):305–12.

———. *Hoi protoi othomanoi.* Athens, 1947.

Artuk, Ibrahim. "Osmanlı Beyliğinin Kurucusu Osman Gâzî'ye Ait Sikke." In *Social and Economic History of Turkey (1071–1920),* edited by O. Okyar and H. Inalcık, 27–33. Ankara, 1980.

Ayverdi, E. H. *Osmanlı Mi'mârîsinde Çelebi ve II. Sultan Murad Devri, 806–855 (1403–1451).* Istanbul, 1972.

———. *Osmanlı Mi'mârîsinin İlk Devri: Ertuğrul, Osman, Orhan Gaziler, Hüdavendigar ve Yıldırım Bayezid, 630–805 (1230–1402).* Istanbul, 1966.

Babinger, Franz. *Die Geschichtsschreiber der Osmanen und ihre Werke.* Leipzig, 1927.

———. "Der Islam in Kleinasien: Neue Wege der Islamforschung." *ZDMG* 76(1922):126–152.

Balivet, Michel. "Un épisode méconnu de la campagne de Mehmed Ier en Macédoine: L'apparition de Serrès." *Turcica* 18(1986):137–46.

———. "L'expédition de Mehmed Ier contre Thessalonique: Convergences et contradictions des sources byzantines et turques." In *Proceedings of CIEPO Sixth Symposium: Cambridge . . . 1984,* edited by J.-L. Bacqué-Grammont and E. van Donzel, pp. 31–37. Istanbul, 1987.

Barcia, J. R., ed. *Américo Castro and the Meaning of the Spanish Civilization.* Berkeley, 1976.

Barkan, Ömer L. "Osmanlı İmparatorluğunda Bir Iskân ve Kolonizasyon Metodu Olarak Vakıflar ve Temlikler." *Vakıflar Dergisi* 2(1942):279–386.

Baron, Salo W. *A Social and Religious History of the Jews.* Vol. 18, *The Ottoman Empire, Persia, Ethiopia, India, and China.* 2d rev. ed. New York, 1983.

Barth, Fredrik. *Nomads of South Persia: The Basseri Tribe of the Khamseh Confederacy.* Boston, 1961.

Barthold, W. *Turkestan down to the Mongol Invasion.* 4th ed. London, 1977.

Bartlett, R., and A. MacKay, eds., *Medieval Frontier Societies.* Oxford, 1989.

Baykara, Tuncer. *Aydınoğlu Gazi Umur Bey.* Ankara, 1990.

———. "Denizli'de Yeni Bulunan İki Kitâbe." *Belleten* 33(1969):159–62.

Bayrakdar, Mehmet. *Kayserili Dâvûd (Dâvûdu'l-Kayserî).* Ankara, 1988.

———. *La philosophie mystique chez Dawud de Kayseri.* Ankara, 1990.

Bayram, Mikail. *Ahi Evren ve Ahi Teşkilâtı'nın Kuruluşu.* Konya, 1991.

———. "Babaîler İsyanı Üzerine." *Fikir ve Sanatta Hareket,* 7th ser., 23(March 1981):16–28.

———. *Baciyan-i Rum (Anadolu Selçukluları Zamanında Genç Kızlar Teşkilâtı).* Konya, 1987.

Bazin, Louis. "Antiquité méconnue du titre d'*ataman?*" *Harvard Ukrainian Studies* 3/4(1979–80):61–70.

Beldiceanu-Steinherr, Irène. "La conquête d'Andrinople par les Turcs: La pénétration turque en Thrace et la valeur des chroniques ottomanes." *Travaux et Mémoires* 1(1965):439–61.

———. "En marge d'un acte concernant le pengyek et les aqıngı," *Revue des Etudes Islamiques* 37(1969):21–47.

———. "Un legs pieux du chroniqueur Uruj." *BSOAS* 33(1970):359–63.

———. "Le règne de Selīm Ier: Tournant dans la vie politique et religieuse de l'empire ottoman." *Turcica* 6(1975):34–48.

———. "La vita de Seyyid 'Alī Sulṭān et la conquête de la Thrace par les Turcs." In *Proceedings of the 27th International Congress of Orientalists . . . , 1967,* edited by D. Sinor, pp. 275–76. Wiesbaden, 1971.

Bergsträsser, G. "Review of F. Babinger, ed., *Die frühosmanischen Jahrbücher des Urudsch,*" *Orientalische Literaturzeitung* 29(1926):433–38.

Berktay, Halil. *Cumhuriyet İdeolojisi ve Fuat Köprülü.* Istanbul, 1983.

———. "The 'Other' Feudalism: A Critique of Twentieth Century Turkish Historiography and Its Particularisation of Ottoman Society." Ph.D. diss., University of Birmingham, 1990.

Bivar, A. D. H. "Cavalry Equipment and Tactics in the Euphrates Frontier." *DOP* 26(1972):281–312.

Bombaci, Alessio. *Histoire de la litterature turque.* Translated by I. Mélikoff. Paris, 1968.

———. *La Turchia dall'epoca preottomana al XV secolo.* Part 1 of A. Bombaci and S. Shaw, *L'impero ottomano.* Turin, 1981.

Bracewell, Catherine W. *The Uskoks of Senj: Piracy, Banditry, and Holy War in the Sixteenth-Century Adriatic.* Ithaca, 1992.

Brown, Peter. "*Mohammed and Charlemagne* by Henri Pirenne," *Daedalus* 103(1974):25–33.

Bryer, Anthony. "Greek Historians on the Turks: The Case of the First Byzantine-Ottoman Marriage." In *The Writing of History in the Middle Ages: Essays Presented to Richard William Southern,* edited by R. H. C. Davis and J. M. Wallace-Hadrill, pp. 471–93. Oxford, 1981.

———. "Greeks and Türkmens: The Pontic Exception." *DOP* 29(1975):113–49.

———. "Han Turali Rides Again." *BMGS* 11(1987):193–206.

Bryer, Anthony, and Heath Lowry, eds. *Continuity and Change in Late Byzantine and Early Ottoman Society.* Birmingham, England, 1986.

Buliett, Richard W. *Conversion to Islam in the Middle Period: An Essay in Quantitative History.* Cambridge, Mass., 1979.

Buluç, Sadettin. *Untersuchungen über die altosmanische anonyme Chronik des Bibliothèque Nationale zu Paris, suppl. Turc 1047, anc. fonds turc 99.* Breslau, 1938.

Cahen, Claude. "Le problème du Shi'isme dans l'Asie Mineure turque préottomane." In *Le Shi'isme imâmite,* Colloque de Strasbourg, 1968, pp. 115–29. Paris, 1970.

———. "Review of Sp. Vryonis, *The Decline of Medieval Hellenism. . . .*" *IJMES* 4(1973):112–17.

———. *La Turquie pré-ottomane.* Istanbul, 1988. The earlier, English edition lacks footnotes (*Pre-Ottoman Turkey* [London, 1968]).

Canard, Marius. "Delhemma, Sayyid Battal et Omar al-Nu'man." *Byzantion* 12(1937):183–88.

———. "Questions épiques: Delhemma, épopée arabe des guerres arabo-byzantines." *Byzantion* 10(1935):283–300.

Cantor, Norman. *Inventing the Middle Ages: The Lives, Works, and Ideas of the Great Medievalists of the Twentieth Century.* New York, 1991.

Cvetkova, Bistra A. "Influence exercée par certaines institutions de Byzance et des Balkans du moyen âge sur le système féodale ottomane." *Byzantinobulgarica* 1(1962):237–57.

———. *Les institutions ottomanes en Europe.* Wiesbaden, 1978.

Daniel, Norman. *The Arabs and Medieval Europe.* 2d ed. London and New York, 1979.

Dankoff, Robert. "Turkic Languages and Turkish Dialects according to Evliya Çelebi." In *Altaica Osloensia,* edited by Bernt Brendemoen, pp. 89–102. Oslo, 1990.

De Jong, Frederick. "Problems concerning the Origins of the Qizilbāş in Bulgaria: Remnants of the Safaviyya?" In *Convegno sul tema: La Shi'a nell'impero Ottomano (Roma, 15 Aprile 1991)* pp. 203–15. Rome, 1993.

Demetriades, Vassilis. "Some Thoughts on the Origins of the Devşirme." *OE,* pp. 23–34.

Demirtaş, Faruk. "Osmanlı Devrinde Anadolu'da Kayılar," *Belleten* 12(1948).

Dennis, G. T. "The Byzantine-Turkish Treaty of 1403." *Orientalia Christiana Periodica* 33(1967):72–88.

De Vries-Van der Welden, Eva. *L'elite byzantine devant l'avance turque à l'époque de la guerre civile de 1341 à 1354.* Amsterdam, 1989.

Dickson, Martin. "Shah Tahmasb and the Uzbeks (The Duel for Khurasan with

'Ubayd Khan: 930–946/1524–1540)." Ph.D. thesis, Princeton University, 1958.

Diehl, Charles. *Byzantium: Greatness and Decline.* Translated by N. Walford. New Brunswick, N. J., 1957).

Doğru, Halime. *XVI. Yüzyılda Eskişehir ve Sultanönü Sancağı.* Istanbul, 1992.

———. *Osmanlı Imparatorluğunda Yaya-Müsellem-Taycı Teşkilatı (XV. ve XVI. Yüzyılda Sultanönü Sancağı).* Istanbul, 1990.

Dumézil, Georges. *Camillus: A Study of Indo-European Religion as Roman History.* Edited and introduced by Udo Strutynski. Translated by A. Aronowicz and J. Bryson. Berkeley, 1980.

———. *The Destiny of a King.* Translated by A. Hiltebeitel. Chicago, 1973.

Eaton, Richard M. *Sufis of Bijapur, 1300–1700: Social Roles of Sufis in Medieval India.* Princeton, 1978.

Erdz, Mehmet. *Türkiye'de Alevîlik-Bektâşîlik.* Istanbul, 1977.

Erzi, Adnan. "Osmanlı Devletinin Kurucusunun İsmi Meselesi." *Türkiyât Mecmuası* 7–8(1940–42):323–26.

Eyice, Semavi. "Çorum'un Mecidözü'nde Âşıkpaşaoğlu Elvan Çelebi Zâviyesi." *Türkiyât Mecmuası* 15(1969):211–44.

Faroqhi, Suraiya. *Der Bektaschi-Orden in Anatolien.* Vienna, 1981.

———. "Seyyid Gazi Revisited: The Foundation as Seen through the Sixteenth- and Seventeenth-Century Documents." *Turcica* 13(1981):90–122.

Febvre, Lucien. "Review of Köprülü, *Les origines de l'empire ottoman.*" *Annales: Economies, sociétés, civilisations* 9(1937):100–101.

Fleischer, Cornell. *Bureaucrat and Intellectual in the Ottoman Empire: The Historian Mustafa Âli (1541–1600).* Princeton, 1986.

———. "Royal Authority, Dynastic Cyclism, and 'Ibn Khaldunism' in Sixteenth-Century Ottoman Letters." *Journal of Asian and African Studies* 18(1983): 198–220.

Flemming, Barbara. *Landschaftsgeschichte von Pamphylien, Pisidien, und Lykien im Spätmittelalter.* Wiesbaden, 1964.

———. "Political Genealogies in the Sixteenth Century." *JOS* 7–8(1988):123–37.

Fletcher, Joseph. "Turco-Mongolian Monarchic Tradition in the Ottoman Empire." *Harvard Ukrainian Studies* 3/4(1979–80):236–51.

Fodor, Pál. "Aḥmedī's Dāsitān as a Source of Early Ottoman History." *Acta Orientalia Hungaricae* 38(1984):41–54.

Foss, Clive. "Byzantine Malagina and the Lower Sangarius." *Anatolian Studies* 40(1990):161–83.

———. "The Defenses of Asia Minor against the Turks. *Greek Orthodox Theological Review* 27(1982):145–205.

———. "The Homeland of the Ottomans." University of Massachusetts, Amherst. Unpublished paper.

Galatariotou, Catia. "Structural Oppositions in the Grottaferrata *Digenes Akritas.*" *BMGS* 11(1987):29–68.

Gallotta, Aldo. "Il Ṣalṣāl-nāme." *Turcica* 21–23(1991):175–90.

Garcia-Arenal, M. "Mahdī, murābiṭ, sharīf: L'avenement de la dynastie sa-'dienne." *SI* 74(1990):77–114.

Gazimihal, Mahmut R. "Savuntoğlu Kösemihal Bahşı." *Türk Folklor Araştırmaları* 113(December 1958):1801–4.

———. "İstanbul Muhasaralarında Mihâloğulları ve Fatih Devrine Ait Bir Vakıf Defterine Göre Harmankaya Mâlikânesi." *Vakıflar Dergisi* 4(1958): 125–37.

Gellner, Ernest. "Flux and Reflux in the Faith of Men." In *Muslim Society*, pp. 1–85. Cambridge, 1990.

———. "Tribalism and the State in the Middle East." In *TSF*, pp. 109–26.

Gervers, M., and R. J. Bikhazi. *Conversion and Continuity: Indigenous Christian Communities in Islamic Lands Eighth to Eighteenth Centuries*. Toronto, 1990.

Gibbons, Herbert A. *The Foundation of the Ottoman Empire*. Oxford, 1916.

Giese, Friedrich. "Einleitung zu meiner Textausgabe der altosmanischen anonyme Chroniken *tewarih-i al-i Osman*." *MOG* 1/2–3(1921–22):49–75.

———. "Das Problem der Entstehung des osmanischen Reiches." *Zeitschrift für Semitistik und verwandte Gebiete* 2(1924):246–71.

Gölpınarlı, Abdülkadir. *Mevlânâ'dan Sonra Mevlevîlik*. 2d ed. Istanbul, 1983.

———. *Simavna Kadısıoğlu Şeyh Bedreddin*. Istanbul, 1966.

———. *Yunus Emre*. Istanbul, 1936.

Gordlevski, V. *Anadolu Selçuklu Devleti*. Translated by A. Yaran. Ankara, 1988.

Göyünç, Nejat. "Osmanlı Devleti'nde Mevleviler." *Belleten* 55(1991):351–58.

Greenblatt, Stephen J. "Improvisation and Power." In *Literature and Society*, edited by Edward W. Said, pp. 57–99. Baltimore, 1980.

Grégoire, Henri. "Autour de Digenis Akritas." *Byzantion* 7(1932):287–302.

Haldon, J. F., and H. Kennedy. "The Arab-Byzantine Frontier in the Eighth and Ninth Centuries: Military Organisation and Society in the Borderlands." *Zbornik Radova Vizantinološkog Instituta* 19(1980):79–116.

Hammer-Purgstall, Joseph von. *Geschichte des osmanischen Reiches*. Vol. 1. Budapest, 1827.

Hartmann, Richard. *Zur Wiedergabe türkischer Namen und Wörter in den byzantinischen Quellen*. Abhandlungen der Deutschen Akademie der Wissenschaften zu Berlin, Klasse für Sprachen, Literatur, und Kunst, no. 6. Berlin, 1952.

Hasluck, F. W. *Christianity and Islam under the Sultans*. 2 vols. Edited by Margaret M. Hasluck. Oxford, 1929.

Hendy, Michael F. *Studies in the Byzantine Monetary Economy, c. 300–1450*. Cambridge, 1985.

Herzfeld, Michael. "Social Borderers: Themes of Conflict and Ambiguity in Greek Folk Song." *BMGS* 6(1980):61–80.

Hess, Andrew. *The Forgotten Frontier: A History of the Sixteenth-Century Ibero-African Frontier*. Chicago, 1978.

Heywood, Colin. "Between Historical Myth and 'Mythohistory': The Limits of Ottoman History." *BMGS* 12(1988):315–45.

———. "Boundless Dreams of the Levant: Paul Wittek, the *George-Kreis*, and the Writing of Ottoman History." *Journal of the Royal Asiatic Society*, 1989, 30–50.

———. "Wittek and the Austrian Tradition." *Journal of the Royal Asiatic Society*, 1988, 7–25.

Hobsbawm, E. J. *Nations and Nationalism since 1780*. Cambridge, 1990.

Hopwood, Keith. "Türkmen, Bandits and Nomads: Problems and Perceptions." In *Proceedings of CIEPO Sixth Symposium: Cambridge . . . 1984,* edited by J.-L. Bacqué-Grammont and E. van Donzel, pp. 23–30. Istanbul, 1987.

Hourani, Albert. "How Should We Write the History of the Middle East?" *IJMES* 23(1991):125–36.

Huart, C. "Les origines de l'empire ottoman." *Journal des Savants,* n.s., 15(1917): 157–66.

———. "Review of H. A. Gibbons, *The Foundation of the Ottoman Empire*." *Journal Asiatique,* 11th ser. 9(1917):345–50.

Humphreys, Stephen R. *Islamic History: A Framework for Inquiry*. Rev. ed. Princeton, 1991.

Imber, Colin. "The Legend of Osman Gazi." *OE,* pp. 67–76.

———. "The Ottoman Dynastic Myth." *Turcica* 19(1987):7–27.

———. *The Ottoman Empire, 1300–1481*. Istanbul, 1990.

———. "Paul Wittek's 'De la défaite d'Ankara à la prise de Constantinople.'" *JOS* 5(1986):65–81.

İnalcık, Halil. "Comments on 'Sultanism': Max Weber's Typification of the Ottoman Polity." *Princeton Papers in Near Eastern Studies* 1(1992):49–72.

———. "The Conquest of Edirne (1361)." *Archivum Ottomanicum* 3(1971):185–210.

———. *Fatih Devri Üzerinde Tetkikler ve Vesikalar*. Ankara, 1954.

———. 'Osmān Ghāzī's Siege of Nicaea and the Battle of Bapheus." *OE,* pp. 77–100.

———. "Ottoman Methods of Conquest." *SI* 2(1954):104–29.

———. "The Ottoman Turks and the Crusades, 1329–1451." In *A History of the Crusades,* edited by K. M. Setton. Vol. 6, *The Impact of the Crusades on Europe,* edited by H. W. Hazard and N. P. Zacour, chap. 7. Madison, 1989.

———. "The Policy of Mehmed II towards the Greek Population of Istanbul and the Byzantine Buildings of the City." *DOP* 23(1970):231–49.

———. "The Question of the Emergence of the Ottoman State." *International Journal of Turkish Studies* 2(1980):71–79.

———. "The Rise of Ottoman Historiography." In *Historians of the Middle East,* edited by B. Lewis and P. M. Holt, pp. 152–67. London, 1962.

———. "The Rise of the Turcoman Maritime Principalities in Anatolia, Byzantium, and the Crusades." *Byzantinische Forschungen* 9(1985):179–217.

———. "The Yürüks: Their Origins, Expansion, and Economic Role." In *Oriental Carpets and Textile Studies*. Vol. 2, *Carpets of the Mediterranean Countries, 1400–1600,* edited by R. Pinner and W. B. Denny, pp. 39–65. London, 1986.

İnalcık, Şevkiye. "İbn Hâcer'de Osmanlılar'a Dair Haberler." *Ankara Üniversitesi Dil ve Tarih-Coğrafya Fakültesi Dergisi* 6(1948):189–95, 349–58, 517–29.

İnan, Abdülkadir. *Tarihte ve Bugün Şamanizm*. 3d ed. Ankara, 1986.

Iorga, N. *Geschichte des osmanischen Reiches*. Vol. 1. Gotha, 1908.

———. *Byzance après Byzance: Continuation de l'"Histoire de la vie byzantine."* Bucharest, 1935.

İz, Fahri. "Makale-i Zindancı Mahmud Kapudan." *Türkiyat Mecmuası* 14(1964): 111–50.

Jennings, Ronald C. "Some Thoughts on the Gazi-Thesis." *WZKM* 76(1986): 151–61.

Johnson, J. T., and John Kelsay, eds. *Cross, Crescent, and Sword: The Justification and Limitation of War in Western and Islamic Tradition.* New York, 1990.

———. *Just War and Jihad: Historical and Theoretical Perspectives on War and Peace in Western and Islamic Traditions.* New York, 1991.

Kafesoğlu, Ibrahim, et al. *A History of the Seljuks: Ibrahim Kafesoğlu's Interpretation and the Resulting Controversy.* Translated and edited by Gary Leiser. Carbondale and Edwardsville, 1988.

Káldy-Nagy, Gyula. "The Holy War (*jihād*) in the First Centuries of the Ottoman Empire." *Harvard Ukrainian Studies* 3/4(1979–80):467–73.

Karamustafa, Ahmet T. *Vāḥidī's Menāḳıb-i Hvoca-i Cihān ve Netīce-i Cān: Critical Edition and Analysis.* Cambridge, Mass., 1993.

Kaygusuz, Ismail. *Onar Dede Mezarlığı ve Adı Bilinmeyen Bir Türk Kolonizatörü: Şeyh Hasan Oner.* Istanbul, 1983.

Kissling, Hans Joachim. *Rechtsproblematiken in den christlisch-muslimischen Beziehungen, vorab im Zeitalter der Türkenkriege.* Graz, 1974.

———. *Die Sprache des ʿĀşıḳpaşazāde: Eine Studie zur osmanisch-türkischen Sprachgeschichte.* Munich, 1936.

Klaniczay, Gabor. *The Uses of the Supernatural.* Princeton, 1990.

Köksal, Hasan. *Battalnâmelerde Tip ve Motif Yapısı.* Ankara, 1984.

Konyalı, Ibrahim H. *Abideleri ve Kitâbeleri ile Sereflikoçhisar Tarihi.* Istanbul, 1971.

———. *Söğüt'de Ertuğrul Gâzi Türbesi ve İhtifali.* Istanbul, 1959.

Köprülü, M. Fuat. "Anadolu Selçukluları Tarihinin Yerli Kaynakları." *Belleten* 7(1943):379–519. Now also see *The Seljuks of Anatolia: Their History and Culture according to Local Muslim Sources,* translated and edited by Gary Leiser (Salt Lake City, 1992).

———. "Anadolu'da İslāmiyet: Türk Istīlāsından Sonra Anadolu Tārīḫ-i Dīnīsine Bir Naẓar ve Bu Tārīḫin Menbaʿları." *Darülfünūn Edebiyāt Fakültesi Mecmūʿası* 2(1922):281–311, 385–420, 457–86.

———. "Bizans Müesseselerinin Osmanlı Müsseselerine Te'siri Hakkında Bâzı Mülâhazalar." *Türk Hukuk ve Iktisat Tarihi Mecmuası* 1(1931):165–313. See also *Some Observations on the Influence of Byzantine Institutions on Ottoman Institutions,* translated by Gary Leiser. Ankara, 1993.

———. *Edebiyat Araştırmaları.* Ankara, 1966. This is a collection of previously published articles.

———. *Influences du chamanisme turco-mongol sur les ordres mystiques musulmans.* Istanbul, 1929.

———. *Les origines de l'empire ottoman.* Paris, 1935. Turkish edition, with a new introduction by the author, *Osmanlı İmparatorluğunun Kuruluşu* (Ankara, 1959). English translation, *The Origins of the Ottoman Empire,* translated and edited by Gary Leiser (Albany, 1992).

———. "Osmanlı İmparatorluğunun Etnik Menşei Meseleleri." *Belleten* 7(1943): 219–313.

———. "Osmanlı İmparatorluğunun Kuruluşu Meselesi." *Hayāt Mecmūʿası* 11(1927):202–3; 12(1927):222.

——. *Türk Edebiyatında Ilk Mutasavvıflar.* 2d rev. ed. Istanbul, 1966.

Kramers, J. H. "Wer war Osman?" *Acta Orientalia* 6(1928):242–54.

Krupp, Alya. *Studien zum Menāqybnāme des Abu l-Wafā' Tāǧ al-'Ārifīn.* Part 1, *Das historische Leben des Abu l-Wafā' Tāǧ al-'Ārifīn.* Munich, 1976.

Kunt, Metin. "Siyasal Tarih (1300–1600)." In *Türkiye Tarihi,* edited by Sina Akşin, vol. 2, pp. 15–144. Istanbul, 1988.

Kuran, Aptullah. "Karamanlı Medreseleri." *Vakıflar Dergisi* 8(1969):209–23.

Kurat, Akdes Nimet. *Çaka Bey: Izmir ve Civarındaki Adaların Ilk Türk Beyi, M.S. 1081–1096.* Ankara, 1966.

——. *Die türkische Prosopographie bei Laonikos Chalkokandyles.* Hamburg, 1933.

Laiou, Angeliki E. *Constantinople and the Latins: The Foreign Policy of Andronicus II, 1282–1328.* Cambridge, Mass., 1972.

Langer, W. L., and R. P. Blake. "The Rise of the Ottoman Turks and Its Historical Background." *American Historical Review* 37(1932):468–505.

Lefort, Jacques. "Tableau de la Bithynie au XIIIe siècles." *OE,* 101–17.

Leiser, Gary, trans. and ed. *A History of the Seljuks: İbrahim Kafesoğlu's Interpretation and the Resulting Controversy.* Carbondale and Edwardsville, 1988.

Levend, Agâh Sırrı. *Gazavât-nâmeler ve Mihal-oğlu Ali Bey'in Gazavât–nâmesi.* Ankara, 1956.

——. *Türk Dilinde Gelişme ve Sadeleşme Safhaları.* Ankara, 1949.

Lindner, Rudi P. *Nomads and Ottomans in Medieval Anatolia.* Bloomington, 1983.

——. "A Silver Age in Seljuk Anatolia." In *Türk Nümismatik Derneğinin 20. Kuruluş Yılında İbrahim Artuk'a Armağan* (Istanbul, 1988), 267–78.

——. "Stimulus and Justification in Early Ottoman History." *Greek Orthodox Theological Review* 27(1982):207–24.

——. "What Was a Nomadic Tribe?" *Comparative Studies in Society and History,* 1982, 689–711.

Lowry, Heath. *Trabzon Şehrinin Islâmlaşma ve Türkleşmesi 1461–1583.* Translated by D. Lowry and H. Lowry. Istanbul, [1981?]. Translation of the author's unpublished Ph.D. thesis, University of California, Los Angeles.

McChesney, R. T. *Waqf in Central Asia: Four Hundred Years in the History of a Muslim Shrine, 1480–1889.* Princeton, 1991.

MacDougall, Hugh A. *Racial Myth in English History: Trojans, Teutons, and Anglo-Saxons.* Montreal, 1982.

Mahdi, Muhsin. "Orientalism and the Study of Islamic Philosophy." *Journal of Islamic Studies* 1(1990):73–98.

Manz, Beatrice F. *The Rise and Rule of Tamerlane.* Cambridge, 1989.

McGeer, Eric. "Tradition and Reality in the *Taktika* of Nikephoros Ouranos." *DOP* 45(1991):129–40.

Mélikoff, Irène. *Abū-Muslim, Le 'porte-hache' du Khorassan dans la tradition épique turco-iranienne.* Paris, 1962.

——. "L'origine sociale des premiers Ottomans." *OE,* pp. 135–44.

——. "Le problème ḳızılbaş." *Turcica* 6(1975):49–67.

Ménage, V. L. "The 'Annals of Murād II.'" *BSOAS* 39(1976):570–84.

——. "Another Text of Uruc's Ottoman Chronicle." *Der Islam* 47(1971):273–77.

———. "The Beginnings of Ottoman Historiography." In *The Historians of the Middle East,* edited by B. Lewis and P. M. Holt, pp. 168–79. London, 1962.

———. "Edirne'li Ruhi'ye Atfedilen Osmanlı Tarihinden Iki Parça." In *Ord. Prof. İsmail Hakkı Uzunçarşılı'ya Armağan,* pp. 311–33. Ankara, 1976.

———. "The Menāqib of Yakhshī Faqīh." *BSOAS* 26(1963):50–54.

———. *Neshrī's History of the Ottomans: The Sources and Development of the Text.* London, 1964.

———. "On the Recensions of Uruj's 'History of the Ottomans.'" *BSOAS* 30(1967):314–22.

———. "Some Notes on the Devshirme." *BSOAS* 29(1966):64–78.

Moravcsik, Gyula. *Byzantinoturcica.* 2d rev. ed. 2 vols. Berlin, 1958.

———. "Türklüğün Tetkiki Bakımından Bizantinolojinin Ehemmiyeti." *İkinci Türk Tarih Kongresi: Istanbul, 1937,* pp. 483–98. Istanbul, 1943.

Mottahedeh, Roy. *Loyalty and Leadership in an Early Islamic Society.* Princeton, 1980.

Ocak, Ahmet Yaşar. "Babaîler İsyanı'nın Tenkidine Dair." *Fikir ve Sanatta Hareket,* 7th ser., 24(September 1981):36–44.

———. "Bazı Menâkıbnâmelere Göre XIII. ve XV. Yüzyıllardaki İhtidâlarda Heterodoks Şeyh ve Dervişlerin Rolü." *JOS* 2(1981):31–42.

———. *Bektaşî Menâkibnâmelerinde Islam Öncesi Inanç Motifleri.* Istanbul, 1983.

———. *Kültür Tarihi Kaynaği Olarak Menâkıbnâmeler.* Ankara, 1992.

———. *Osmanlı İmparatorluğunda Marjinal Sûfîlik: Kalenderîler (XIV–XVII. Yüzyillar).* Ankara, 1992.

———. *La revolte de Baba Resul, ou la formation de l'hétérodoxie musulmane en Anatolie au XIIIe siècle.* Ankara, 1989. Dissertation completed in 1978, Université de Strasbourg. Abridged Turkish translation published under the title *Babaîler Isyanı* (Istanbul, 1980).

Oğuz, Burhan. *Türkiye Halkının Kültür Kökenleri.* Vol. 2. Istanbul, 1988.

Oğuz, Mevlut. "Taceddin Oğulları." *Ankara Üniversitesi Dil ve Tarih-Coğrafya Fakültesi Dergisi* 6(1948):469–87.

Okiç, Tayyib. "Bir Tenkidin Tenkidi." *Ankara Üniversitesi İlâhiyat Fakültesi Dergisi* 2(1953):219–90.

———. "Sarı Saltuk'a Ait Bir Fetva." *Ankara Üniversitesi İlâhiyat Fakültesi Dergisi* 1(1952):48–58.

Orhonlu, Cengiz. *Osmanlı İmparatorluğunda Aşiretlerin İskânı.* 2d enl. ed. Istanbul, 1987.

Özdemir, Hasan. *Die altosmanischen Chroniken als Quelle zur türkischen Volkskunde.* Freiburg, 1975.

Paret, Rudi. *Die legendäre Maghāzī-Literatur: Arabische Dichtungen über die muslimischen Kriegszüge zu Mohammeds Zeit.* Tübingen, 1930.

Pertusi, Agostino. "I primi studi in Occidente sull'origine e la potenza dei Turchi." *Studi Veneziani* 12(1970):465–552.

Peters, Rudolph. *Islam and Colonialism: The Doctrine of Jihad in Modern History.* The Hague, 1979.

———. *Jihad in Medieval and Modern Islam.* Leiden, 1977.

Philippides-Braat, Anna. "La captivité de Palamas chez les Turcs: Dossier et commentaire." *Travaux et Mémoires* 7(1979):109–221.

Ranke, Leopold. *The Turkish and Spanish Empires in the Sixteenth Century, and Beginning of the Seventeenth.* Translated by W. K. Kelly. Philadelphia, 1845.

Richards, J. F. "Outflows of Precious Metals from Early Islamic India." In *Precious Metals in the Later Medieval and Early Modern Worlds,* edited by J. F. Richards, pp. 183–205. Durham, N.C., 1983.

Ritter, Helmut. *Das Meer der Seele: Mensch, Welt, und Gott in den Geschichten des Fariduddin 'Attar.* Leiden, 1978.

Romilly, Jacqueline de. *The Rise and Fall of States according to Greek Authors.* Ann Arbor, 1977.

Runciman, Steven. "Teucri and Turci." In *Medieval and Middle Eastern Studies in Honour of Aziz Suryal Atiya,* edited by S. Hanna, pp. 344–48. Leiden, 1972.

Şahin, Ilhan. "Osmanlı Devrinde Konar-Göçer Aşiretlerin Isim Almalarına Dâir Bâzı Mülâhazalar." *Tarih Enstitüsü Dergisi* 13(1983–87):195–208.

Searle, Eleanor. *Predatory Kinship and the Creation of Norman Power, 840–1066.* Berkeley, 1988.

Sezen, Lütfi. *Halk Edebiyatında Hamzanâmeler.* Ankara, 1991.

Shaw, Stanford J. *History of the Ottoman Empire and Modern Turkey.* Vol. 1, *Empire of the Gazis: The Rise and Decline of the Ottoman Empire, 1280–1808.* Cambridge, 1976.

Spencer, Terence. "Turks and Trojans in the Renaissance." *Modern Language Review* 47(1952):330–33.

Srivastava, A. L. "A Survey of India's Resistance to Medieval Invaders from the North-West: Causes of Eventual Hindu Defeat." *Journal of Indian History* 43(1965):349–68.

Strohmeier, Martin. *Seldschukische Geschichte und türkische Geschichtswissenschaft: Die Seldschuken im Urteil moderner türkischer Historiker.* Berlin, 1984.

Sümer, Faruk. *Kara Koyunlular (Başlangıçtan Cihan-Şah'a Kadar).* Ankara, 1976.

———. *Oğuzlar (Türkmenler): Tarihleri-Boy Teşkilâtı-Destanları.* 3d enl. ed. Istanbul, 1980.

Taeschner, Franz. *Eine Mesnevi Gülschehris auf Achi Evran.* Leipzig, 1930.

———. "Der Weg des osmanischen Staates vom Glauberkämpferbund zum islamischen Weltreich." *Welt als Geschichte* 5(1940):206–15.

Taneri, Aydın. *Mevlânâ Âilesinde Türk Milleti ve Devleti Fikri.* Ankara, 1987.

Tapper, Richard. "Anthropologists, Historians, and Tribespeople on Tribe and State Formation in the Middle East." In *TSF,* pp. 48–73.

Tekin, Şinasi. "XIVüncü Yüzyıla Ait Bir İlm-i Hâl: Risâletü'l-İslâm." *WZKM* 76(1986):279–92.

Todorov, Nikolai. *The Balkan City, 1400–1900.* Seattle, 1983.

Togan, A. Zeki Velidî. "Moğollar Devrinde Anadolu'nun İktisadî Vaziyeti." *Türk Hukuk ve İktisat Tarihi Mecmuası* 1(1931):1–42.

———. *Umumî Türk Tarihi'ne Giriş. Cild I: En Eski Devirlerden 16. Asra Kadar.* 3d ed. Istanbul, 1981.

Turan, Osman. *Doğu Anadolu Türk Devletleri Tarihi.* 2d reprint ed. Istanbul, 1980.

———. "L'islamisation dans la Turquie du moyen âge." *SI* 10(1959):137–52.

———. "Selçuk Türkiyesi Din Tarihine Dair Bir Kaynak: *Fusṭāt ul-ʿadāle fī ḳavāʿid is-salṭana.*" In *Fuad Köprülü Armağanı,* pp. 531–64. Istanbul, 1953.

——. *Selçuklular Zamanında Türkiye*. Istanbul, 1971.

——. *Türk Cihân Hâkimiyeti Mefkûresi Tarihi*. 2 vols. in 1. 6th reprint ed. Istanbul, 1980. Summarized in Turan's "The Idea of World Domination among the Medieval Turks," *SI* 4(1955):77–90.

Uluçay, Çağatay. *Saruhan Oğulları ve Eserlerine Dair Vesikalar*. 2 vols. Istanbul, 1940–46.

Ursinus, Michael. "Byzantine History in Late Ottoman Turkish Historiography." *BMGS* 10(1986):211–22.

——. "From Süleyman Pasha to Mehmet Fuat Köprülü: Roman and Byzantine History in Late Ottoman Historiography." *BMGS* 12(1988):305–14.

——. "'Der schlechteste Staat': Ahmed Midhat Efendi (1844–1913) on Byzantine Institutions." *BMGS* 11(1987):237–43.

Uzunçarşılı, I. Hakkı. *Anadolu Beylikleri ve Akkoyunlu, Karakoyunlu Devletleri*. Ankara, 1937.

——. *Çandarlı Vezir Ailesi*. Ankara, 1974.

——. "Gazi Orhan Bey Vakfiyesi, 724 Rebiüelevvel–1324 Mart." *Belleten* 5(1941):277–88.

——. "Orhan Gazi'nin Vefat Eden Oğlu Süleyman Paşa için Tertip Ettirdiği Vakfiyenin Aslı." *Belleten* 27(1963):437–51.

——. *Osmanlı Tarihi*. Vol. 1. Ankara, 1947.

——. "Osmanlı Tarihine Ait Yeni Bir Vesikanın Ehemmiyeti ve Bu Münasebetle Osmanlılarda İlk Vezirlere Dair Mütalea." *Belleten* 3(1939):99–106.

Varlık, Çetin. *Germiyanoğulları Tarihi (1300–1429)*. Ankara, 1974.

Vryonis, Speros. *The Decline of Medieval Hellenism in Asia Minor and the Process of Islamization from the Eleventh through the Fifteenth Century*. Berkeley, 1971.

——. "The Decline of Medieval Hellenism. . . ." *Greek Orthodox Theological Review* 27(1982):225–85. Response to reviews of his 1971 book.

——. "Evidence of Human Sacrifice among Early Ottoman Turks." *Journal of Asian History* 5(1971):140–46.

Werner, Ernst. *Die Geburt einer Grossmacht—Die Osmanen (1300–1481): Ein Beitrag zur Genesis des türkischen Feudalismus*. 4th enl. ed. Vienna, 1985.

——. "Panturkismus und einige Tendenzen moderner türkischer Historiographie." *Zeitschrift für Geschichtswissenschaft* 13(1965):1342–54.

Werner, E., and K.-P. Matschke, eds. *Ideologie und Gesellschaft im hohen und späten Mittelalter*. Berlin, 1988.

Wittek, Paul. "De la défaite d'Ankara à la prise de Constantinople." *Revue des Études Islamiques* 12(1938):1–34.

——. "Deux chapitres de l'histoire des turcs de Roum." *Byzantion* 11(1936): 285–319.

——. *Das Fürstentum Mentesche: Studie zur Geschichte Westkleinasiens im 13.–15. Jahrhundert*. Istanbuler Mitteilungen 2. Istanbul, 1934.

——. *The Rise of the Ottoman Empire*. London, 1938.

——. "Le rôle des tribus turques dans l'empire ottoman." In *Mélanges Georges Smets*, pp. 665–76. Brussels, 1952.

——. "Der Stammbaum der Osmanen." *Der Islam* 14(1925):94–100.

——. "The Taking of the Aydos Castle: A Ghazi Legend and Its Transformation." In *Arabic and Islamic Studies in Honor of Hamilton A. R. Gibb*, edited by G. Makdisi, 662–72. Cambridge, Mass., 1965.

Wolff, Robert Lee. "Review of G. G. Arnakis, *Hoi protoi othomanoi.*" *Speculum* 26(1951):483–88.

Woods, John. *The Aqquyunlu: Clan, Confederation, Empire.* Minneapolis and Chicago, 1976.

Yerasimos, Stéphane. *La fondation de Constantinople et de Sainte-Sophie dans les traditions turques.* Paris, 1990.

Yınanç, Mükrimin H. *Türkiye Tarihi Selçuklular Devri.* Vol. 1, *Anadolu'nun Fethi.* Istanbul, 1944.

Yınanç, Refet. *Dulkadir Beyliği.* Ankara, 1989.

Yörükân, Yusuf Ziya. "Bir Fetva Münasebetiyle Fetva Müessesesi, Ebussuud Efendi ve Sarı Saltuk." *Ankara Üniversitesi İlâhiyat Fakültesi Dergisi* 1/2–3(1952):137–60.

Yüce, Kemal. *Saltuk-nâme'de Tarihî, Dinî ve Efsanevî Unsurlar.* Ankara, 1987.

Yücel, Yaşar. *Anadolu Beylikleri Hakkında Araştırmalar I: Çoban-oğulları Beyliği, Candar-oğulları Beyliği, Mesalikü'l-ebsar'a Göre Anadolu Beylikleri.* 2d ed. rev. Ankara, 1991.

———. *Anadolu Beylikleri Hakkında Araştırmalar II: Eretna Devleti, Kadı Burhaneddin Ahmed ve Devleti, Mutahharten ve Erzincan Emirliği.* Ankara, 1989.

Zachariadou, Elizabeth A. "The Emirate of Karasi and That of the Ottomans: Two Rival States." *OE,* 225–36.

———. "Marginalia on the History of Epirus and Albania (1380–1418)." *WZKM* 78(1988):195–210.

———. "The Neomartyr's Message." *Bulletin of the Centre for Asia Minor Studies* 8(1990–91):51–63.

———. "Notes sur la population de l'Asie Mineure turque au XIVe siècle." *Byzantinische Forschungen* 12(1987):223–31.

———. "Pachymeres on the 'Amourioi' of Kastamonu." *BMGS* 3(1977):57–70.

———. "S'enrichir en Asie Mineure au XIVe siècle." In *Hommes et richesses dans l'empire byzantin.* Vol. 2, *VIIIe–XVe siècle,* edited by V. Kravari, J. Lefort, and C. Morrison, pp. 217–24. Paris, 1991.

———. *Trade and Crusade: Venetian Crete and the Emirates of Menteshe and Aydın (1300–1415).* Venice, 1983.

———. "Yahshi Fakih and His Menakib." In *Proceedings of the Turkish Historical Association Congress, 1989.* Forthcoming.

Index

Abbasids, 63
abdāl, 176n94
'Abdül'azīz (Bedreddīn's grandfather), 183n150
'Abdül'azīz (dream interpreter), 132–33
'Abdül'azīz (Persian author), 177n96
'Abdülḥamīd II, Sultan, 74, 185n9
'Abdü'l-vaṣī Çelebi, 95
Abū'l-Wafā', Sheikh, 172n44
Abū Muslim, tale of, 63, 65
accommodationism: frontier cultures, 79–84, 144; Ottoman, 11, 146. *See also* cooperation, Christian-Muslim; inclusivism
Acropolites, 89
administrative apparatus, Ottoman, 16–18, 104, 111–14, 131–53 passim; Byzantine influences, 24, 39, 41, 140; Ilkhanid legacy, 40, 45; Seljuk institutions, 40, 142; Turco-Muslim origins, 10, 24, 42. *See also* fiscal policies
aḫī brotherhoods, 7, 34–35, 45, 176n94, 187n26; autonomy lost, 141; land given to, 181n136, 187n26
Aḫī Evren, 7, 93, 154, 172n43
Aḥmedı, 93–94, 102; and Ertoġrıl's sons, 107; *ġazā* thesis and, 38, 42, 51, 55; and Kayı genealogy, 122
Aḥmed III, Sultan, 149
'*aḳā'id*, 64
Akdağ, Mustafa, 45–46, 160–61
Akkoyunlu, 69, 94, 122, 178n101. *See also* Uzun Ḥasan
akritai, and gazis, 48, 56. *See also* Digenis Akritas
al-Aḳsarāyī, Karīm al-Dīn Maḥmūd, 130
Aḳşemseddīn, 87
'Alā'eddīn (Orḫān's brother), 106, 108, 136–37, 180n126, 189n46
'Alā'eddīn (Seljuk sultan), 147
'Alā'eddīn Beg, Karamanoğlu, 177n96
'Alā'eddīn Keyḳubād, 66, 169n14
Alanya, 6
'Alevī Turks, 54, 75, 172n44
Alexios III Comnenos, Emperor of Trebizond, 69
Algiers, 83
'Alī (cousin and son-in-law of Muḥammad the Prophet) tales of, 63, 75, 176n94
'Alī Amourios, 126, 130, 142
alliances: Christian-Muslim, 19; Ottoman/proto-Ottoman, 15, 71, 74, 104, 122–38, 140. *See also* cooperation, Christian-Muslim
altèrhistoire, 114–17
Anatolia, 14–15, 36–37, 39; invasions, xiii, 2–4, 5, 23–24; migrations into, xiii, 2, 3, 5, 23–24, 45; Ottoman symmetrical expansion, 17; politically divided, 2–7, 14–15, 48–49. *See also* frontier; Rūm; Seljuks; Turco-Muslim society; Turkey
Ancient Slavery and Modern Ideology (Finley), xiii

Andronicus II, 134, 188n38
Andronicus III, 186n15
Angiolello, Giovanni Maria, 191n66
Ankara: Battle of (1402), 18, 94, 96; Turkish capital, 149
Annales (French historical journal), 39
'Antarnāme, 63
appanage, 136–38, 189n45
Apz ('Āşıkpaşazāde), 54, 96–114 passim, 179n118, 181n137, 183n146; and Ede Bali, 129, 187nn25,26; education, 177n97; and *ġazā,* 86–87, 145, 146, 179–80, 190n59; and Kayı genealogy, 122; and Orḥān's succession, 137; orthodoxy, 144; on 'Osmān and Christians, 126; on 'Osmān's dream, 132; and 'Osmān's sons, 189n46; and sword-document, 60
Arabic: histories in, 63, 93, 96; names, xiv, 53, 61, 124–25, 167n62; transliterations, xiv
Arabs: Anatolian, 2, 45, 62–63, 67–68, 87; Cem and, 190–91; historians, 182n142
architecture: gazi milieu, 147; House of Aydın, 134
archives, xii, xiii, 42
Ardabil, Sheikh Ṣafī al-Dīn of, 8
'Ārif 'Alī, 176n95
'Ārif Çelebi, 77
Arık, Fahriye, 164n31
Armenians, 3, 26
armies, 30; Battle of Bapheus, 129–30; Christians in Ottoman, 26, 52–53; Janissary (yeñi çeri), 17, 18, 112, 139, 149; Karasi warriors in, 116, 138; *ḳul,* 83–84, 116, 146, 148–49, 182n142; Ottoman strategies, 145; *uc begleri,* 142–43. *See also* Ankara: Battle of; gazis; march environment; navy, Ottoman; political-military events
Arnakis, George G., 42–44, 50, 51, 55
Artuḫı, 67–68
Artuḳ, 166–67
Artuk, İbrahim, 168n3
'aṣabiyya, 114, 182n142
'Āşıḳ Paşa, 74, 93, 101
'Āşıkpaşazāde. *See* Apz
'Aşkar, 63
'askerī class, 112, 142, 190n57
Aspurça Ḫātūn, 168n1
astrologers, *taḳvīm* by, 96
Atatürk, Mustafa Kemal, 41, 91
Aydın, House of, 69–78 passim, 89, 130, 134, 138, 139. *See also* Umur Beg
Aydınoğlu Meḥmed Beg, 77
Aydos fortress, in gazi epic, 70, 103, 104
'ayyārūn, 56

Baba Ilyās, 5, 73–75, 109, 172nn43,44
Baba'īs, 74–75, 144; Ede Bali and, 74, 124, 128–29; Revolt, 74–75, 109, 124; as Shi'is, 171n40. *See also* Vefā'īs
babas, 141
Babinger, Franz, 34
bāc, 104
bacis, 176n94
Baghdad, 2, 9
Balabancık, 135
Balivet, Michel, 175n90
Balkans, 17, 34, 113, 145–47, 160n23; battles, 17, 116, 145; gazi warlords mostly based in, 18; "metadoxy," 76; and national historiography, 21; Ottoman benefits to, 32, 165n46; political ideologies, 23; Ṣalṭuḳ and, 64, 190n63; scholarly community, 42; Serbian losses, 17, 116, 139; Thracian towns leading to, 117
Bapheus, Battle of, 129–30
Bari (Italy), 3
Barthold, W., 55–56, 167n71
Bashkiria, 44
Batatzes, 16
Baṭṭālnāme, 67–68
Bayatlı Maḥmūdoğlı Ḥasan, 106–7
Bayburt: law code, 131; walls, 77
Bāyezīd I (the Thunderbolt), 18, 97, 114, 140, 183n145; and chronicles, 100, 106; and fratricide, 95, 136, 137; intra-Muslim conflicts, 88; and Muslim quarter in Constantinople, 40; son-in-law, 115; son's name, 124; and Timur/Timurids, 18, 85, 94–95, 112, 128, 185n5
Bāyezīd II, 97
Bazin, Louis, 186n13
Bedreddīn, Sheikh, 143, 145, 171n40, 183–84
beg/beglik, 14–15, 17, 125, 143
Bektāşī order, 7, 30, 97–98, 139; cultic sites, 184n152; radicalization, 144; Shi'ism and, 75. *See also* Ḥācī Bektaş Velī
Beldiceanu-Steinherr, Irène, 104, 116, 139, 182–83

Belgrade, 147
Bergama, 116
Beyatlı, Yahya Kemal, 179n115
Bilecik, 126; lord of, 85, 105, 126, 129
Birgi, conquest of, 77, 170n24
Bithynia, 47, 118, 125, 167n72, 188n31; archeology, 104; Baba'īs, 124, 129; Byzantine, 7, 10, 15–16, 133–34; Christians, 10, 26, 85, 107, 114, 142; 'Oṣmān's tribe, 7, 10, 15–16, 118, 122–36 passim, 142; Ottoman, 16, 43–44, 53–54, 90, 135–36; Palamas in, 90. *See also* Bursa; Sögüt
Blake, Robert P., 35
Bodin, Jean, 31
Borges, Jorge Luis, 157n3
Bosnia, 21
Bryer, Anthony, 169–70, 174n70
Bulgaria, 17, 21
Burhāneddīn, Ḳāḍī, 177n96, 178n102
Bursa: Emir Sulṭān and, 183n147; Ottoman conquest, 16, 43, 136; siege of, 125, 135, 186n15. *See also* inscription (1337)
Busbecq, 33
Byzantines, 14, 117, 119, 160–61; administrative influences, 24, 39, 41, 140; Anatolian hinterland and, 37; vs. Arab-Muslim armies (seventh century), 2–3; Bithynia, 7, 10, 15–16, 133–34; capital moved to Constantinople, 5–6; chroniclers, 51, 61, 89, 129–30, 170n28, 174n76, 175n87, 189nn40,46; Crusades, 3, 6; factions, 16, 71, 135, 138; foreign origins of rulers, 41; frontier authority, 125; and *ġazā*, 51, 89; in gazi epics, 67–71, 81–82, 84–85; inclusive tribalism, 51; Karasi emirate near, 16; national historiography and, 24, 38; 'Oṣmān's first conflict with, 61; as Ottoman heritage, 24, 33, 34, 39; Ottoman power established over, xiii, 46, 146; Ottoman warfare with, 134–35, 146; Plethon persecution, 90; and Seljuks, 3, 4; *tekvur*, 14–15, 68; Trebizond, 20, 68–69; weakness in Anatolia, 15, 48, 49, 133–34; weakness internally, 45. *See also* Constantinople

Çaka Beg, 3
Cakü Beg, 128
calendars, annalistic, 96, 98, 102
Cām-i Cem-Āyīn (Bayatlı), 106–7
Çandarlı 'Alī Paşa, 111, 112
Çandarlı family, 18, 111, 140, 146
Çandarlı Ḫalīl Paşa, 97, 146
Çandarlı Ḳara Ḫalīl (Ḫayreddīn) Paşa, 16, 100, 112, 129, 140
Cantemir, Dimitrie, 183–84
Cantor, Norman, 12
caravanserai, 6
Castro, Américo, 20, 21
Catalan mercenaries, 188n39
causality, and cultural history, 58
Çavdar Tatars, 128
Cem, Prince: books written for, 71, 107, 147–48, 190–91; and brother, 97, 137; son's name, 124
census registers, xiii
Charalambos, Saint, 74
charity, wealth and, 87
Charles V, 20
Chingisids, 2, 9, 10, 29–30, 122; Altunorda, 45; and economic globalization, 6; inheritance practices, 136; Ottoman vassals, 147; and Tatars, 122, 127–28; Timurids and, 137, 183n151. *See also* Ilkhanids
Christians, 19–20, 122, 141; Anatolian, 2–4, 14–15, 52–53, 79–84, 89, 126, 160–61; Bithynian, 10, 26, 85, 107, 114; chronicles and, 107; commingling with Muslims, 20, 56; conversions to Islam, 10–11, 19–45 passim, 51, 67–74 passim, 160n22, 174n77; Crusades, 3, 6; dervishes and, 15; gazis, 52–53, 81–82; Göynük, 186n21; Karakeçili, 185n9; in Ottoman armies, 26, 52–53; Ottoman marriage alliances, 135; vs. Ottomans, 98, 128; punishment for sins of, 30; saint-sharing with Muslims, 74. *See also* Byzantines; cooperation, Christian-Muslim; *ġazā*
chronicles of House of 'Oṣmān, xii, 13–14, 48, 90–117, 181n137; anonymous, 96, 102–16 passim, 131, 143, 145, 181n137, 183n146; and court history, 98–100, 114; differences among, 99–103; as fiction, 13, 33, 44; Karamānī Meḥmed, 96, 102, 107; and Karasi, 116, 138; Kemalpaşazāde, 114; and Marmara-basin economy, 45; Neşrī, 102–3, 105, 107, 108, 109; and Orḫān's brothers, 136; Şükrullāh, 96, 102, 107,

chronicles of House of ʿOsmān *(continued)* 114, 122; Uruç, 96, 100, 106, 107, 109; and wealth, 86–87, 111–12; Yazıcızāde, 94, 96, 122. *See also* Aḥmedı; Apz
class struggle: Werner history and, 46. *See also* ruling class
Çobanoğlu family, 76–77, 130
coins, 168n3; gazis of Rūm, 147; Kayı symbol, 184n4; Orḫān's, 164n31, 184n4; ʿOsmān's, 16, 60, 123, 186n13
colleges *(medrese)*, 16, 77, 177n97
colonization, Ottoman policy of, 45, 145
Constantinople: Byzantine capital moved to, 5–6; Church of Hagia Sophia, 71; Muslim quarter, 40; new Ottoman capital, 97, 148, 152; Ottoman conquest, xi, 14–20 passim, 96, 100, 146–52 passim; siege (1422), 183n147
conversions to Islam, 160n22; Christian, 10–11, 19–45 passim, 51, 67–74 passim, 160n22, 174n77; in frontier narratives, 65–68, 71–75; Jewish, 74; *ḳul,* 83–84; Mongol, 74; ʿOsmān, 10, 33, 34–35, 55, 124; ʿOsmān's partners, 26, 127, 135; Ottoman lack of pressure for, 45, 51, 145, 190n57. See also *ġazā*
cooperation, Christian-Muslim, 11, 19, 114, 145, 160–61; Bedreddīn Revolt and, 143; in gazi epics, 66, 68–72, 79–84
corporate organizations: *aḫī,* 7, 34–35, 141; gazi, 56, 167n71, 176n92
Coşan, Esad, 172n43, 180n130
Cossacks, Zaporozhian, 186n13
Crusades: First, 3; Fourth, 6
cultural history, and causality, 58
culture: fluidity of identities, 19–28, 81–82; frontier, 61, 62, 64, 84, 89, 147; national historiography and, 20–28, 159–60; Ottoman written, 93; western Turkish "classic," 7, 94–95. *See also* ethnicity; literacy; political culture; religion; Turco-Muslim society

La dame aux camélias, 82
Dānişmend Gazi, Melik, 3, 63–71 passim, 78, 116
Dānişmendids, 3–4, 48, 57, 64, 66
Dānişmendnāme, 63, 66, 68, 93, 95–96, 141
dānişmends (schoolmen), 110–14
Dede Korkut, 68–69, 94, 177–78
Dehhānī, poet, 93
Deny, Jean, 186n13
dervishes, 7, 15, 35, 45, 188n37; ʿAlāʾeddīn, 136; Apz, 54, 60, 86–87, 101–2; changing standing with Ottomans, 120; chroniclers, 97; Ede Bali and, 187; and gazis, 13, 64–90, 101–2, 109, 110, 115–17; Geyikli Baba, 53–54; hagiographies, 62–93, 115–17; land ownership, 97, 181n136; Mevlevī, 7, 75, 77, 130, 172n43; networks, 101–2; Ottoman alliances with, 135; Ottomans alienated from, 143–44, 150; radicalization, 144; Safavids and, 141; and schoolmen, 110; Seljuks and, 66; *taḳvīm* produced by, 96; and wealth, 86–88. *See also* Babaʾīs; Bektāşī order; Sufis
desire, in frontier narratives, 68
De Vries-Van der Welden, Eva, 175n89
devshirme, 141
Diehl, Charles, 34
Digenis Akritas, 81–82, 84, 85, 174n72
Dimetoka (Dhidhimoteichon), 184n152
Disraeli, Benjamin, 179n115
Douglas, Mary, 82
dream: interpreters, 132–33; Murād I's, 151; ʿOsmān's, 8–9, 10, 29–30, 33, 104, 128, 132–33
Dumézil, Georges, 29, 161n1, 181n134
Dündar, 105–9, 123, 180n124
Durkheimian tradition, 39, 163n23
Düstūrnāme, 65, 69–70, 71, 73

Eastern Roman Empire, xi, 1–2, 3, 8
Ebāmüslimnāme, 63
Ebū'l-ḫayr-i Rūmī, 71
Ebūssuʿūd Efendi, 154
Eco, Umberto, xii–xiii, 157n3
economy: chronicles and, 111–12; globalization of Eurasian, 6–7; Marmara basin, 45–46. *See also* administrative apparatus, Ottoman; fiscal policies; trade; wealth
Ede Bali, Sheikh, 87, 128–29, 187nn25,26; and Babaʾīs, 74, 124, 128–29; cult, 144; descendants, 187n26; dream interpreter, 132–33; as ʿOsmān's father-in-law, 87, 123, 129; wealth, 87, 187n25
Edirne, 148–49, 191n67
Efromiya, 67–68
Elbistan, Battle of, 76
El Cid, 182n143

Ellisaeus, 90
Elvān Çelebi, 73–74, 75, 101, 128–29
Emecen, Feridun, 166n56
emir/emirates, 14–15. See also *beg/beglik*
Emir Sulṭān, 115–16, 183n147
endowment deeds: by Bāyezīd, 183n145; Foss study, 188n31; by Orḫān (1324), 61, 136, 189n47; by Orḫān's wife (1323), 168n1; ʿOsmān's polity issuing, 16
Enverī, 69–70
epics, gazi, 62–90
Ertoġrıl, 45, 53, 105, 123–24, 184n3, 185n9, 186n14; brothers, 106–7; historicity, 60, 123; lineage, 96, 122, 181n134; and ʿOsmān's dream, 30; and Sögüt, 74, 95, 124; and Tatars, 128
Erzi, Adnan, 186n13
ethnicity, 4, 10–11, 12; fluidity of identity and, 19–28, 81–82, 140–41; national historiography and, 10, 20–42 passim, 159–60. *See also* Arabs; Europeans; Jews; nationalism; tribalism; Turks
Europeans: "anti-Turkish" leagues, 18; Crusades, 3, 6; Habsburg, 7–8, 20, 33, 150; historiography, 30–31; Iberian, 19–21, 89; *jihad* and colonialism by, 79; refugees in Ottoman administration, 90. *See also* Balkans; France; Greeks
Evrenos family, 151
Evrenos Gazi, 74
exclusiveness: *ġazā*, 50, 51; Ottoman state, 121

faḳīhs, 110, 135, 181n136
Ferando, Captain, 83
feudal system, Ottoman, 46
Fevbre, Lucien, 39
fiction, chronicles dismissed as, 13, 33, 44
Finley, Moses, xiii
Firdevsī, 180n130
fiscal policies: Ottoman, 15, 100, 111–14, 131–33, 145. *See also* monetary system; taxes
fitra, 84
Foss, Clive, 104, 187–88
France: *Annales* school of, 39; historiography on, 22, 25
Franks, Crusades, 3
fratricide, 95, 105–9, 136–37
frontier, xiii–xiv, 1–3, 10, 14–18, 39–40; authority layers, 14–15, 125–26, 142–43; culture, 61, 62, 64, 84, 89, 147; hinterland vs., 37; "historical" narratives, 62–90, 139–40, 177n96; "in operation," 65; "metadoxy," 76; mobility and fluidity, 140–41; Ottoman alienation/conflicts, 94, 113–14, 139–50, 151–52; political culture/wilderness, 14–15, 125, 141, 173n59; Turco-Muslim, 1–3, 13–15, 37–38, 52, 62–90, 125–28; *uc begleri,* 142–43; vogue, 61. *See also* Bithynia; dervishes; gazis; nomads; Ottoman state
frontier narratives, 62–90, 139–40, 177n96. *See also* chronicles of House of ʿOsmān; history
futuwwa, 34–35, 176n92

Ġarībnāme (ʿĀşıḳ Paşa), 93
ġazā, 11–12, 13, 45–59, 91–92, 176n94; chronicles and, 101–2, 109–14, 145, 179–80; definition, xii, 56–57, 80; exclusiveness, 50, 51; "historical" narratives, 62–90, 139–40; vs. *jihad*, 79–80; "motive force" confused with "sufficient cause," 57–58; Ottomans/proto-Ottomans and, 10–11, 47–59, 89–97, 110–24 passim, 140, 144–46, 179–80; Safavids and, 53, 93, 145, 176n94, 181n135; schoolmen and, 109–14, 140; and sedentarization, 54, 113–14, 140, 142, 147, 181n135; standing up to salute, 146, 152, 190n59; true, 52, 145; and wealth, 85–88, 111–12. *See also* Wittek, Paul/*ġazā* thesis
Ġāzī Çelebi, 78
gazis, 11, 13–14, 45–49, 91–92, 165–66; Bedreddīn Revolt and, 143; Byzantine authors and title of, 89; and central government, 16–18, 111–14, 120, 138–53; chronicles and, 100–103, 110, 111–17; corporate organizations, 56, 167n71, 176n92; depiction, 55–57, 58–59; epics, 62–90; formalization, 176n92; heterodoxy, 11, 53, 143–44; as historiographical creation, 57; and *"hochislamisch"* tendencies, 49; honor, 84–86, 174n72; identity, 78; inclusivism, 38, 68–70, 82–84; joy, 179n115; most illustrious, 135; Muslimness of, 12, 52, 55, 66–67, 75–90, 167n67; Mustafa Kemal Atatürk, 91; networks,

gazis *(continued)*
101–2, 176n92; ʻOṣmān as, 38, 51–52, 70, 77, 84–85, 150; Ottoman/proto-Ottoman, 38, 48, 51–53, 78, 90–93, 99, 120, 127–50 passim; Ottomans alienating/subjugating, 16–18, 112–13, 120, 138–53; and *pençik* tax, 112–13, 114, 142; Safavid, 93, 176n94; and Thrace, 16–17, 114–17, 138–44 passim; tribal leaders, 190n57; "true," 52; *uc begleri*, 142–43, 146; wars between, 88–89; and wealth, 85–88, 111–12. See also *ġazā*
Gelibolu, 184n152; earthquake, 145; gazis taxed in, 112–13; Ottoman capture of, 16, 113; Ottoman loss of, 17, 139
gender: gazi epic inclusiveness, 67–69, 70; inclusiveness in genealogies, 40
genealogy, Ottoman, 29–30, 104–5, 181n134; Kayı, 37–42 passim, 49, 96, 122, 164nn31, 37, 184–85; tribes and, 50–51
generosity: Ottoman, 131; wealth and, 87
genetic method, historiographical, 32
geographic location: Karasi, 16; and Ottoman rise to power, 15–16, 36, 45, 58, 120, 130–34; Sögüt, 130–31, 187–88. *See also* Bithynia; frontier
George, Saint, 74
Germiyan, House of, 76–77; Aḥmedı attachment, 93–94; House of Aydın's autonomy and, 139; vs. Ottomans/proto-Ottomans, 104, 107, 123–24, 128–29, 135; Tatars and, 128, 135
Die Geschichte des osmanischen Reiches (Hammer-Purgstall), 32
Geyikli Baba, 53–54
Gianitsa (Yenice Vardar): Gazi Baba of, 74; Ḥayretī of, 190n62
Gibbon, E. F., 161n3
Gibbons, Herbert A., xi, 9–10, 32–35, 42–43, 44; Byzantines compared with Osmanlis, 162n12; and chronicles, 13, 33, 44, 98; and ʻOṣmān as Muslim, 10, 33, 34–35, 54, 124; and ʻOṣmān's dream, 10, 33, 132; and Wittek critics, 50
Giese, Friedrich, 34, 187n26
Gökalp, Ziya, 163n23
Gökyay, Orhan Şaik, 143
Gölpınarlı, Abdülkadir, 75, 171n40, 180n130
Göynük, 40, 128, 186n21
Granada, Spanish conquest, 20
Greeks: conversions to Islam, 33; Meḥmed II and, 9; and national historiography, 21, 24, 25–26; vs. Turks, 84. *See also* Byzantines
Greenblatt, Stephen J., 72, 170–71
Gregoras, Nicetas, 170n28, 175n87
Grousset, R., 34
Gülşehrī, 93
Gündüz, 105, 107–8

Habsburgs, 7–8, 20, 33, 150
Ḥācī Bektaş Velī, 94, 97, 107, 108, 141, 172n43, 177n95; dream interpreter, 132–33; and Ḳızıl Deli, 115; order, 7, 30, 75, 97–98, 139, 144, 154, 184n152; and ʻOṣmān's name, 124; and rulership, 30; as Saint Charalambos, 74. *See also* Bektāşī order
Hagia Sophia, 105
hagiographies, 13–14, 62–92, 102, 114–17, 176–77
Ḥalīlnāme (ʻAbdü'l-vaṣī Çelebi), 95
Hammer-Purgstall, Joseph von, 32, 132
Ḥamza (the uncle of Muḥammad, the Prophet), 63, 94
Ḥamzanāme, 63, 190n63
Ḥamzavī, 94
al-Harawī, 169n14
Harmankaya, 127
Ḥārūn, Seyyid, 177n95
Ḥātūn, Nilüfer, 40
Ḥayreddīn Paşa (Barbarossa), 83, 84, 170n30
Ḥayretī, poet, 190n62
Hellenism, Byzantines and, 90
heterodoxy: gazi, 11, 53, 143–44; Islamic, 52, 53–54, 71–76; networks, 176n92; Ottoman, 11–12, 51, 53, 54; Türkmen, 75–76
historical linguistics, xii
historiography, xi–xv, 9–13, 14, 21–59; European, 30–31; generational cycles, 11; genetic method, 32; international, 160n21; "lid model," 21–22; national, 10, 20–47 passim, 159–60; Ottoman onion/garlic, 99, 102, 114; and political-military events, 10, 32, 36, 38, 39, 174n70; trends in, xii–xiii; Turco-Muslim Anatolian, 93–95; Turkish, 10,

23, 41, 42, 44–46. *See also* chronicles of House of 'Oṣmān
history: cultural, 58; narrative, 39–40; sociological, 39, 46–47, 163n23. *See also* archives; historiography
Ḥıżır Beg (Aydınoğlu), 75
honor, gazi code of, 84–86, 174n72
Hopwood, Keith, 84, 174n70
hospitality, wealth and, 87
Houtsma, M. Th., 35, 42
Huart, C., 35
Ḫüdāvendigār district, 108
human sacrifice, 54
Hungarians: "anti-Turkish" leagues, 18; refugees in Ottoman administration, 90
ḫünkār, 143. *See also* sultanate
ḫurūc, 63, 118–19
Ḥüsāmeddīn, 76
ḫuṭbe, 104, 147, 179–80

Iberia, 19–21, 89
Ibn 'Arabshāh, 85, 88
Ibn Baṭṭūṭa: and *aḫī* associations, 187n26; at Göynük, 40, 186n21; and hospitality in Anatolia, 87; and Jew in Anatolian court, 77; on Orḫān, 135
Ibn Hājar, al-'Asḳalānī, 182n142
Ibn Kemāl (Kemālpaşazāde), 105, 108, 114
Ibn Khaldūn, 16–17, 114, 182n142
Ibn Sīnā (Avicenna), 166n59
Iconium (Konya), 4
ideals: *ġazā* thesis and, 49–50; and wealth and glory, 87. *See also* ideology
identities, 190–91; explanatory value, 35; fluidity of cultural/national, 19–28, 81–82, 140–41; gazi, 78, 81–82; as Turks, 95. *See also* culture; ethnicity; nationalism
ideology: conflicting norms, 81; in historiography, xiii, 99–105. See also *ġazā*
İlbegi, Ḥācī, 114–17, 143, 183–84; death, 100, 106, 116–117, 139
Ilkhanids, 6, 14, 122, 130; influences on Ottomans, 40, 44–45; and "king of Artana," 186n22; Oljaitu of, 75
İnalcık, Halil, 45, 47, 58, 163n23, 179n108; and Apz version, 180n127; and Meḥmed II's policy, 104; and 'Oṣmān-Miḫal, 145; and 'Oṣmān's military logic, 136; and *uc begleri*, 146
inclusivism, xii, 13; gazi, 38, 68–70, 82–84; gender, 40, 67–69, 70; of Ottoman elite, 90; Ottoman state, 120, 121; redefined, 120; tribal, 38, 50–51. *See also* cooperation, Christian-Muslim; heterodoxy
India, 21, 159n18
influence, historiography on, 24–25, 39
inscription (1337), Bursa, 61, 77, 109, 120; produced later, 52, 55; Wittek thesis and, 38, 42–43, 51, 52, 55
Interregnum (1402–13), 18, 101, 102, 137
Iorga, Nicolae, 32, 34, 145, 162n7
Islam. *See* Muslims
Ismailām'īl, Shah, 75–76, 176n94
Istanbul. *See* Constantinople
Italy, Bari, 3
Iznik. *See* Nicaea
'İzzeddīn, 66

Janissaries (yeñi çeri), 17, 18, 112, 139, 149
Jennings, Ronald C., 51–52
Jews: Anatolian, 74, 77; conversions to Islam, 74; in Ottoman court, 90
jihad, vs. *ġazā*, 79–80
Johnson, Samuel, 30–31, 161n3

ḳāḍī'asker, 112, 142, 190n53
kadis, 104, 135
Káldy-Nagy, Gyula, 51–52, 53, 186n14
Kallipolis. *See* Gelibolu
Kantakouzenos, John, 16, 89, 175n87, 189n46; alliance with Orḫān, 71, 89, 104, 138, 169–70; and Umur Beg, 70, 170n28
ḳapıḳulu. See *ḳul*
Ḳara, Rüstem, 112–13
Karacahisar, 104, 109–10, 126
Karakeçili, 123, 185n9
Karakoyunlu, 122
Karamanids, 94, 178n102, 185n5
Karamānī Meḥmed Paşa, 96, 102, 107
Karasi emirate/warriors, 16, 113, 116, 138, 139
Kastamonu, 76–77
Kayı branch, Oğuz Turks, 184–85; Köprülü and, 37–42 passim, 49, 122, 164nn31,37, 184n3; Yazıcızāde and, 96, 122, 184n4

Keykā'ūs II, 66
Khorasan, gazis of, 55–56, 115
Kilia-Akkirman victory (1484), 96
Kilij Arslan II, 77
Kipchak influences, 164n37
ḳızılbaş, 92–93
Ḳızıl Deli (Seyyid 'Alī Sulṭān), 114–17, 139, 183, 184n152; cult, 115, 117
Knolles, Richard, 30–31, 161–62
Konya, 4
Köprühisar village, 108
Köprülü, Mehmet Fuat, xi, 10, 35–44, 54, 171n40; and Ḥācī Bektaş, 172n43; İnalcık as student of, 163n23; and Kayı genealogy, 37–42 passim, 49, 122, 164nn31,37, 184n3; and philology, xii; political career, 165n48; on religious syncretism, 75; on Sufis, 171n41; Werner and, 46–47; and Wittek, 10–11, 35–44, 50, 55, 163n26, 164n31
Kösedağ, Mongols defeating Seljuks, 5
Kramers, J. H., 35
ḳul, 83–84, 116, 146, 148–49, 182n142
Kurds, 2, 172n44
Kütahya, 77

Laiou, Angeliki E., 188n38
Lamprecht, Karl, 32
Langer, William L., 35
language: of endowment deeds, 61, 136; of historical writing, 93. *See also* Arabic; Turkish language; writing
Lascarids, 48, 127, 133
latitudinarianism, xii, 13, 66, 72. *See also* cooperation, Christian-Muslim
law codes, Ottoman, 131–32, 190n53
leaders, 14–15, 125–26, 142–43; *beg,* 14–15, 17, 125, 142–43; *emir,* 14–15; *hetman,* 186n13; *tekvur,* 14–15, 68. *See also* sultanates
Lefort, Jacques, 104
De la legislation (Bodin), 31
Leunclavius, 109
Lewis, G., 178n101
"lid model," historiographical, 21–22
Lindner, Rudi Paul: and Byzantine Bithynia, 133; and chronicles, 89, 98–99, 102, 103–4; and *ġazā* thesis, 50–57, 109, 110; and 'Oṣmān's dream, 132, 133
literacy: and orality, 64; Ottoman, 16, 93, 177n97. *See also* colleges; writing
Luṭfī Paşa, 184n1

Machiavelli, Niccolò, 31
maġāzī, 63
Maghrib, 188n35
Mahdi, Muhsin, 166n59
Maḥmūd II, 149
Maḥmūd Paşa, 69
Malatya, 4, 64, 87
Malkoçoglu family, 151
Mamluks, 53, 76, 125
Mantzikert, 3, 4
march environment, 48, 122; heterodoxy, 53, 72; oral lore, 65; and Ottoman state building, xi, 12, 14, 37, 131. *See also* Anatolian frontier; gazis; nomads
"Marmara-basin economy," 45–46
Marquart, J., 35
marriages, as possible political strategy, 15, 71, 129–30, 135, 169–70
Marxism-Leninism, 46, 165n46
Massignon, Louis, 35, 176n92
medrese, 16, 77, 177n97
Meḥmed I, 18, 95, 101, 137, 178n105
Meḥmed II (the Conqueror), 37, 104, 146–47, 148, 152; and Cem's enthronement attempt, 191n66; expropriation drive, 115; and factions, 18–19, 96–97, 146; fiscal policies, 100; and fratricide, 108, 136, 137; and *ġazā* salute, 146, 152, 190n59; imperial project, 96–97; navy, 69; son, 115; Sufi mentor, 87; at Troy, 9
Meḥmed Beg, Aydınoğlu, 77
Meḥmed Çelebi, 137
Ménage, V. L., 99, 179n108; and gazi resentments, 114; and 'Oṣmān's dream, 104; and Rūḥī's chronicle, 191n67; and Yaḫşi Faḳīh's *menāakib,* 99, 181n137
menāḳib. *See* hagiographies; Yaḫşi Faḳīh
Menāḳibü'l-ḳudsiye (Elvān Çelebi), 73–75, 93, 109
Mengli Giray, 147
Menteşe emirate, 36, 38, 48, 78, 134
Mes'ūd I, 4
"metadoxy," 76–78
Mevlānā Celāleddīn Rūmī, 7, 77, 93
Mevlevī order, 7, 75, 77, 130, 172n43
migrations, 160n22; into Anatolia, xiii, 2, 3, 5, 23–24, 45
Miḫal, House of, 127, 151
Miḫal, Köse (Mikhalis the Beardless), 26, 40, 101, 127, 145
Miḫaloğlu 'Alī Beg, 150

Miḫaloğlu Meḥmed Beg, 101–2
Miżrāb, 63
Momen, Moojan, 171n40
monetary system: Ottoman, 16, 100, 111, 114. *See also* coins
Mongols, 6, 14, 30, 45; conversions, 74; frontier authority, 125; vs. Seljuks, 5, 48; "Tatars," 127–28
Moravcsik, Gyula, 89
Mordtmann, J. H., 35
Morocco, 188n35
Mottahedeh, Roy, 132
Mübārizeddīn, 77
Muġīṣeddīn Ṭoġrılşāh, Melik, 77
Muḥammad (the Prophet), 63, 94, 115, 190n63
mulūk al-ṭavā'if, 19–20
Müneccimbaşı, 109
Murād I, 17, 111, 137; dream, 151; fiscal policies, 111, 112, 113; fratricide, 95, 137; and İlbegi's death, 116, 139; institutionalization of central power, 141–43; mother, 40; sultanic attitude, 143
Murād II, 18, 101, 137, 146, 184n4
music, martial, 146, 152
Muslims, xi, 1–4, 141, 166n59, 170n30; Baghdad caliphate, 9; cooperation and commingling with Christians, 11, 19, 20, 56; epics, 63; European history and, 31; *futuwwa* organizations, 34–35; gazi, 12, 52, 55, 66–67, 75–90, 167n67; heterodox, 52, 53–54, 71–76; Islamic political culture, 61, 140, 188n37; *jihad* vs. *ġazā*, 79–80; metadoxy, 76–78; military skills, 30; *mulūk al-ṭavā'if,* 19–20; names, 53, 61, 124, 167n62, 186n14; 'Oṣmān, 10, 33, 34–35, 54–55; Ottomans not "fanatic," 11–12, 44, 45, 51–54, 89–90, 145, 165n38, 190n57; Ottoman wars with other, 8, 51, 73; Ṣalṭuḳ's role, 7; saint-sharing with Christians, 74; Shi'i, 73, 75–76, 141, 171–72; "true," 52; *umma*, 52. *See also* conversions to Islam; cooperation, Christian-Muslim; dervishes; *ġazā;* orthodoxy; Sunni; Turco-Muslim society
Muṣṭafā (the Imposter), 101, 146
Muṣṭafā II, Sultan, 149
Muẓaffereddīn Yavlaḳ Arslan, 76–77
Myriokephalon, 4

Nācī, Mu'allim, 185n9
Name of the Rose (Eco), xii–xiii
names: Arabic, 53, 61, 124–25, 167n62; Byzantine, 124; Digenis, 82; and fluidity of identity, 141; in hagiographies, 75; Muslim, 53, 61, 124, 167n62, 186n14; 'Oṣmān's, 61, 124–25, 158n1, 185–86; Turkic, 51, 53, 147, 167n62, 186n13; Turkish, 124, 186n14
narrative history, 39–40
narratives, xiii; Anatolian frontier, 62–90, 139–40, 177n96; oral, 62, 65, 71, 98; theme, 65–66. *See also* chronicles of House of 'Oṣmān; historiography
naṣīrü'l-ġuzāt, 77
Nasreddin Hoca (Naṣreddīn), 7
nationalism, 10; and frontier inclusivism, 84; historiography, 10, 20–47 passim, 159–60; Turkish, 10, 26, 32, 46, 75–76, 164n31
navy, Ottoman, 69, 170n22
Neşrī, 102–3, 105, 107, 108, 109
Nicaea (Iznik): Byzantine capital in, 6, 133; crusaders recapturing, 3; Ottoman conquest and first *medrese* built in, 16
Nicopolis (Niğbolu), Battle (1396), 94
Nihālī, Ca'fer of Galata, 150
Nogay, Prince, 45
nomads: 'Oṣmān and tribe as, 2, 10, 16, 33, 78, 123, 126; and Ottoman alienation/sedentarization, 140, 147, 150; Safavids and, 181n135; and sectarianism, 76; sedentary dispositions, 54; vs. sedentary farmer, 174n70; symbiosis with farmers/townsmen, 126. *See also* frontier; march environment
Normans, 3, 25
Noyan, Bedri, 180n130

Oġuz, son of Prince Cem, 124, 147
Oġuz Ḫān, 96
Oġuz Turks, 37, 45, 94, 96, 184–85; Dede Korkut tales, 68–69, 94, 177–78; dialect, 2. *See also* Kayı branch
orality: and literacy, 64; narratives, 62, 65, 71, 98
Orḫān, 52, 61, 90, 135, 142; and booty, 15, 86; and brother, 106, 108, 136–37, 180n126, 189n46; Bursa and Iznik conquests, 16; and Byzantine factions, 138; and chronicles, 96, 99–100; coins, 164n31, 184n4; endowment deed

Orhān *(continued)*
(1324), 61, 136, 189n47; epithet, 61; and *ġazā*, 109–10, 113; imam's son, 96, 99, 101, 124, 131; inheritance, 136–37, 180n126, 189nn46, 47; Kantakouzenos alliance, 71, 104, 138, 169–70; and Karasi, 16, 116; marriages, 15, 71, 129, 168n1, 169–70; name, 186n14; son, 17, 139

Les origines de l'empire ottomane (Köprülü), 36, 47

orthodoxy, 54, 72–76; gazis and, 66–67; Ottoman, 11, 90, 92, 99, 109–14 passim, 144–45. *See also* Muslims

Oruç Re'īs, 170n30

'Osmān, xi, 1, 7–9, 15–16, 122–38; and *ahīs*, 34–35, 187n26; ancestors, 2, 5, 37, 122; coins, 16, 60, 123, 186n13; conversion to Islam, 10, 33, 34–35, 55, 124; death, 16, 180n126, 189n47; dream, 8–9, 10, 29–30, 33, 104, 128, 132–33; entourage, 10, 127; epithet, 61; father, 60, 123; frontier narratives and, 77–78, 84–85; and *ġazā*, 11, 65, 179–80; as gazi, 38, 51–52, 70, 77, 84–85, 150; location of beglik, 15, 36, 45, 58, 120, 130–34; marriage, 128–29; names, 61, 124–25, 158n1, 185–86; political acumen, 15, 34, 126; religion, 10, 33, 34–35, 53, 54–55; rise to power, 15, 103–5, 118, 128–38, 184n1; as "self-made man," 34; Sögüt base of power, 65, 130–31; sons, 11, 15, 16, 52, 61, 136, 189n46; and uncle, 105–9, 123, 180n124. *See also* genealogy, Ottoman; 'Osmān, House of

'Osmān, House of, xi, 4, 7–9, 10, 15–17, 36, 117; absolute power of, 151–52; and Aydınoğlu family, 69; and Baba'īs, 74, 129; and chronicle authors, 95–96, 110–14; diverse elements, 33–34; entering competition, 119, 129–30; frontier narratives and, 77–78, 84–85, 139–40; heterodoxy of, 11–12, 51, 53, 54; and House of Mihal, 127; inclusive tribalism, 51; *kul* system, 83–84, 146, 148–49, 182n142; loss of purity, 110–14; and "Marmara-basin economy," 45–46; nomads, 2, 10, 16, 33, 78, 123, 126; Safavids vs., 93; Timur's land divisions, 94; tribal factor, 10–11, 37–42 passim, 50–51, 99, 104, 164nn31,37, 167n72; Turkic names, 53; *yeñi çeri*, 112, 139. *See also* chronicles of House of 'Osmān; genealogy; Ottoman state

'Osmān II, 149

'Osmāncık, 35

Ottoman state, xi–xv, 3–19, 21–59, 118–53; alliances, 15, 71, 74, 104, 122–38, 140; Byzantine heritage, 24, 33, 34, 39; capitals, 97, 148–49, 152; centralizing, 16–19, 97, 111–14, 120–21, 137–53; centrifugal vs. centripetal tendencies, 14, 121, 139; classical Ottoman system, 96–97; "corrupt" phase, 10; *devshirme* in, 141; factions, 18–19, 92–98 passim, 143–44, 146; fragmentation, 117; and *ġazā*, 10–11, 47–59, 89–97, 110–24 passim, 140, 144–46, 179–80; gazis of, 38, 48, 51–53, 78, 90–93, 99, 120, 127–46 passim; gazis alienated / subjugated, 16–18, 112–13, 120, 138–53; generosity and justice, 131; geographic location and, 15–16, 36, 45, 58, 120, 130–34; Ibn Khaldūnian paradigm and, 16–17, 114, 182n142; Interregnum (1402–13), 18, 101, 102, 137; legitimation, 95, 96; length of, xi; lid model and, 21–22; and Maghrib, 188n35; "Romanesque" quality, 1; ruling class, 4, 142, 190n57; ruling traditions (higher Islamic / Persianate), 61, 140, 188n37; succession, 120, 136–38. *See also* administrative apparatus, Ottoman; archives; religion; sedentarization

Pachymeres, 61, 129–30, 174n76, 175n87, 189n40

Palaeologus, Michael, 134

Palamas, Gregory, 90, 175n89

Paphlagonia, 35, 130, 134

Pazarlu Beg, 189n46

"peace party," Ottoman faction, 18–19, 146

pençik, 100, 112–13, 114, 142

Persians: documents in language of, 61, 136; histories, 93, 96, 130, 177n96, 178n102; ruling traditions, 61, 140

Petropoulos, Elias, 25–26

Philadelphia, siege of, 126–27

Philanthropenos, Alexios, 126–27

philology, xii, 39

Pīr Sulṭān Abdāl, 92–93, 184n152

Plethon, 90

poetry, 118, 176n94; Beyatlı, 179n115; Dehhānī, 93; Yūnus Emre, 5, 7
Polish refugees, in Ottoman administration, 90
political culture: Anatolia, 2–7, 14–15, 48–49, 125, 173n59; Bithynia, 125; frontier, 14–15, 141, 173n59; Islamic/Persianate ruling traditions, 61, 140, 188n37; Seljuk Anatolia, 121. *See also* administrative apparatus, Ottoman; alliances; Ottoman state; political-military events
political-military events, 4, 173n60; historiography and, 10, 32, 36, 38, 39, 174n70; in Ottoman rise to power, 138–50 passim. *See also* armies; gazis; march environment; navy, Ottoman; revolts; *specific events*
politics: international, 7–8, 138; tripartite taxonomy, 144; writers of comparative, 31. *See also* political culture; political-military events
Polo, Marco, 6
positivism, 13, 29, 72
power: in frontier narratives, 68; House of 'Oṣmān absolute, 151–52; legitimacy of, 188n37. *See also* politics
pseudo-Lachanes, 133

al-Qā'im, Muḥammad (Moroccan ruler), 188n35

racialism, 10; in historiography, 30, 160n22. *See also* ethnicity
Raḥāmn, Gazi, 70
Rashīd al-Dīn, 130
religion: babas, 141; and gazi legitimization, 56; "metadoxy," 76; 'Oṣmān and tribe, 10, 33, 34–35, 53, 54–55; pagan Hellenism, 90; pagan Tatar, 128; pre-Islamic, 10, 53–54, 71, 72, 75; "shamanistic," 53–54, 75, 99; syncretistic, 15, 53, 72, 74–75, 89–90, 143; Zoroastrians, 45. *See also* Christians; dervishes; heterodoxy; Muslims; Sufis
republic, Turkish, 10, 149
revolts: Baba'īs, 74–75, 109, 124; Bedreddīn, 143, 145; ḳul army, 146
Romans, 1, 181n134; Eastern Roman Empire, xi, 1–2, 3, 8
Romulus, 1, 8
Rudolf of Habsburg, 7–8
Rūḥī of Edirne, 148, 191n67
ruling class: frontier sociopolitical order and, 141; Ottoman, 4, 142, 190n57. *See also* 'Oṣmān, House of
ruling traditions: higher Islamic/Persianate, 61, 140, 188n37. *See also* political culture
Rūm, 1–2, 4; gazis of, 112–13, 147–48, 149; Seljuks of, 3–5, 66, 115. *See also* frontier; Rūmī Turks
Rūmī Turks, 1–2, 4, 28. *See also* Turco-Muslim society
Rüstem, Ḳara, 112–13

sacredness, ambiguity and impurity, 82
Sa'dian dynasty, 188n35
Safavids, 8, 94, 141; and *ġazā*, 53, 93, 145, 176n94, 181n135; and Ottoman factions, 144, 145; Shi'i, 73, 75
Ṣafī al-Dīn, Sheikh, 8
Şahin Paşa, Lala, 86
Sahlins, Marshall, 8, 181n134
saint-sharing, Muslim-Christian, 74
Salāḥ al Dīn al-Ayyūbī (Saladin), 127, 186n18
Saljan, Princess, 68–69
Ṣalṭuḳ, Ṣarı, 7, 94, 115, 149, 177n95; and Balkans, 64, 190n63. See also *Ṣalṭuḳnāme*
Ṣalṭuḳnāme, 63, 65, 71–72, 147–49, 190–91
Şamşa Çavuş, 123
Sasa Beg, 70, 77
schoolmen, Ottoman, 18, 90, 110–14, 129, 140
sectarianism: Turkish, 75–76. *See also* Shi'i; Sunni
sedentarization, 140; and dream legend, 133; and *ġazā*, 54, 113–14, 140, 142, 147, 181n135. *See also* administrative apparatus, Ottoman
Selīm, Sultan, 75–76, 148, 191n67
Seljuks, 2–9 passim, 14, 66, 122, 184n1; administrative apparatus, 4, 40, 142; and Baba'īs, 129; descendants, 116, 183–84; frontier authority, 125; and gazis, 48; Germiyan tribe and, 124; histories in medieval times, 94, 96; inheritance practices, 136; Iorga on significance of, 32; juridical system, 190n53; Köprülü on, 39, 40; 'Oṣmān as vassal, 147; Persian chronicles of, 178n102;

Seljuks *(continued)*
political culture, 121; power disintegrating, 30, 38; Türkmen tribes vs., 5, 73–74; Yazıcızâde history, 94, 96, 178n101
Serbia, 17, 116, 139
Seyyid 'Alī Sulṭān. *See* Ḳızıl Deli
Seyyid Baṭṭāl Gazi, 63–68, 78, 94; shrine, 92–93, 154
Shāhrūḫ, 137
shamanism, 53–54, 75, 99
Shi'i, 73, 75–76, 141, 171–72
Şihābeddīn Gazi, 76
Şikārī, 177n96
Sinān, 26
Sinop, 6, 78
Sisiya, 66–67
slaves, 135, 139; *ḳul,* 83–84, 146, 148–49, 182n142; tax on, 112, 142
Sofia, 170n24
Sögüt, 108, 187–88; Ertoğrıl and, 74, 95, 124; Meḥmed I mosque, 95, 178n105; 'Oṣmān base of power, 65, 130–31; and 'Oṣmān-Ede Bali relations, 129
Soviet Union, 21, 44
Spain, 20–21
Stone, Lawrence, 11
subaşı, 104
succession, Ottoman, 120, 136–38
Sufis, 92, 171n41; Aḳşemseddīn, 87; and dream interpretation, 133; *futuwwa* organizations and, 34–35; Ottoman preferences, 141; Sheikh Ṣafī al-Dīn, 8. *See also* Baba'īs; Bektāşī order; dervishes; Mevlevī order; Vefā'īs
Şükrullāh, 96, 102, 107, 114, 122
Süleymān, Prince, 94
Süleymān Paşa, 115
Süleymān the Magnificent, 20, 33, 83, 90, 150, 154
sultanates, 186n22; Mamluk, 125; Ottoman, 17–18, 137, 139, 143, 148–49; Seljuk, 2, 9, 125
sun-language theory, 41, 163–64
Sunni, 144–45, 171–72; and heterodoxy, 54, 75–76; Ottoman defender of, 73, 92
sword-document, 60
syncretism: religious, 15, 53, 72, 74–75, 89–90, 143. *See also* cooperation, Christian-Muslim; heterodoxy; latitudinarianism

Tāceddīn-i Kürdī, 86, 129
Taeschner, Franz, 168n1, 176n92
taḳvīm, 96, 98, 102
Tarsius (Tersiye/Terzi Yeri), 134
Ṭaşköprīzāde, Aḥmed, 54, 86
Tatars, 85, 122, 127–28, 135
taxes, 16, 131–32, 145; *bāc,* 104; *pençik,* 100, 112–13, 114, 142
Tekin, Şinasi, 166n56
tekvur, 14–15, 68
Tevārīḫ-i Āl-i 'Oṣmān, 149. *See also* chronicles of House of 'Oṣmān
Thrace, 16–17, 71, 114–17, 138–44 passim; Beldiceanu-Steinherr on, 104, 116, 139, 182–83
Timur (Tamerlane)/Timurids, 9, 18, 88, 93–96 passim; and Bāyezīd I, 18, 85, 94–95, 112, 128, 185n5; Bursa departure, 183n147; Chingisid relation, 183n151; son, 137; and Tatars, 85, 128
Todorov, Nikolai, 160–61
Togan, A. Zeki Velidî, 44–45, 123, 164–65
Toktagu Khān, 45
trade, 126; routes, 6–7, 17, 45–46, 188n31
transliteration, xiv
treasury, Ottoman, 100, 111, 112
Trebizond, 20, 68–69
tribalism, 12, 16–17, 130, 132, 167n72; *ġazā* superseding, 120, 165–66; Ibn Khaldūnian paradigm and, 16–17, 114, 182n142; inclusive, 38, 50–51; 'Oṣmān and, 10–11, 37–42 passim, 50–51, 99, 104, 164nn31,37, 167n72. *See also* ethnicity; Türkmen tribes
Trojans, Turks as, 9, 159n11
Troy, Meḥmed II at, 9
Turahanoğlu family, 151
Turalı, Kan, 68–69, 178n101
Turan, Osman, 160n22
Turco-Muslim society, 10–11, 35–44 passim, 117, 151–52, 165–66; and administrative apparatus, 10, 24, 42; authority layers, 125; in Balkans, 145; and centrifugal vs. centripetal tendencies, 121; classics of, 7, 94–95; frontier milieux, 1–3, 13–15, 37–38, 52, 62–90, 125–28; and *ġazā,* 62–90, 91, 165–66; heterodox, 52, 73; historiography, 93–95; House of 'Oṣmān entering competition in, 119; Knolles history and, 31; leaders, 14–15, 125–26; nonsectarian, 76; proto-Ottoman identity with, 78;

Turkish historiography's tendencies with, 46; and unigeniture, 120. *See also* Anatolia; gazis; Ottoman state
Turkestan (Barthold), 55–56
Turkey: Akdağ imprisonment, 45–46; Atatürk inscriptions, 41; and chronicles, 98; identity, 23; Köprülü's political career, 165n48; as locally recognized entity, 4; republic, 10, 149; scholarly community, 42; Togan, 44. *See also* Anatolia; Turkish nationalism
Turkic names, 51, 53, 147, 167n62, 186n13
Turkish historiography, 10, 23, 41, 42, 44–46
Turkish language, 4, 5; histories in, 63, 93; names, 124, 186n14; Oğuz dialect, 2; as Ur-language, 163–64. *See also* Turkic names
Turkish nationalism, 10, 26, 32, 46, 75–76, 164n31
Türkmen tribes, 3, 5, 73–76, 93–94, 160n22. *See also* Turks
Turks, 12, 122, 160–61; 'Alevī, 54, 75; Battle of Bapheus, 129–30; Cem identification with, 147, 190–91; historiography on, 10, 23–46 passim; inclusive tribalism, 51; maturing identification of, 95; and Philanthropenos, 126–27; racialism toward, 30; "real," 23, 95; Rūmī, 1–2, 4, 28; Sunni, 54; "Tatars," 127–28. *See also* Oğuz Turks; Ottoman state; Seljuks; Turco-Muslim society; Türkmen tribes

uc begleri, 142–43, 146
ulema, 110–14
Ulu Cami (built by Aydınoğlu Meḥmed Beg in 1312), 77, 134
al-'Umarī, 124, 128, 134, 135
Umayyads, 63
umma, Muslim, 52
Umur Beg, Aydınoğlu, 65–71 passim, 94, 135, 170; and Kantakouzenos, 70, 170n28; ship "Ġāzī," 78; tax abolished by, 132
unigeniture, 120, 136–38
Uruç bin 'Ādil, 96, 100, 106, 107, 109
Uzunçarşılı, I. Hakkı, 164n31, 171n40, 189n47
Uzun Ḥasan, Akkoyunlu, 94, 131, 178n101

vassalage, 146–47
Vefā'īs, 74, 128–29, 144. *See also* Baba'īs
Veled, Sulṭān, 93
Vietnam War, 50
Voltaire, F. M. A. de, 29
Vryonis, Speros, 46, 54

waqf deeds. *See* endowment deeds
"war party," Ottoman faction, 18–19, 146
warriors. *See* armies; gazis
wealth: Ede Bali, 87, 187n25; *ġazā* and, 85–88, 111–12; Ottoman ventures bringing, 15, 16, 86. *See also* taxes
Werner, Ernst, 46, 165n46
Wittek, Paul/*ġazā* thesis, xi–xii, xiii, 10–11, 13, 35–59, 164n31; and chronicles, 103, 104, 109–14, 180n127; and cooperative undertakings, 82–83; critics, 13, 49–59, 91, 163n26, 164n31; and formalization of gazis, 176n92; and Köprülü, 10–11, 35–44, 50, 55, 163n26, 164n31; and tribalism, 10–11, 37, 38, 50–51, 164n31, 167n72
women, in gazi epics, 67–69, 70
World War I, 32, 36
writing, 60, 64; blooming of historical, 93–95; of oral narratives, 63. *See also* language

xiónai, 90, 175n90

Yaḫşi Faḳīh (YF), 96–106 passim, 110, 124, 131, 183n146; and *ġazā,* 179–80; and *ġazā* salute, 190n59; and Kayı genealogy, 122; and Orḫān's inheritance, 137; on 'Oṣmān and Christians, 126; and 'Oṣmān's sons, 189n46
Yarcānī, 177n96
Yarhisar, 129
Yazıcıoğlu, M. S., 171n40
Yazıcızāde 'Alī: and Oğuz/Kayı, 122, 184n4; Seljuk history, 94, 96, 178n101; and tribal electoral process, 180n124
Yerasimos, Stéphane, 104–5, 178n107, 191n67
Yınanç, Mükrimin Halil, 160n22, 185–86
Yūnus Emre, 5, 7, 93

Zachariadou, Elizabeth A., 104, 174n77
Zaporozhian Cossacks, 186n13
Zoroastrians, 45

Compositor: Keystone Typesetting, Inc.
Text: 10/13 Galliard
Display: Galliard
Printer: IBT
Binder: IBT